Wisconsin's Best
Beer Guide

A Travel Companion
SECOND EDITION

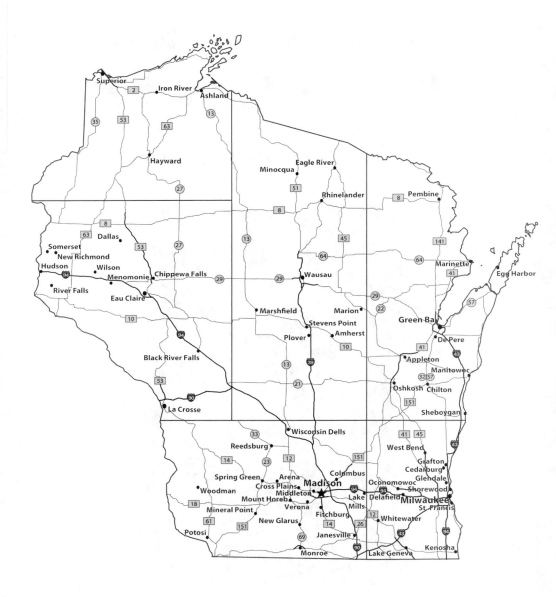

Wisconsin's Best
Beer Guide

A Travel Companion
SECOND EDITION

by Kevin Revolinski

Thunder Bay Press

Holt, Michigan 48842

Wisconsin's Best Beer Guide, 2nd edition
by Kevin Revolinski

Published by
Thunder Bay Press
Holt, Michigan 48842

First edition June 2010
Second edition November 2012

16   15   14   13   12   1   2   3   4   5

ISBN: 978-1-933272-34-4
Library of Congress Control Number: 2012952701

Note: Prices, special offers, hours, availability, etc. listed in this guide are
subject to change.

Photographs are by the author except where credited.
Book and cover design by Julie Taylor.

Printed in the United States of America by McNaughton & Gunn, Inc.

MIX
Paper from
responsible sources
FSC® C011935

For Grandpa Louie

He told me this joke once and I said I'd put it in the next edition of this book...

Two guys sitting at the bar. One guy sips his beer and makes a face. "I think there's something in my beer." His buddy tells him, "Well, why don't you send it to a lab to be tested." So he does. About a week later he gets a letter. "What's it say?" asks his friend. "Says here I should rest that horse for two weeks and it should be fine."

TABLE OF CONTENTS

Table of Contents

Table of Contents

PREFACE

In 2006 I wrote my first version of this book finding a brewing scene that included just over 60 breweries. By the first edition of the newly titled *Wisconsin's Best Beer Guide* in 2010, there were over 70. Now in just two years that number has leapt over 90. This is not a fad, but a return to the heyday of Wisconsin's brewing history.

The Wisconsin reputation for beer is well known. In September 2011 when the *Today Show* came to Green Bay to broadcast live from Lambeau Field on the opening day of NFL football, I was invited on to line up a few samples for Al Roker at 8 AM. Beer for breakfast? Sure, why not? And a bit of cheese and bratwurst on the side that day.

More and more people aren't interested in just drinking any old thing. There is an increased expectation of quality and a call to support your local businesses. More and more, the average beer drinker is taking a good long look at the local beers. Craft beer perhaps intimidates some drinkers who aren't accustomed to some of the bolder styles or who have gotten used to the "lawnmower" beers of summer. But there is no question that people's palates are getting more sophisticated. Just note the most popular beers listed for each of the breweries. Back in 2006 it was strictly the pilsners or whatever had "Light" tacked on at the end of the beer name. That's not always the case anymore, and even in cases where it is, other styles are creeping up on these. Many breweries see their Scotch ales, stouts, and Belgian-style brews taking the lead. A growing number of hopheads are putting the India Pale Ales out in front.

Yes, a few breweries went under since the last edition for various reasons, but Wisconsin still has a net gain of almost a couple dozen, and there are more to come. The list of the fallen is short, but a tip of the hat to them:

Black Forest Dining and Spirits, Green Bay
Brown Street Brewery at Bugsy's in Rhinelander is closed indefinitely
Farmers Brewing Co., Shawano never opened
Hops Haven, Sheboygan
Log Jam Brewery, Unity
Pioneer Haus at the University of Wisconsin-Platteville

I put a few breweries in this edition that weren't open when we went to print but would be a month or three after that. I wanted to make sure this book would be up-to-date for as long as possible after its release. Just be sure to phone first or check a website if you're making a long pils-grimage. This is a static guidebook (until the next edition) and changes can happen overnight.

Drive safely and don't drive at all when you've had too much. The mission here is to have fun exploring, trying new brews and revisiting favorites. Go enjoy the great brews Wisconsin has to offer and stop at a few other cool places along the way. Lift a pint and let the pils-grimage begin!

INTRODUCTION

We live in "God's Country" with water from when the earth was pure, when glaciers melted and left artesian wells that would create the foundation of a land of lagers, an empire of ales, where Schlitz made Milwaukee famous, Pabst got blue ribbons, and Miller called its beer "champagne" and put its name on that time when we just needed a good brewsky. (It's Miller time!) Even our baseball team is the Brewers. This is a Beer State. Where *kraeusening* is tantamount to breathing and a brewed beverage is something akin to a fine French wine or Scotch whiskey. We are only considered Cheeseheads because Beerheads seemed inappropriate for prime-time television—what with the kids watching and all—and frankly the cheese wedge was simply more aerodynamic than a beer mug when they designed the hats—not to mention spillage.

At one time before the Dark Ages of 1919 to 1933 (Prohibition), Wisconsin had a brewer at practically every crossroads with farmers doing their own little operations and bigger bottle works setting up in town. You couldn't swing a cat without hitting one. When consumption of our veritable holy water became a mortal and legal sin, many were the breweries that went beer belly up. The larger ones survived, a few got by on root beer and soda (Pabst survived with cheese), and for this we can lift a pint. Miller, Pabst, Schlitz, G. Heileman, Blatz, the list of Hall of Famers is long in Wisconsin, but we live in a new golden age. Since the late 1980s, we have witnessed a rise in the number of local breweries. Places that love beer for beer's sake. Places that aren't necessarily looking to send a keg to a tavern in Hoboken, New Jersey or a million cases to a liquor store in L.A. Point Beer always claimed, "When you're out of Point, you're out of town." Nowadays, they might be getting a little more distance on shipping, but they have a good... er... point: many of Wisconsin's beers are personal, and unless you take your glass outside the screen door behind the bar, you won't find some of these brews beyond a good dart toss from the tap handle. Many of us Wisconsinites are fortunate to have someone looking out for us with a handcrafted lager or ale. Who in this state should not have their own personal hometown beer? (My condolences to those who don't, but don't worry—this book can help you adopt.) Designate a driver (or pack your sleeping bag in the trunk), turn the page, and set off on a *pils*-grimage to the breweries of Wisconsin.

BUT I HATE BEER

When I took on the first edition of this book back in 2006, I didn't even like beer. I can already hear the collective gasp of horror, but let me explain: beer was social lubricant, something you sipped at with friends at a cookout, bought for the cute woman at the other end of the bar, or beer-bonged on occasion. I didn't like the taste so much and—oh the humanity—often didn't even finish them. I killed many a houseplant at parties and have gotten hordes of bees drunk at picnics with the remains of a bottle of Something-or-Other Light.

But consider this: what better person to send around on a beer discovery journey than the person who knew absolutely nothing? I'd be learning from scratch and whatever I found would be useful for a beginning beer drinker or at least commiserating confirmation for the connoisseur. And since Wisconsin is my home state, there was more than a little pride involved as well, like I might be introducing my family to friends or fellow travelers.

Beer experts already know and commercial beer drinkers might be leery of the fact that outside of the mass-produced impersonal brews, beers are as different as people. They have tremendous character and the people who dedicate their lives to brewing are characters as well. Going to visit a brewery—what I like to call a *pils*-grimage—is as much about appreciating the subtleties and variations of beer, as it is about taking a peek into local communities and beer's place in them. What makes Wisconsin great and what makes brewing great, is the sense of the little guy. All respects to the giants of the massive beer industry, but how cool is it to see the brewmaster standing at the bar sharing suds with the guy next door?

This book is a compilation of all the places that brew their own beer in Wisconsin. That means from the megabrewer MillerCoors all the way down to the little nanobrewery Black Husky in Pembine. The list changes often as pubs close and others pounce on the used equipment and open up elsewhere. After the first edition in 2007, eight microbreweries left us, Miller became MillerCoors in a merger and is owned by South African Breweries, and the Central Waters brewpub in Marshfield became the independent Blue Heron. And a nice list of newcomers joined the list. Since the last edition, we lost six (including the campus brewery at Pioneer Haus at University of Wisconsin-Platteville) and gained 22!

Using the very latest cutting edge state-of-the-art rocket-science-level technology, I established the locations of all of the breweries in the state.

OK, actually it was a Sharpie and a free Wisconsin highway map paid for with tax dollars and available at www.travel-wisconsin.com or 800-432-8747. I sat down with the list and divided the state into six zones. Each of those zones is listed in the Where's the Beer At? section and shows the brewtowns alphabetically. If you already know the name of the brewery you are seeking, look for it in the cross referenced lists at the beginning of Where's the Beer At? The center brewery of each zone is generally no more than an hour's drive from any of the surrounding breweries in that same zone. Make sense? Worked for me!

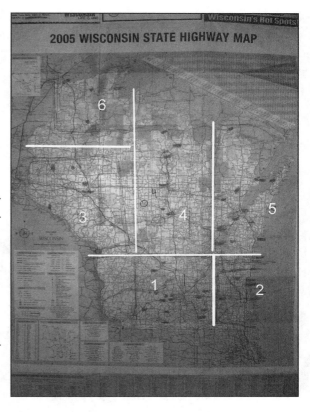

And do I still hate beer? Not on your life! Just characterless beer maybe. I am a convert. I gained about ten pounds from my research the first time around and chose to write *60 Hikes Madison* right after that to wear it off. You may notice *Best Easy Day Hikes Milwaukee* appeared on the market at the same time the second book was released. And this one? Well, let's just say I need some exercise. I call it the guidebook-writing weight-control program. Results may vary.

WHAT IS BEER?

Beer is produced by fermenting some sort of starch product. In many cases this is barley, wheat, oats or rye, but even corn, rice, potatoes, and certain starchy roots in Africa have been used. In parts of Latin America, corn is chewed, spit out, and left to ferment and become a sort of corn beer called *chicha*. I've tried it… *before* my traveling companion told me about the chewing process. We are no longer on speaking terms. Don't expect MillerCoors to be rolling it out in mass quantities very soon. And since you don't hear anyone advertising "brewed from the finest Senegalese cassava roots" you can guess barley is still the primary grain of choice. (If you've tasted some of those commercial non-Wisconsin beers though, you've gotta wonder.) There's no distilling for beer—that would make it some kind of liquor, and it's not strictly sugars or fruit juices—which is where your wine comes from.

THE HISTORY OF BEER

MANNA FROM HEAVEN

Yes, beer is pure brewed right here "in God's country" (Wisconsin, or so claimed G. Heileman's Old Style Beer), but it wasn't always so. Egyptians loved it long before, Sumerians wrote down recipes for it on stone tablets, and you can imagine the drunken bar brawls over at the Viking lodge. Beer dates way back beyond 5000 BC, which is before *writing* even. (I think Ernest Hemingway, F. Scott Fitzgerald, and many other writers have also put the one before the other.)

The word itself comes to us by way of Middle English *ber*, from Old English *bEor* which goes to show you just how difficult life must have been without spellchecker. The English version surely comes from *bior* which was Old High German which became Old Low German by the end of a serious night of drinking.

BEER IN WISCONSIN

In 1998, I traveled to Czech Republic to see a bit of the land my forefathers left behind for the sake of Wisconsin. I landed in Frankfurt, Germany (cheaper flight!) and with a rental car drove to Prague. Remember the movie *Stripes* with Bill Murray? His character said this about getting into Czechoslovakia: "It's like going into Wisconsin – you drive in, you drive out." Well, it is. In fact, as I bundled up in a jacket and faced an unseasonably cold June in Plzen, this is pretty much what struck me. My great grandparents had packed up all they had into small trunks or had a big garage sale perhaps, left behind everyone they knew on this earth—friends, family, perhaps a few creditors—spent much of their remaining money on ocean liner tickets, braved the long and sometimes dangerous Atlantic crossing, had their names misspelled at Ellis Island[*]

---

[*] 'Hey Bucko?' —one of the family surnames had an unfortunate pronunciation with the English spelling so we had to add the 'h' after the 'c' (Buchko) to get everyone to pronounce it right, otherwise anyone addressing us felt they were potentially getting a little surly. Fuggetabout 'Lajcak,' many of us just let people say it as they will.

and went overland halfway across a continent to settle in the same damn place they left behind. Seriously. Change the highway signs to English and set up some road construction detours and I may as well have been driving down County Trunk C outside of Stevens Point. But these immigrants' absurd notions of improving their lots worked to our benefit: conditions were perfect here for making the same great German, Belgian, Czech, etc. beers of Northern Europe—and so they did.

The brewing equation in Wisconsin goes like this:

Immigrants

+

cold (frozen tundra)

+

water (unfrozen tundra)

+

grain (that flat sort of boring part near my hometown)

+

happy hour

=

beer!

Or even more simply:

Cold thirsty immigrant farmers = beer.

BEER TERRITORY

How serious were the European settlers about beer? Consider this: Wisconsin became a state in 1848. 1856 was the first kindergarten. The first brewery? 1835 in Mineral Point founded by John Phillips. The Welsh, coming to work in the lead mines, really started things off. Milwaukee's first brewery was Milwaukee Brewery (never would have thought of *that* name), founded in 1840. Despite our reputation for lagers, this brewery was doing English-style ales and porters. The name changed to Lake Brewery (interestingly we have Lakefront and Milwaukee Brewing Co. again these days), but the locals knew it by the surname of one of the founders: Owens' Brewery. The competition in town led Milwaukee to be the great brew city that it is. They had almost *fifty* breweries only twenty years later. And of course the state itself also blossomed with breweries. Most of this was due to the massive German immigration. *Prosit!* (A German toast to your health. Sometimes also *prost!*)

PROHIBITION

Just before the ratifying of the 18th Amendment in 1919, people were as bitter as an IPA on mega-hops about the Germans, what with the World War and all, and of course it was the German-Americans running most of the breweries in Wisconsin! So we had some beer hate on the brew. A: Americans hate Germans. B: Germans make beer. C: Americans hate… now wait a minute! Why can't we all just get along? But the Prohibitionists had been on the boil already since the middle of the nineteenth century for religious and social motivations.

So the fat lady was singing you might say, but not in Wisconsin. Thirty-two states already had Prohibition in their state constitutions—Wisconsin was one of sixteen that did not.

Well, in 1917 Congress passed a resolution to shut down sales, transportation, and production of all forms of alcohol. States signed off on it and the amendment went into effect on July 1, 1919. And if you were looking for loopholes, the Volstead Act in October defined alcoholic beverages as containing over one-half percent of alcohol. So do the math here. At best, you'd need about NINE BEERS to drink the equivalent amount of alcohol as a normal picnic beer! Even the most ambitious drinkers weren't going to be getting a buzz.

Beer was one of the top industries in the state and it had just been banned.

SO I MARRIED AN AXE-PROHIBITIONIST: CARRIE A. NATION

Imagine a six-foot, 175-pound teetotaler woman with an axe and an attitude. And you thought *your* marriage was rough. Once married to an alcoholic, Nation went on a rage against alcohol in the 1890s and until her death in 1911. Often joined by a chorus of hymn-singing women, she is known for marching into taverns and busting up the place with a hatchet. A resident of then dry-state Kansas, she did wander up to Wisconsin on occasion to lecture us. If you find yourself passing through Fond du Lac sometime (Zone 5), stop by J.D. Finnagan's Tavern and you'll find the "Historic Schmidt Sample Room, Scene Of The Famous Carrie Nation Hatchet Swinging Episode, July 18, 1902" where she smashed up a bottle of whiskey offered as a peace gesture by someone she was arguing with. The fighting words? "Every German in Wisconsin should be blown up with dynamite." Now *that's* harsh.

The best way to make something attractive? Prohibit it. This also goes a long way to making it profitable on the black market. Stories of Al Capone and bootleggers and the mob in Chicago are widely known. But Wisconsin played the backyard to this story. Capone had his hangouts in the Northwoods and there are old escape tunnels he allegedly employed below Shipwrecked Brewpub in Door County. Something as crazy as outlawing beer was doomed to fail, and when Prohibition was repealed by the Twenty-first Amendment in 1933, there was much celebration. Miller sent a case to President Roosevelt. Many communities such as Cross Plains even had parades (see Cross Plains Brewing).

Not long after, the University of Wisconsin-Madison decided to serve beer on campus. This just seems normal to a Wisconsinite, but apparently there are a lot of colleges that still do not. What's *that* all about? Wisconsin even has a university named for beer: UW-Stout. OK, that's just coincidence actually, but I like the idea.

BEER COMMERCIALS

Advertising wasn't a big deal right away. Who needed an ad to know where the brewery was across the street? But as breweries got bigger and started shipping over distances (Milwaukee's population in the 19th century was too small to drink all the beer, and so they shipped to Chicago), there was a rise in beer propaganda. It started with newspapers of course and then on into the radio age. When the beloved radio show *Amos 'n' Andy* went to TV in 1951, Milwaukee's Blatz Beer was the sponsor.

Thanks to all the advertising, the names of Wisconsin's old beers are widely known. Think of Schlitz, "the beer that made Milwaukee famous."

RETRO BEER: SCHLITZ RETURNS!

Jos. Schlitz Brewing was a powerhouse which started when Mr. Schlitz took over the 1849 brewery of August Krug. Schlitz beer was a huge success and became known as "the beer that made Milwaukee famous." Schlitz dominated the market for years (and waited on hold throughout Prohibition), but then a strike at the brewery tripped them up. A certain St. Louis brewery stepped in and has dominated since. Schlitz suffered when the reins were no longer kept in the family. The thirst for expansion may have outweighed the thirst for good beer and in pushing to brew faster, the quality went down.

The beer got flat and to try to compensate, an additive was used to help produce a head. As that additive aged, it solidified! Schlitz became a bit like peanut butter—do you prefer creamy or chunky style? That didn't go over too well and by 1981 the owners stopped brewing and sold off the brand to Stroh's in Detroit. Now Pabst Brewing, also a former Milwaukee brewer which now contracts breweries to make its namesake Blue Ribbon Beer and several other old-school brews, owns the Schlitz brand.

In 2008 Pabst brought the old legend back. They spent some time going over old brewery notes and interviewing the former brewers to come up with what they believe to be the old-school top-notch recipe: The Classic 60's Formula. Fans seem to agree. Schlitz is back in bottles and tap lines all around Wisconsin. Here's the craziness of mass-market beer: Schlitz is owned by Pabst but brewed by MillerCoors (formerly Miller) at a non-Wisconsin brewery facility. Hats off to them all for bringing back a nostalgic beer but it sure would be nice if it came home to be brewed. Crack open a 16-oz. (used to be 24) Tall Boy and take yourself back to the 1960s.

Laverne and Shirley worked at the fictional Milwaukee equivalent "Schotz" brewery. "Schlemiel! Schlimazel! Hasenpfeffer* Incorporated!" Old Style was "pure brewed in God's country" with waters from when the earth was pure (over in La Crosse at G. Heileman Brewing). Pabst Blue Ribbon: "PBR me ASAP." Old Milwaukee which "tastes as great as its name" boasted in their ads, "It doesn't get any better than this." Always an ad with some guys fishing in Alaska or eating crawdads in the bayou or whatever

---

* Hasenpfeffer is a traditional German stew made from marinated rabbit.

and the voiceover about New Orleans or someplace and Milwaukee being a thousand miles apart and it didn't make any difference to these guys who knew good beer. I wasn't really convinced that people would go so far out of their way for an Old Mil until I saw it appeared to be the import of choice in Panama when I lived there in 2003! "Welcome to Miller Time" "when it's time to relax, one beer stands clear" (the champagne of beers). And of course the "Tastes great, less filling" debates of Miller Lite. My favorite Lite commercial was the one with Bob Uecker, voice of the Milwaukee Brewers baseball team, being moved from his seat by an usher to the worst bleacher seat—"I must be in front row!" Classic.

Well, despite surviving the dry years on soda or near beer (or in the case of Pabst, cheese!), most of the breweries hit hard times by the late 60s, and some even crawled into the 70s before giving up the ghost. Rhinelander, Marshfield, Oshkosh, Rahr Green Bay, Potosi, Fauerbach—all these breweries bit the dust. One of the survival strategies of the big guys was to buy up the labels of the sinking ships and thus acquire the loyalists who went with them. So, for example, places like Point continued to brew Chief Oshkosh, and for years Joseph Huber Brewing (now Minhas Craft Brewery) produced Rhinelander and Augsburger.

A handful of the giants made it a bit further through the troubled times. Schlitz, once America's largest brewer, made it to the 80s (still at number three in size) when Stroh's of Detroit bought them out. G. Heileman did some label buying (they bought Blatz in 1969) and then was passed around itself in the late 80s and early 90s until it was bought by Pabst in 1999. When all Heileman's breweries were shut down, City Brewery took over the original La Crosse facilities and kept the previous brewmaster. Now City Brewery does a pretty sizeable business with contract brews. They even repainted the famous World's Largest Six Pack grain silos. Pabst closed in Milwaukee in 1996 and the last of its breweries shut its doors in 2001. The offices moved to San Antonio, Texas, but recently came closer to home as they returned to the Midwest—suburban Chicago, in fact. They own the labels for a variety of old Wisconsin beers including Old Style, Special Export, Old Milwaukee, and Schlitz, but now they contract brew, many of them at Miller.

Who's left standing after all this? It's hard to say and depends on one's definition. Miller, of course, remains but has been bought and merged a couple times and is now MillerCoors in the United States. Point Brewery still lives, and though Leinenkugel was bought by Miller, they still operate independently and retain their classic integrity. Gray's Brewing in

Janesville is an old timer as well, but Prohibition switched them to a successful line of sodas, and it wasn't until the 90s that they started producing beer again.

Even as a few old-school brewers lay there bleeding, a few fresh upstarts were putting down roots and starting a trend that continues to grow and gives this book a reason for being. Randy Sprecher was working at Pabst when the blade of downsizing swept through. With a bit of inspiration, a modest sum of capital, and a whole lot of used equipment, Sprecher founded a "microbrewery" in 1985, the first in the state since Prohibition. Of the original small breweries to start up in the 80s, Capital Brewery (1986) and Lakefront (1987) are still up and running, and continuing to grow in popularity.

The history of Wisconsin brewing continues as we speak, with new brewpubs opening every year and a few unfortunates falling by the wayside. But you can play your part in making history: support your local brewers!

WHEN FARM BREWERIES WERE KING

One of the most overlooked breweries in your typical history of brewing is the farm brewery. OK, perhaps you get the image of Old Farmer Braun brewing up a batch of bad brewsky in the kitchen sink, but such is certainly not the case. On farms all across the state, from the 1830s to the 1860s, the good stuff was being made. These brewers—primarily German immigrants—knew their craft. Wisconsin had just become a state in 1848 and a revolution in the same year over in Germany was driving some people to seek a better life. And what's a better life without beer, pray tell?

Location was key. To brew, farmers needed a property with an artesian well, and since they were all lager brewers, they needed a freezable water source—such as a stream that could be dammed—for the ice needed to keep the beer below 40 degrees while it fermented (though most brewing was simply done in the winter when air conditioning was already amply provided).

Don't compare the farm breweries to sly moonshiners or bootleggers; these were legitimate businesses and tax records for many of them still exist. The German brewers adhered to the strict German Purity Law. Doing it all yourself, from the crops to the stein, was by no means a simple job. The farmers grew all their ingredients—hops and barley—and then needed to malt the grain. This part of the process took up about three-quarters of the facility. The actual brewing, in fact, took a much smaller portion of the space and labor. It was done typically in open top, iron brew kettles over an open wood flame. Imagine sweating over a smoky fire and then crossing the yard through a Wisconsin subzero winter to get to the 40-degree beer cellar. Lager was called Summer Beer, and if the temperature was too high in the cellars either the

PHOTOGRAPH COURTESY OF WAYNE KROLL

fermentation would blow up the kegs or the beer itself would spoil. Ice blocks and straw, however, could last long into the summer. Ever wonder why your grandparents referred to the freezer portion of your refrigerator as the ice box? The same method was at work on a smaller scale in homes.

But by the end of the 1870s, most farm brewers were already out of business. Better transportation and the discovery of pasteurization meant that city brewers could ship beer farther without spoilage. Some of them had chemists on staff. Advertising made a contribution as well. And then, of course, there was just plain competitive big business strategies—the big city guys could come into town and court the saloons by offering whatever the saloons needed—new set of tables? Chairs? Maybe a new roof? Plus they could just drop prices to drive off the local competition. Then dairy farming went big and farmers saw better money (the cities didn't do so well raising milk herds).

Few are the remains of the farm breweries today; most of the structures have been worked into other more modern buildings or simply dismantled completely. These were pretty big operations in little townships and in rural sites (and the locations of remains are often still out in the country). Roman arches that mark old lagering cellars can still be found here and there. Most were never recorded in history books so it takes an expert to identify them. Wayne Kroll of Fort Atkinson is one such person dedicated to the preservation of the record and has spent a lot of time searching them out. To date he has confirmed 150, but there are surely more. Wayne estimates there were once 25-30 farm breweries in the average county, one in nearly every township. Production was probably 100 to 300 barrels per year.

Some of the city breweries started as farm operations. Fred Miller was initially rural, though he bought some of his ingredients so was not quite a true farm brewery. And yes, nowadays Dave's Brew Farm operates in a wind-powered barn, and Sand Creek was founded in a farm shed, but these modern brewers aren't farm breweries in the strictest sense either.

Want to know more? Check out *Wisconsin's Frontier Farm Breweries* by Wayne Kroll, self-published. Order it from the Wisconsin Historical Society in Madison or Wayne Kroll himself at W3016 Green Isle Drive, Fort Atkinson, WI 53538, kroll@centurytel.net.

BARRELS OF FUN

Remember pull tops*, those little throwaway raindrop-shaped openers from beer cans that you used to cut your foot on at the beach? Prior to the pull tops and the modern apparatus that thankfully stays attached, some cans needed an opener like you'd use for a tin can of condensed milk. Thus some great collectibles in the beer can world are the first pull-top cans which boasted No Opener Needed. There were also cone-tops, cans that opened like a bottle with a cap and had heads like the Tin Man. But before all this, and before the advent of the aluminum kegs, there were wooden barrels. The cooper—the guy who tended them—was almost as important as the brewer. He had to choose the right wood and get a tight fit in a world without duct tape and crazy glue. Imagine! Gone, you might say, are *those* days. But not so! Some of the craft brewers still age some of their beers in wood. Especially popular are the recycled bourbon barrels which give that whiskey aroma to the beer. Look for a barrel-aged brew at your local brewpub and see what all the buzz is about.

---

*   Point Brewery was the last brewery to use pull tabs.

The Wisconsin Historical Society at Old World Wisconsin (www.wisconsinhistory.org/oww, S103 W37890 Hwy 67, Eagle, WI, 262-594-6300) has been toying with the idea of building a reconstruction of the farm brewery. It is still just rumor and speculation and hey, where's the money gonna come from?? If it happens it will be unique. They will be operational, grow all the barley and hops, and use horses. They'll brew the same recipes in an open kettle over wood fires. Surely volunteers will be many. Cross your fingers that it happens!

HOPS

Pioneers in Wisconsin found their new home to be an agricultural haven, and in the middle of the 19th century many farmers had success growing wheat. After that market peaked for them and prices dropped, many moved on to dairy farming which contributed to a great cheese industry and our future reputation as cheeseheads. Others found another crop that was in high demand locally and paying big prices: hops.

The first hops in Wisconsin were planted at what is now Wollersheim Winery near Prairie du Sac. Prior to the Civil War much of the nation's hops were being grown in the east, but problems with a destructive pest, the hop louse, took their toll. Wisconsin, um, "hopped on the bandwagon," and by the end of the 1860s the crop had grown to over 50 times its yield at the beginning of that decade. Sauk County led the state and was one of the top growing regions in the United States. Much of the hops got on

the rails in Kilbourn City and was shipped to other parts of the country. (Kilbourn City became Wisconsin Dells and you can still find some local hops in Dells Brewing's Kilbourn Hop Ale.)

A blight, however, in 1882 put the smackdown on Wisconsin hops. That, combined with dropping hop prices, was the end of hoppy times and the industry eventually found itself backed into a corner of sorts in the Washington State region.

A recent hop shortage in 2008 had brewers extremely concerned about where they could get hops in a timely manner and without breaking open piggy banks to afford them. The hops availability has gotten better, but the scare has inspired more and more Wisconsin growers to look at growing them. Brewers, however, have committed to buy what the farmers grow. Hops are a sensitive plant, and the risks—from pests to rainfall to blight—are numerous. But hops, I mean, *hopes* are high that this is a slight return to the heyday of Wisconsin hops.

INGREDIENTS

Hops
Malt
Water
Yeast
Other

THE DIVINE PROCESS

The first step in brewing beer is *MASHING*, and for this you need a malted grain, such as barley, and it needs to be coarsely ground. In Wisconsin we are fortunate to have our very own source of malt in Chilton (see Briess later in the book and check out the malting process). The brewer will add hot water to the malt to get the natural enzymes in the grain to start converting the starches into the sugars necessary for fermentation. Think of your bowl of sugared breakfast cereal growing soggy and then making the milk sweet. It's kind of like that, only different.

The next step is *SPARGING* when water ("from when the earth was pure") is flushed through the mash to get a sweet liquid we call *WORT*, which in all caps looks like a great alternative radio station we have in our capital, Madison. See? I told you we're all about beer here. The wort is sent to the brew kettle and filtered to remove the barley husks and spent grain.

Wort then needs to be boiled to kill off any unwanted microcritters and to get rid of some of the excess water. This generally goes on for about an hour and a half. It is at this stage that any other flavoring ingredients are generally added, including hops.

Once this is all done, the fermentation is ready to begin. A brewer once told me, "People don't make beer, yeast does." Yes, yeast is the magical little element that monks referred to as "God is Good" when they were making their liquid bread in the monasteries. If you wanted to grab a brewsky in the Middle Ages (and believe me you didn't want to drink the water), the best place to stop was the local monastery. The monks made beer, the travelers spent money, the church got along. Everyone happy. How the Church ended up with Bingo instead of beer we may never know. Bummer.

Yeast eats sugars like the little fat boy in *Willie Wonka and the Chocolate Factory* and as we all know from a long afternoon of drinking and stuffing our faces, what goes in must come out. As Kurt Vonnegut once put it and as unpleasant as it may seem, beer is yeast excrement: alcohol and a little bit of gas. Reminds me of a night of Keystone Light, actually.

And what is *kraeusening*? No idea.

ALES VS. LAGERS

There are two basic kinds of beer: ales and lagers. It's all about yeast's preferences. Some yeasts like it on top, some prefer to be on bottom. Up until now, yeasts have not been more creative in their brewing positions, but we can always fantasize.

Ale yeasts like it on top and will ferment at higher temperatures (60–70 °F) and so are quicker finishers than lagers (1–3 weeks). Usually ales are sweeter and have a fuller body, which really starts to take this sexual allusion to extremes.

Lagers, on the other hand, use yeasts that settle in at the bottom to do their work and prefer cooler temps of about 40–55 °F. They take 1–3 months to ferment. Lagers tend to be lighter and drier than ales and are the most common beers, often easier to get along with for the average drinker and they don't mind if you leave the seat up. (In fact, you may as well, you'll be coming back a few times before the night is done.) For lager we can thank the Bavarians who—when they found that cold temperatures could control runaway wild yeasts in the warm summer ale batches—moved them to the Alps. The name lager comes from the German "to store."

Wisconsin, being the frozen tundra that it is in the wintertime, was ideal for this type of beer, and we have the German immigrant population to credit for getting things started here. Oh, they'll tell you that it was because of our cold water, winter and great farmland, but then I have to ask myself: how could they have chosen any other place when we count Germantown, Berlin, *New* Berlin, and Kohler among our communities? It's like we knew they were coming! Did you know there are also two Pilsens in Wisconsin? My grandfather, in fact, was a Pilsner and made a point of supporting pilsners quite well over the years.

Ale is the first real beer that was made and it was sort of a mutation of another alcoholic drink called mead. This was made with fermented honey. Remember the mead halls when you read *Beowulf* in high school? OK, I didn't read it either, but the Cliffs Notes mentioned it some. This is the sweet and potent concoction that put the happy in the Vikings as they raped, pillaged and plundered. Someone added a bit of hops, and later some malt, and the hybrid *brackett* evolved. You can still find both of these here in Wisconsin (see White Winter Winery in Iron River) along with the ales and lagers. We don't discriminate like that. Equal opportunity drinkers we are.

THESE ARE NOT YOUR MALTED MILKBALLS

Malting is a process of taking a grain, such as barley or wheat, getting it to start germinating, and then drying it quickly to cut off that process. I like to call this *germinus interruptus,* but then I like to make a lot of words up, so take that with a grain of barley.

So the malting process is 1: get grain (seeds) wet; 2: let it get started; 3: roast it in a kiln until dried. And here's where the specialty malts come in. You can roast the malted grains to different shades, a bit like coffee beans, and you can even *smoke* the stuff for a real twist on flavor (check out Rauchbier). I mean like you smoke bacon, not like you smoke tobacco—don't get any ideas.

Why is barley the most common grain? It has a high amount of those enzymes for beer. So although corn, wheat, rye, even rice can be used, you'll see that barley is the king of the malts. If you have gluten troubles, this is bad news because barley has it, but fear not—Wisconsin to the rescue. Check out Lakefront Brewery's gluten-free brew made with yet another grain called sorghum.

I know you're wondering, because I was too: What about malted milk balls? There *is* a connection, in fact. William Horlick of Racine, Wisconsin, sought to create a food for infants that was both nutritious and easy to digest. He mixed wheat extract and malted barley with powdered milk to form malted milk. Walgreen's Drugstores almost immediately started selling malted milkshakes, and *Voila!* another great Wisconsin idea entered the world.

REINHEITSGEBOT!

Gezundtheit! Actually, it's not a Bavarian sneezing; it's the German Purity Law. Want to know how serious the Germans were about beer? By *law* dating back to 1516, beer had to be made using only these three ingredients: barley, hops, and water. (The law later added yeast to the ingredient list once Louis Pasteur explained to the world the role of the little sugar-eating microorganisms in the process.) But this meant you wheat or rye or oat lovers were out of luck. Barbarians! Bootleggers! Outcasts! Why so harsh on the alternative grains? Because these grains were necessary for breads and these were times of famines and the like. Fortunately, times got better and we have the wide variety of ales and lagers that we see today. Nevertheless, the Germans came to Wisconsin quite serious about beer (see Farm Breweries). In the end, the law was used more to control competitors and corner a market—so much for its pure intentions.

But there's more to beer quality than a list of ingredients anyway; it's the *purity* of those ingredients that makes all the difference. It's also the time, patience and care of the brewer that lifts the brew to a higher level. Am I talking about craft brewing here? I most certainly am!

WHAT'S HOPPENIN', HOP STUFF?

So why the hops? It's a plant for cryin' out loud; do you really want *salad* in your beer?? Actually, without refrigeration beer didn't keep all too well. The medieval monks discovered that hops had preservative properties. The sun never set on the British Empire which meant it never set on the beer either. So the Brits hopped the ale hard to get it all the way to India and thus India Pale Ale was born. (No, the color is not really pale, but compare it to a porter or a stout, and the name makes sense.)

The point in the process when you put the hops in makes all the difference, and generally it goes in the boil. Boil it an hour and it's bitter; half an hour and it's less bitter with a touch of the flavor and aroma; toward the end of the boil and you lose the bitter and end up with just the aroma and flavor, making it highly "drinkable." (You will hear people describing beer as very "drinkable," and it would seem to me that this was a given. Apparently not.) There is another way to get the hoppiness you want. Dry hopping—which sounds a lot like what some of yous kids was doin' in the backseat of the car—is actually adding the hops after the wort has cooled, say, in the fermenter, or more commonly in the keg.

But let me tell you this, when I first sipped a beer I only stared blankly at brewers when they asked me, "Now, do ya taste the hops in this one?" How was I to know? I mean, if someone from Papua New Guinea says, "Do you get that little hint of grub worm in that beer?" I really have nothing to go on. Before touring or on your brew tour, if you aren't already hops-wise, ask someone if you can have a whiff of some. I did, and suddenly the heavens parted and Divine Knowledge was to me thus imparted. I could then identify that aroma more accurately and I have to confess I'm still not sure I taste it in those mass market beers.

THERE'S SOMETHING FUNNY IN MY BEER

So you know about the German Purity Law and the limits on what goes into a beer, but obviously there is a whole range of stuff out there that thumbs its nose at boundaries. Some of this is a good thing, some of it not so much. These beyond-the-basics ingredients are called *adjuncts*.

Let's talk about the type of adjunct that ought to make you suspicious and will elicit a curse or look of horror from a beer snob. In this sense an adjunct is a source of starch used to beef up the sugars available for fermentation. It is an ingredient, commonly rice or corn, used to cut costs by being a substitute for the more expensive barley. Pale lagers on the mass market production line commonly do this. It doesn't affect the flavor and often cuts back on the body and mouth feel of the brew, which is why if you drink a mass market beer and then compare it to the same style (but *without* adjuncts) from a craft brewer you will taste a significant difference.

You may hear beer snobs use the word adjunct when ripping on the mass produced non-handcrafted brews, but there are other ingredients which are also adjuncts that we can't knock so much.

Wheat, rye, corn, wild rice, oats, sorghum, honey—many are the options that don't just serve to save a buck or two on the batch ingredients but rather bring something to the beer. Maybe a longer lasting head, a silkier mouth feel or a sweeter taste. And in the case of a wheat beer can one really call wheat an adjunct? Most would say no. Word dicers will say yes. Whatever.

Fruits and spices are also friendly adjuncts. Think of cherry, orange or pumpkin flavors in certain brews, or spices such as coriander in Belgian wit beers, ginger, nutmeg, or even cayenne pepper like Valkyrie Brewing's

Hot Chocolate Stout or the Great Dane's Tri-Pepper Pils. Brewers can add chocolate, milk sugar, or even coffee as in the case of Lakefront's Fuel Café Stout or Stone Cellar's Caffeinator Doppelbock. I had mint in a stout from South Shore. Furthermore puts black pepper in their IPA. By German Purity Law, of course, this is a big no-no, but there's nothing wrong with pushing the envelope a bit for some new tastes. It's not cutting corners, but rather creating new avenues.

Are you gluten-sensitive? Well, bummer for you, beer has that. But an alternative grain called sorghum does not and Lakefront is making beer with it. Adjunct? I'd say not. Point Brewery took a Specialty Ale gold at the 1991 Great American Beer Festival for its Spud Premier Beer—made with the starch from Wisconsin potatoes!

THE MAN BEHIND THE BARRELS

When Wisconsinite Tom Griffin tasted his first whiskey-barrel-aged beer, it was a life changing event. It was at a beer festival in Milwaukee and it had been brought in from someone out of state. So there was no way he could pick it up on a regular basis. But if he could get it locally… So he had an idea: convince brewers in the neighborhood to start making it as well. "Great idea, Tom, but we can't get barrels." "What if I can get the barrels for you?" This was the beginning of something special.

PHOTOGRAPH COURTESY OF SETH JOVAAG, UNIFIED NEWSPAPER GROUP

Tom had a background in bio-chemistry and had worked building bio-reactors. What's that? "Basically it looks like a giant stainless steel pressurized coffee pot that costs $25,000 to $250,000 depending on the size and bells and whistles," he says. "Bio-reactor" is a system that degrades contaminants in groundwater and soil with microorganisms which can be used as pharmaceuticals or food flavorings. I like the coffee pot answer better.

Tom's "coffee pot" work had taken him to Kentucky, a land of whiskey, and he knew where he could get the used barrels that would lend their unique character to an aging beer. He had no idea just how well his idea and efforts were going to be received. Soon he was delivering the barrels to more than 90% of the breweries across the entire country that wanted them. Now it may be down to a lot less than that, but nevertheless, this is a man the brewers call friend and his basement is stocked with the delicious "thank yous" of brewers.

Most of the old barrels have been used for 10 to 15 years. He took some to Tyranena Brewing Co. that are as old as 25 years. (Older than some of the drinkers of the beer!) Most of the barrels held whisky, rye or brandy. Tom is always looking for new types of barrels to expand the palette of flavors. It's up to the brewers, of course, to see what can be done with them.

How long does a beer have to wait? Tom suggests one month of aging per alcohol percentage point. So seven months for a 7% alcohol beer. The beer takes on some of the bourbon flavors but also develops a relationship with the charred wood. "You have to get to that stuff, and that takes time. You can't just pour it in and pour it out." Just like wine, beer can mellow and age, and some beers might be best drunk fresh, while others just keep getting better over time.

If you are drinking a barrel-aged brew, odds are Tom had something to do with it. He makes various road trips throughout the year, sometimes sleeping in his car or in a brewhouse. Tom holds the record for most showers taken with a brewery hose. Cheers to the barrel guy!

GREEN BEER

It may sound like I'm talking about St. Patrick's Day but this is about local brewers doing their part to work toward a cleaner, energy-efficient future while keeping us well stocked in suds. One of the first brewers to go "green" was Central Waters Brewing Company. They have solar panels heating water, providing power, and saving them money. The system pays for itself in roughly seven years and the savings over the lifetime of it are enormous. Dave's BrewFarm has some wind and solar power going as well and the Grumpy Troll in Mt. Horeb installed solar panels at the beginning of 2010. Milwaukee Brewing Company uses vegetable oil from the Milwaukee Ale House to heat their boiler thus reducing fuel consumption, repurposing the old oil and reducing bad exhaust gases.

Having a grain silo eliminates the need for bags of malt. Heat exchangers recapture the heat of cooling wort. Cooling water can be used to clean the tanks. In fact, New Glarus Brewery's expanded brewhouse uses the heat from a previous brew by pumping the wort on to another tank and bringing in the next.

Using recycled equipment is another method of minimizing a brewery's impact on the environment. So many have used old dairy equipment in the past, but many more have purchased another brewer's systems.

Keeping the ingredients local is another great contributor to Wisconsin's economy that also cuts down on the energy required to bring grains in from far away. Capital Brewery made a buzz when they worked with growers on Washington Island to get the wheat for their Island Wheat beer. It was a shot in the arm for a struggling industry, and other brewers around the state—Lakefront Brewery and South Shore Brewery to name a couple—have followed suit. South Shore now grows all its own grain. Lakefront makes a beer brewed with *all* ingredients produced within 100 miles of the brewery. The recent hops shortages have inspired more growers to invest in hops production and cooperatives.

Not only are more and more brewers using local ingredients, but many more are also recycling the spent grain, sending it out to area farmers as feed for farm animals. As Bo Belanger of South Shore says, "Essentially we're paying the farmer to grow his own feed. I just borrow it for a moment for the sugars."

The latest trend has been in packaging: the aluminum can. Milwaukee Brewing Co. still does bottles but has greatly increased their use of cans. The lighter weight saves energy and money on shipping/transportation, and aluminum doesn't let the beer-spoiling light in like glass. Plus it's easier to recycle.

And let's not forget, if you are drinking at your local brewpub, there's a bottle or can that was never needed. Pack a growler for carry-out purposes!

TASTING YOUR BEER

Back in the days of youth I suppose savoring the taste of your beer meant you belched after pouring it down your throat. Since you have evolved to drinking craft beers, you may take a bit more time to savor it. Here are a few pointers for savoring the stuff:

Sniff it for aromas. Remember your nose works with your tongue to make you taste things. Kids plug their noses to eat liver for a reason! Get a bit of that beer in your sniffer before you sip by swirling it around in your glass to raise that aroma like you would with wine.

OK, now sip it. Swirl it a bit around on your tongue. Gargling is generally frowned upon, however. Is it watery or does it have a bit of body to it? Squish it against the roof of your mouth with your tongue to appreciate the "mouth feel."

Swallow! Wine tasters can spit it out during a tasting but beer has a finish that you can only get at the back of the tongue where the taste receptors for bitterness are. The most graceful option is to swallow. (Remember what I said about gargling!)

Everyone's tastes are different, of course, and some may prefer a bitter IPA to a sweet Belgian tripel, but the test of a good beer is that bittersweet balance. Now if you want to be good at this tasting business, you need to practice. I know, I know, oh the humanity of it all! But you can suffer all this drinking if it really matters to you. Repeat the process with various craft brews and you will start to see how different all the beers are. Is this one too bitter? Too malty? Is the hops aroma strong, fair to middlin', barely

SOME FOOD WITH YOUR BEER

PAIRING AND PALATES with Lucy Saunders

Think about your tastebuds, and what you savor: the five elements of taste - salty, sweet, bitter, sour and savory umami – are foremost. Pour a glass of beer and ponder its possible pairings.

But start with sniff, not a sip. In tasting beer, often aromatics can suggest herbs, spices or other ingredients that might make a bridge for a potential food pairing.

Hops can be piney and resinous – which suggests rosemary or juniper berries. Citrusy hops meld well with tropical flavors such as mango or lemons and limes.

Witbiers brewed with coriander and orange zest bring out the best in seafood and many salads. Malty, bready notes suggest caramelized flavors and meld well with rind-washed cheeses. Peppery, high ABV brews will extend the heat of chiles and spicy foods. Yeasty dark ales balance the acidity in dark chocolate.

Since everyone's palate and threshold of sensitivity differs, know how to approach a pairing.

I interviewed Chef Jonathan Zearfoss, a professor at the Culinary Institute of America, about pairing tips. "The standard approach to flavors is to complement, contrast, or create a third new flavor through the synergy of flavor," he says.

For example, Zearfoss read a menu description of a rauchbier that suggested pairing it with smoked foods. "I had the rauchbier with a lentil salad made with smoked bacon and a vinaigrette. On my palate, the acidity of the vinegar cut through the smoke. But my friend, who was eating a pasta with cream sauce, found that the smoky taste coated her palate and became cloying."

"The taste memory is composed of the synergy between the drink and the food," says Zearfoss, "and that's especially true with beer since it has a definite aftertaste." Texture elements in beer—carbonation, residual yeast—also contribute to flavor.

When tasting a beer that's new to you, try sampling both bottled and draft versions of the same beer. Fresh beer tastes best, and be sure you know what the brewer wanted the beer to taste like. For more tips on beer and food pairing, plus free recipes, visit BeerCook.com. Cheers!

© 2012, Lucy Saunders

Lucy Saunders *is the author of five cookbooks and has written about craft beer and food for more than 20 years. One of my favorites of her books is Grilling With Beer!*

noticeable? Hints of chocolate? Coffee? Caramel? Is it citrusy? Creamy? Crisp? Even smoky? (See "rauch beer" in the glossary.)

Is that *butterscotch* I'm tasting?!?

Shouldn't be! Beware of diacetyl! This natural byproduct of yeast is actually used in artificial butter flavoring. At low levels diacetyl gives a slippery mouth feel to the brew. A bit more and the butterscotch flavor starts to appear. Brewers need to leave the yeast a couple days or so after the end of fermentation and it will reabsorb the flavor-spoiling agent. The warmer temp of ale brewing makes this happen faster.

Here's something that will sound crazy: a good beer will even taste good when it has gone warm in your glass. (Some will even taste better!) Now try THAT with your crappy picnic beer!

BEER ENGINES AND NITRO

On your exploration of the brewpubs you may find a beer engine. No, I'm not talking about an alternative motor for your car that runs on brewsky. The beer engine looks suspiciously like a tap handle, but not exactly. Normally, beer is under pressure from carbon dioxide—or air you pumped into the keg at a party—which pushes your pint out at the tap. Now this can affect your beer, of course. Air will eventually skunkify it (which is why pubs aren't using it; at a party you will probably finish the keg in one go, so it doesn't matter anyway), and too much CO_2 increases the carbonation of the brew, sometimes beyond what is desirable. There are a couple of tricks that can avoid all this.

The beer engine is one. It is a piston-operated pump that literally pulls the beer up from the barrel or holding tanks. So when it looks like the barkeep is out at the water pump in an old western, he or she is actually using a beer engine. When you use this, the beer gets a cascading foam going in the glass (very cool and hypnotic, really) and a meringue-like head. Look for the tap with the long curved swan-neck spout that delivers the beer right against the bottom of the glass to make that special effect.

In Ireland, the Guinness people came up with an alternative to the barkeep arm wrestling the pump handle. They put the beer "under nitro." This was not some sort of IRA terrorist plan (talk about hitting the Irish where it hurts!), it meant nitrogen. Unlike CO_2, nitrogen does not affect the natural carbonation of the beer and yet it still provides the pressure to get the brew up the lines and into your glass. You'll mostly see Irish-style stouts coming out this way, though a few exceptions are out there, such as the Great Dane's red lager, Dells Brewing's IPA and Hinterland's pale ale.

PRESERVING YOUR BEER

You probably know enough to cool your beer before you drink it, but remember that many craft brews are not pasteurized. Yes, hops are a natural preservative, but let's face it, we are not sailing round the Cape of Good Hope to India eating hardtack and hoping for the best for the ale. This is fine beer, like fine wine, and needs some tender loving care.

LOUIS PASTEUR CHANGED BEER FOREVER

Well, and milk too I suppose. But really, which one is more important? Louis demonstrated that there wasn't any sort of magic mumbo jumbo going on in the brewing process and that, actually, fermentation was brought about by microorganisms (that'd be the yeast). Prior to this the theory was spontaneous generation, that things just happened, but he figured out it was airborne yeasts that got into the brew kettles. The alcohol, of course, comes as a byproduct as the little buggers went about eating the sugar. (Author Kurt Vonnegut once described alcohol as "yeast excrement," but that's kind of a gross thought, so let's forget it.)

But it wasn't just yeast getting in there—there were other little critters messing up things and making people sick or simply skunking up the beer. Solution? Pasteurize it. (Notice the name is from Louis. I'm just pointing it out in case you are four or five beers in on that case you bought already.) Pasteurization was heating the liquid (milk, beer, etc.) and killing off the nasty bits that would eventually spoil the beverage (or worst case, such as with milk, make the drinker quite sick!)

If on your brewery tour you pick up a growler, put that thing on ice! If you don't refrigerate unpasteurized beer, you are getting it at less than its best and perhaps at its worst. And if your local grocer thinks stacking bottled six-packs of the unpasteurized stuff in fancy geometric designs on the floor is a good marketing strategy, have a word with that guy. Get that beer to a fridge!

If you are picking some up on a longer road trip, please, take a cooler along. The longer you leave good beer exposed to light and heat, the more likely the taste will deteriorate until you have the infamous beer of Pepé Le Pew.

Living yeast? Treat it like milk!

BREW YOUR OWN

OK, I know what you're thinking: if so many of these brewmasters started in their basements, why can't I? Well, truth is, you can!

Check your local yellow pages under BEER to find a place near you that sells what you need.

A basic single-stage brew kit includes a 6.5 gallon plastic bucket with a lid and fermentation lock, a siphoning tube, bottle brush, handheld bottle capper and caps, and hopefully, instructions. You then need a recipe pack and about 50 returnable-style bottles (not twist-offs). (Grolsch bottles with the ceramic stopper also work great; you only need to buy new rubber rings for the seal.) The kit starts around $50.

A two-stage kit throws in a hydrometer, thermometer and a 5-gallon glass "carboy" where the brew from the bucket goes to complete fermentation. Now you can watch it like an aquarium. Don't put any fish in it though.

Ingredient kits have all you need for a certain recipe. Simple light ales might start around $25 while an IPA with oak chips can get up around $50. Each makes about 50 bottles of beer. In many cases you are using malt extracts thus skipping the grinding of grain in the wort-making process. As you go deeper into the art you will likely want to do this yourself as well.

If your future brewpub patrons are really slow drinkers or Mormons, this basic kit will do you fine. That said, the pros are by no means always using the state-of-the-art equipment either. Remember Egyptians and Sumerians were already making beer over 5000 years ago and they didn't even have toilet paper yet. Um… my point is, big brewers might have the funds to get the fancy copper brew kettles made in Bavaria and a microbiology lab, while others, like the guys at Central Waters at least got their start with used equipment that had other original purposes. Old dairy tanks are popular. And Appleton Beer Factory is actually making and welding their own tanks. Talk about hardcore.

But before you get all excited about naming your beers and what the sign on the pub is going to look like, consider Tom Porter's thoughts on the challenges of starting a brewery.

ON STARTING A BREWERY: TOM PORTER

If you want to start a brewery, use somebody else's money. Because you can go big to start, big enough to make it a profit-able minimum, and then if it goes belly up you just tell them, "Sorry, guys, I did the best I could!" I'm on the hook for it, win or lose. It *does* give you tremendous impetus to not fail. There's no doubt about it. "Hey, you gotta make good beer." That's a given. There's nobody out there making really crummy beer anymore, they all went belly up and we all bought their used equipment. It's a given that the beer is pretty darn good. Yeah, there are dif-ferent interpretations of style, but it's really all about costs.

I could be in the muffler business, or I could be in the hub cap business; I could be making paper clips for chrissakes, as long as the paper clip quality is as good as everybody else's, it doesn't matter. The reality is you better be darn good on cost control and you better know business, and I didn't. I was an engineer. Engineers sit way in back of a great big company. Someone else goes and sells it, someone else decides if there is profit in it. By the time the paper ever gets to your desk, it's a done deal. I went from the engineering business to having to *do* the business, the books, the capital decisions, the sales... *inventory* control. All those things: debt amortization, accounting... ggarrggh, accounting? Man! I never went to accounting classes. I got out of those thinking they were like the plague to me. "A credit is a debit until it's paid?!?" *What?!?*

My accounting system that started out when I started this brewery is I had a bucket of money. And every time I get some more I put it in the bucket. And when I need it, I take it out of the bucket. When the bucket's empty I got to stop taking money out until I get some more to put in. Well, that system still works here, but there's a WHOLE—SERIES—OF BUCKETS now! There's literally *dozens* of buckets. It gets hard to remember which one do I put it into and which one do I take it out of. And sometimes you don't notice one's empty. So business and accounting—that's really been my learning curve. I went from going "What's a balance sheet?" to a profit and loss statement, and now I work off cash flow statements and sometimes I split them up. I want to know where the push and pull is of my cash flow, because that's really what makes a good businessman. And I'm learning this because I HAVE to. And it has had NOTHING to do with

making good beer. The good beer part is a given. You've gotta have it. If you don't have it, don't even think about it. But having that is not enough. I have a lot of people here coming through the door on tours and such saying, "I'm thinking of starting a brewpub. Gees, I make really good homebrew." And I say, "That's a really good first step." But the second through fortieth steps are... how are your plumbing skills? How're your carpentry skills? Can you pour concrete? Can you weld? And then can you balance a balance sheet every thirty days?

Where's The Beer At?
(INTRO TO THE LISTINGS)

The listings for all the commercial brewers in Wisconsin are divided here into the six zones I mentioned before. Each section has a map of that portion of the state with the brewtowns marked. Within each zone the communities are listed in alphabetical order with the brewpubs and breweries below the town heading. Watch for a few extra non-brewing but brewing related attractions and other interesting bits you can read during your journey.

HOW TO USE THE LISTINGS:

OK, this isn't rocket science but let's go over a brief summary of the finer points of the listings.

Brewmaster: So you know who to ask brewing questions.

Staple Beers: Always on tap.

Rotating Beers: Like roulette only with beer, the beers that may come and go, often seasonal brews.

Special Offer: This is something the management of the place you're visiting agreed to give to a patron who comes in and gets **this book** signed on the signature line of that particular brewer. This is a one-time bonus and the signature cancels it out. You must have a complete book—photocopies or print-outs don't count. I didn't charge them and they didn't charge me; it's out of the goodness of their hearts, so take it as such and don't get all goofy on them if the key chain turns out to be a bumper sticker or something. And if they are offering beer, it is assumed that it is the brewer's own beer, not Bud Light or some such non-Wisconsin stuff or that fancy import you've been wishing would go on special. If they are giving you a free beer, be a good fella and spend a little money while you're there too! *The brewer reserves the right to rescind this offer at any time and for any reason.* Legal drinking age still applies of course.

Stumbling Distance: Two or three cool things that are very local, very Wisconsin or just plain cool. Some may be more of a short car ride away. If you really *are* stumbling, get a designated driver for those.

Notes on Terminology (not found in the glossary): Kirby Nelson over at Wisconsin Brewing Co. hates the term 'microbrewery.' He believes—and I agree—that it sounds condescending or implies that what is going on there is of small significance. Plus it just sounds so trendy. I met a drunk from Washington when I made the rounds for the first edition of this book who boasted that the first "microbreweries" (ugh!) were in his home state. I pointed out that during the 1800s nearly every community had its own little brewery and that if anything Washington was about 100 years behind on the trend.

Now there are also some terms that are very Wisconsinite in nature, and for those you may need to consult the fellow at your elbow at the bar. You might hear, "I grew up in Mahwaukee," which translates to "Milwaukee." In the unlikely event that a fellow beer drinker asks for the nearest "bubbler," he seeks water from a drinking fountain. There is argument over where the geographical line is between the folks who say "soda" instead of "pop." I myself have adopted "soda pop" just to cover all bases. And "ainahey?" is particular to Mahwaukee; if people lay it on you, just nod—they are seeking agreement (ain't it though?).

And that's about it, the rest should be self-explanatory. Enjoy the ride! Last one all the way through the breweries is a rotten egg. Or a skunk beer.

LISTINGS BY BREWER

LISTINGS BY BREWTOWN

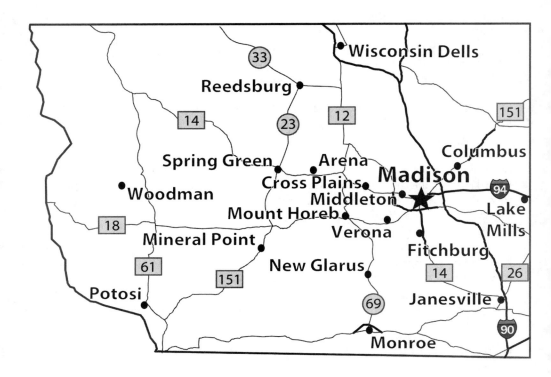

ZONE 1

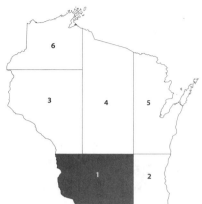

Arena: Lake Louie Brewing
Columbus: Hydro Street Brewery
Cross Plains: Cross Plains Brewery
Fitchburg: Great Dane Pub and Brewery
Janesville: Gray's Brewing Co.
Lake Mills: Tyranena Brewing Co.
Madison: Ale Asylum
Madison: Granite City Food and Brewery
Madison: Great Dane Pub and Brewery
Madison: Great Dane Pub and Brewery—Hilldale
Madison: House of Brews
Madison: Karben4 Brewing
Madison: One Barrel Brewing
Madison: Vintage Brewing Company
Middleton: Capital Brewery
Mineral Point: Brewery Creek Brewpub
Monroe: Minhas Craft Brewery
Mount Horeb: Grumpy Troll Brew Pub
New Glarus: New Glarus Brewing Co.
Potosi: Potosi Brewing Co.
Reedsburg: Corner Pub
Spring Green: Furthermore Beer
Verona: Gray's Tied House
Verona: Wisconsin Brewing Co.
Wisconsin Dells: Moosejaw Pizza and Dells Brewing Co.
Wisconsin Dells: Port Huron Brewing Co.
Woodman: Woodman Brewery (Whistle Stop Restaurant)

Lake Louie Brewing

Founded: 2000
Brewmaster: Tim Wauters
Address: 7556 Pine Road • Arena, WI 53503
Phone: 608-753-2675
Website: www.lakelouie.com
Annual Production: 5500 bbls
Number of Beers: 13

Staple Beers:
» Arena Premium Pale Ale
» Coon Rock Cream Ale (named after the local Coon Rock Cave where legend has it there be treasure)
» Kiss the Lips India Pale Ale
» Tommy's Porter
» Warped Speed Scotch Ale (sweet and malty)

Rotating Beers:
» Brother Tim's Tripel
» Dino's Dark Porter
» Louie's Reserve (a limited batch of Scotch Ale with higher alcohol, see story below)
» Milk Stout
» Mosquito Beach
» Mr. Mephisto's Imperial Stout (I get goosebumps even typing it)
» Prairie Moon Belgian Farmhouse Wit (with blood orange)
» Radio Free India Black Ale

Most Popular Brew: Warped Speed Scotch Ale

Brewmaster's Fave: "The next one we haven't made yet."

Tours? In July 2012 they started doing tours again, each Saturday at noon and 1:15 PM. Email a reservation via the form on the website.

Where can you buy it? Lake Louie beer can be found statewide in bottled six-packs (four-packs for specialty brews) and as tap accounts in various bars some of which are listed on the website. If your local pub doesn't have it, request it.

Special Offer: Not participating. Tours and samples are already free!

Directions: From US Hwy 14 go north on Oak Street in Arena. Turn left where it ends and becomes Elizabeth St/Pine Dr. Follow this until it too takes a right angle turn to the right. Just about 1000 feet past this on the right you will see the Porter mail box and the driveway to the brewery.

The Beer Buzz: Another engineer gone brewing, founder/owner Tom Porter quit his job, cashed in the 401K, and made his garage into a brewery. "I figured I'd fail, but fail small and recover." Not so much. He brewed it all himself, produced about 200 gallons every two weeks, and then did all the deliveries as well. And it caught on. Tom used to get his parents in to pack boxes sometimes. Then Tim Wauters joined Tom to keep up with growth. They once had a waiting list for wannabe customers. Limited releases would sell out in less than two days, and it wasn't uncommon to see serious fans following the delivery truck on release dates. Now Tim is head brewer and they hired Asa Derks (a film school grad) as their cellar chief. They no longer have to deliver their own beer, and a brewery expansion has helped them keep ahead of demand—just barely. It's popular stuff.

Tom bought the original brewing system from a microbrewery that gave up its ghost in Eugene, Oregon. It took four semi-trucks to get it to Wisconsin. The brewery is on twenty acres Tom got from his uncle. The name comes from the pond there where he and some friends used to go skinny dipping when they were in high school. Uncle Louie would come and chase them out of the "lake."

Louie's Reserve, for those in the know, is Liquid Reefer as it was dubbed when Tom tried the first batch out on the locals. They changed the name so as not to antagonize the ATF, what with them brewing in the middle of the woods and all!

Want to do what Tom did? Read his "On Starting a Brewery" in the History of Beer section.

Stumbling distance: Get your cheese curd fix at *Arena Cheese* (arenacheese. com, 300 US Hwy 14, 608-753-2501), the place with the big mouse out front. There's a window into the production area so you can watch.

Hydro Street Brewery

Founded: December 22, 2011
Brewmaster: Aaron Adams
Address: 152 West James Street
        Columbus, WI 53925
Phone: 920-350-0252
Website: www.hydrostreetbrew.com
Annual Production: 300 barrels
Number of Beers: 11 on tap

Staple Beers:
» Campfire Porter
» Seven Sisters Scotch Ale
» Throwback Pale Ale
» Twist And Shout Stout

Rotating Beers:
» Aaron's Altbier
» Newport Red
» Old Pappy Pale Ale
» Summer Rescue Amber
» Truancy IPA
» also a changing R&D tap

Most Popular Brew: Seven Sisters or Throwback Pale Ale.

Brewmaster's Fave: Altbier, Summer Rescue. It changes seasonally.

Tours? The brewery is open to see, but he ferments in the basement. Call ahead.

Samples: Yes, five samples for $8.50

Best Time to Go: Always open until at least 11 PM seven days a week. Happy hours run 9-10 AM, 3-6 PM, and 10 PM-close! Local live music can happen anytime.

Where can you buy it? In growlers at the bar and a few regional draft accounts (see the website).

Got food? Yes! Pickled eggs at the bar, but then a really nice menu of almost entirely local meat, cheese and veggies. French onion soup, a beef sandwich, and chocolate pudding all use beer in the recipes. Spent grain even ends up on a salad. Aaron's wife Sandye is executive chef. They serve breakfast too for you early drinkers.

Special Offer: Half off the price of an appetizer.

The Beer Buzz: Aaron started homebrewing while he was going to school for his PhD in forest entomology. He met Sandye and they took up the hobby, escalating from extract to grain, from a 5-gallon to a 10-gallon, etc. He had a job with University of Wisconsin but when the grant funding ran out, he had trouble finding something. So they decided they'd just dive into brewing and working for themselves. In the beginning, everyone told them Columbus probably couldn't support a brewpub. A place in Washington looked very good but even as they were packed up and ready to go, the deal fell through. Northern Michigan was an option, but nothing looked solid. So they shunned conventional wisdom and settled on Columbus anyway.

The building, located in the historic downtown, is an 1895 former men's clothing store, and when they moved in, it had been storing horse carriages (from a llama-carriage builder next door). The old wood floor and tongue-and-groove ceiling are still in place. Aaron built the bar himself. Um, A+ for the effort! There's an open kitchen and a small beer garden out back. Local art for sale adorns the walls, and the front space is coffee-shop tables. They want this place to be a community center, a good meeting place. They make their own root beer. There is free WiFi.

Tip: they make a nice sort of shandy with the pale ale and grapefruit juice. Try it!

Stumbling Distance: Right across the street is a 1919 bank building designed by the famous architect Louis Sullivan. It was used as a set in Johnny Depp's 2009 Dillinger flick *Public Enemies*. Looking for good cheese? Watch for *Schultz's Cheese Haus* (schultzscheese.com, N6312 Hwy 151, Beaver Dam, 920-885-3734) on your way to Columbus, selling Wisconsin's finest since 1962.

Photographs courtesy of Preamtip Satasuk

ESSER'S CROSS PLAINS BREWERY

Founded: 1863
Brewmaster: Stevens Point Brewery
Address: 2109 Hickory Street • Cross Plains, WI 53528
Phone: 608-798-3911
Website: www.essersbest.com
Number of beers: 2

Staple Beers:
» CROSS PLAINS SPECIAL (lighter pilsner)
» ESSER'S BEST (hearty lager, caramel color)

Tours? Drop in 8:30-12 weekdays or by appointment. It's a good idea to call first.

Samples: Yes

Best time to go: Not Badger game days!

Where can you buy it? In area stores and bars throughout Wisconsin.

Got food? Go to Main Street for restaurants.

Special Offer: Bring your book for a signature and get a free sample and an Esser's Best patch.

Directions: Come into Cross Plains on US Hwy 14 (Main Street) and turn north on Hickory Street and they're right there on your left.

The Beer Buzz: George Esser came all the way from Cologne, Germany in 1852 and started brewing beer for us in 1863, beating out his buddy Heinrich Leinenkugel to get a brewery started in Cross Plains. Esser's Best was brewed until 1910 when the Essers gave up brewing in favor of being a distributor. Six generations later, the family has taken the recipe from George's German diary and is producing the original with the help of the Point Brewery. The "brewery" has a collection of cool odds and ends from the old-school brewing days as well as an old hack

(horse-drawn carriage) that they pull out for special events. Cross Plains threw one helluva parade in '33 when Prohibition ended and the Essers were part of the 75 year anniversary in 2008. They will throw another big party and parade in 2013 to celebrate 80 years of legal beer. This is one of the oldest family businesses in the USA with the 5th and 6th generations running the show now. Great stories here and Wayne and Larry love to chat it up. If no one's there in the morning, wait fifteen minutes.

Stumbling distance: Check out *Coach's Club* (1200 Main St, 608-413-0400) which uses Esser's Best to beer batter some fish for an excellent Friday night fish fry. *Sheltons Bar and Restaurant* (1821 Main St., 608-798-3621) does the same! Nearby Black Earth Creek offers some world class trout fishing. The Table Bluff Segment of *The Ice Age National Scenic Trail* (iceagetrail.org, 2110 Main St, 800-227-0046) is just outside of town and the Ice Age Trail Alliance's office is in Cross Plains. Pack some beer for the hike!

The Great Dane Pub and Brewery

Founded: 2002
Brewmaster: Pat Keller
Address: 2980 Cahill Main • Fitchburg, WI 53711
Phone: 608-442-9000
Website: www.greatdanepub.com
Annual Production: 1400 bbls
Number of Beers: 11-12

Staple Beers:
  » Black Earth Porter on beer engine
  » Crop Circle Wheat
  » Jon Stoner's Oatmeal Stout
  » Landmark Lite Lager
  » Old Glory American Pale Ale
  » Texas Speedbump IPA
  » Verruckte Stadt German Pils

Rotating Beers:
  » Amber Lager (summer)
  » Bock
  » Doppelbock (winter)
  » Foxy Brown
  » Maibock (spring)
  » Oktoberfest

Most Popular Brew: Crop Circle Wheat or Texas Speedbump IPA

Brewmaster's Fave: Texas Speedbump or Maibock

Tours? By chance or appointment but always welcomed.

Samples? Yes, a couple 2-ounce tasters, side by each, dontcha know, or sampler platters of as many 4-ounce tasters as you want for $1.50 each.

Best Time to Go: Happy hour is 4-6 weekdays and offers beer discounts

Where can you buy it? On-site growlers, pub kegs, and half barrels (with 24-hour notice), but see their other locations near Hilldale Mall (also a brewpub), at the airport, and the original downtown Madison location. The Duck Blind at Madison Mallards Northwoods-League baseball games is fueled by 4 specially brewed Great Dane beers. In 2012 the Dane did its first limited bottles with Imperial Red Ale, available in house. And for something farther afield, find the Dane in Wausau, WI. 100+ tap accounts around the state.

Got food? Yes, a full menu of soups, salads, burgers, and entrees. The bratburger (created on a dare) is an original with bacon on a pretzel bun. Beer, brat and cheese soup is Wisconsin in a bowl. Beer bread is standard, fish and chips available, and a load of other great dishes. Friday night pilsner-battered fish fry!

Special Offer: A free 10 oz. beer!

Directions: From the Beltline Hwy 12/14/18/151, go south just over 1 mile on Fish Hatchery Road and the brewpub is in the complex to the right, across from the fish hatchery.

The Beer Buzz: You can change the scenery, but the beer remains the same. With a few beers unique to this location, this Dane is a nice option for those who don't want to go all the way downtown for their great beer. In the upper level of a strip mall across from the Fish Hatchery on Fish Hatchery Road just south of Madison, this place draws more of the after-work crowd and families on the weekends.

Inside you'll find dark hardwood floors around a horseshoe-shaped bar in a high-ceiling room with a large projection screen TV. (Packer and Badger games!) To the right along the wall under glass is the brewhouse on both the first floor and mezzanine, and copper brew kettles greet you by the door. The rooftop terrace is partly canopied in case of summer sprinkles and has a bar of its own. The mezzanine with four pool tables (free pool with food purchase 11-2 Mon-Fri!) and shuffleboard rests over a quieter dining area with spacious booths and windows looking out over the parking lot toward the greenery of the Fish Hatchery across the road.

Brewmaster Pat did a career in the Coast Guard, and when that ended a friend told him, "Find something you do for free and get them to pay you for it." It was serendipity: his resume arrived at the Dane downtown the same day someone quit. "Can there be a better job? I love the immediate reaction of the people in the pub. It's pretty much my life." There's Wii at the bar, and WiFi throughout.

From the parking lot out front you will see the sign on the pub upstairs, but look to the left (if you're facing it) for the white grain silo and a black arrow to find the outdoor stairs up the hill to get in. There is an access road behind the mall and ramp parking if you want to avoid the steps. Smoking is allowed out on the patio.

Stumbling Distance:

Liliana's (www.lilianasrestaurant.com, 2951 Triverton Pike, 608-442-4444) is a New Orleans-themed fine-dining restaurant with a stellar wine list, *all* of which are available by the glass. Well, it's not a fish fry, it's a fish *hatchery*: *Nevin Hatchery* (3911 Fish Hatchery Road, 608-275-3246,), the oldest in the state dating back to 1876, raises 550,000 trout each year, mainly for Wisconsin inland waters. Stop for a self-guided tour or make a reservation for larger groups and they'll provide a guide.

Gray Brewing Co.

Founded: 1856
Brewmaster: Fred Gray
Address: 2424 W Court Street •
      Janesville, WI 53548
Phone: 608-754-5150
Website: www.graybrewing.com
Annual Production: 3500 bbls
Number of Beers: 7

Staple Beers:
» Bully Porter
» Busted Knuckle Irish-Style Ale
» Gray's Light
» Honey Ale
» Oatmeal Stout
» Rathskeller Amber Ale
» Wisco Wheat

Rotating Beers:
» Limited production beers may come up once in a while

Most Popular Brew: Oatmeal Stout

Brewmaster's Fave: Oatmeal Stout

Tours? No. The brewery is no longer open for public visits.

Where can you buy it? Major liquor stores in Wisconsin, Illinois, and Pennsylvania.

The Beer Buzz: Founded by Irish immigrant Joshua Gray in 1856, this was the first all-ale brewery in Wisconsin, and Fred is the fifth generation of the Gray family to operate it. Only 15% of the production is actually beer, the rest is some very popular sodas—especially the root beer. Soda is what carried the brewery through Prohibition and the Grays stuck with it until the plant was burnt down by arson in 1992. When they decided to press on, it was with the plan of their forefathers: beer and soda. The malt beverage is the raspberry-flavored Rock Hard Red. The lobby has a nice collection of breweriana and there's a gift shop. Gray's Tied House in Verona is a great brewpub showcasing Gray's beers.

Tyranena Brewing Co.

Founded: November 1998
Brewmaster: Rob Larson
Address: 1025 Owen Street (PO Box 736) • Lake Mills, WI 53551
Phone: 920-648-8699
Website: www.tyranena.com
Annual Production: 4500 bbls
Number of Beers: 6 year-round, 6 seasonal, a variety of specialties

Staple Beers:
- » Bitter Woman IPA
- » Chief Blackhawk Porter
- » Headless Man Amber Ale
- » Rocky's Revenge (bourbon-barrel aged brown ale)
- » Stone Tepee Pale Ale
- » Three Beaches Honey Blonde

Seasonal & Specialty Beers:
- » Down 'n Dirty Chocolate Oatmeal Stout
- » Fargo Brothers Hefeweizen
- » Gemuetlichkeit Oktoberfest
- » Painted Ladies Pumpkin Spice Ale
- » Scurvy IPA with Orange Peel
- » Sheep Shagger Scotch Ale

"Brewers Gone Wild!" is a series of limited batches of "big, bold or ballsy beers." Past brews include: Who's Your Daddy? Bourbon Barrel-Aged Imperial Porter, Bitter Woman from Hell Extra India Pale Ale, HopWhore Imperial India Pale Ale, Spank Me Baby! Barley Wine-Style Ale, The Devil Made Me Do It! Imperial Oatmeal Coffee Porter, High Class Broad Imperial Brown Ale Aged in Brandy Barrels, Stickin' It To The Man Extra India Pale Ale, Dirty Old Man Imperial Rye Porter Aged in Rye Barrels, Devil Over A Barrel Imperial Oatmeal Coffee Porter Aged in Bourbon Barrels, Scurvy IPA brewed with orange peel *(now an early summer seasonal)*, Paradise by the Dashboard

Lights Doubly Blessed Cherry Porter, Bitter Woman In The Rye... an India Pale Ale brewed with rye malt, Benji's Smoked Imperial Porter Brewed with Chipotle Pepper.

Most Popular Brew: Bitter Woman IPA

Brewmaster's Fave: Bitter Woman IPA

Tours? Yes, free tours most Saturdays at 3:30 PM, but check the website for exact dates.

Samples? No, but you can buy some in the tasting room. Occasionally there is a fun beer only available on tap here.

Best Time to Go: In summer there is a beer garden; in winter you don't have anything better to do—tour breweries. Wed–Sun is when the tasting room is open: 4:30 PM to 11:00 PM Wed & Thurs; 3:00 PM to Midnight Fri & Sat; noon to 8 PM Sun. (The tasting room has additional hours in summer months.) Live music every Saturday and in summer on Fridays as well.

Where can you buy it? All over Wisconsin and in goodly portions of Minnesota, Indiana, and the Greater Chicago area.

Got food? No, but you can carry-in or have it delivered from area restaurants. (No outside beverages though! That'd be rude and insensitive.)

Special Offer: Not participating

Directions: From the 259 Exit on I-94 head south towards Lake Mills and take the first left (east) at Tyranena Park Road (Cty Hwy V). The first right after Cty Hwy A is Owen St.

The Beer Buzz: What does Brewmaster Rob love about this job? "At the end of the day, sitting down to a beer that I brewed." When Rob left his previous job, he had to sign a 5-year non-compete agreement which meant essentially he was bound for a career change. Life's little curveball worked to the benefit of the rest of us because Rob decided to open this brewery. It takes its name from a native name for the nearby lake. Settlers came up with the inventive moniker Rock Lake for the rocks along the shore and Lake Mills for the town's grist mill. For a while in the 1870s, the town tried out the name Tyranena but it was soon changed back, perhaps for spelling difficulties. Rob's favorite legend of the origin of the name is that it was given to the Ho Chunk tribe by a "foreign tribe" that had lived there before them. Could it have been the same pyramidal mound-building tribe of Aztalan down the road? Who knows?

The tasting room is decorated with some historical photos of Lake Mills and offers glassware, apparel, and samples for purchase. There's outside seating and even a gas grill that patrons can use.

Stumbling Distance: *Aztalan Inn* (920-648-3206, W6630 Hwy B at Cty Hwy Q) is a local favorite for Friday fish fries. *Carp's Landing* (920-648-3005, 103 S. Main St) boasts in-house smoked brisket and pork as well as outdoor seating and craft beer on tap. *Hering's Sand Bar* (920-648-3227,

345 Sandy Beach Rd) is only open in the summer but also offers the fish fry as well as cheese curds, with outdoor seating and a view of the sunset. Locally loved and arguably dangerous are the "sliders," yummy greasy burgers at the *American Legion Post 67 Hamburger Stand* (133 N Main St, only in summer—locals freeze them for winter). Rinse the arteries with some Tyranena products afterward*. *Town and Country Days* are the last full weekend in June and as with any great Wisconsin festival, there is a beer tent. First Saturday in October is the *Tyranena Oktoberfest Bike Ride* at the brewery, with food, live music, and… well, you know—beer.

---

* Not actual medical advice, consult a heart specialist and don't sue me.

Ale Asylum

Founded: May 2006
Brewmaster: Dean Coffey
Address: 2002 Pankratz Street • Madison, WI 53704
Phone: 608-663-3926
Website: www.aleasylum.com
Annual Production: 14,000 bbls and rising
Number of Beers: 10 to 16

Staple Beers:
  » Ambergeddon Amber Ale
  » Contorter Porter
  » Hopalicious (APA)
  » Madtown Nutbrown Ale

Rotating Beers:
  » Ballistic IPA
  » Bedlam! IPA
  » Mercy Grand Cru
  » Satisfaction Jacksin Double IPA
  » Sticky Mcdoogle (Scotch Ale)
  » Tripel Nova

At Taproom Only:
  » Bamboozleator (Doppelbock)
  » Big Slick Stout (Oatmeal Stout)
  » Diablo (Belgian Duppel)
  » Gold Digger Blonde Ale
  » Happy Ending (Belgian Abbey)
  » Hatha-Weizen (Hefeweizen)

Most Popular Brew: Hopalicious

Brewmaster's Fave: "I can't choose one of my children above the others. That'd be rude!"

Tours? Every hour on the hour from noon to 6 PM. First come, first served. Additional tours may be added on Sundays.

Samples? Of course.

Best Time to Go: Friday nights are busiest. Open Sunday–Thursday 11:00 AM to midnight; Friday–Saturday 11:00 AM to 2:30 PM.

Where can you buy it? Growlers, six-packs and cases on site. Six-packs, twelve-packs, cases and kegs are available from Madison and Milwaukee craft-beer retailers. On tap in many Madison and Milwaukee area bars.

Got food? Falbo Bros. Pizzeria pizza, sandwiches and limited light fare.

Special Offer: A free beer.

Directions: From Hwy 151/East Washington Ave, take First Street north a block to where it ends at Packers Avenue. Go right here and follow it to International Lane, the road to the airport. You'll see the brewery on the corner on your right, but you'll need to go down International to the next right (Anderson St) to get to Pankratz, your next right.

The Beer Buzz: Located just west of Dane County Regional Airport (Truax Field) is one of Madison's hottest contributors to the art of brewing. On how he started homebrewing, Brewmaster Dean offers this about his college days: "I was too poor to buy good beer and too proud to drink cheap beer." So he took matters into his own brew kit. He made a name for himself in his ten years at the now defunct Angelic Brewpub, and when he broke out on his own Dean was without limits. "Some places

have strict rules about what remains on tap. I just want to play." *Fermented In Sanity* is the motto here. The name Ale Asylum acknowledges this as a refuge to pursue the art of beer. All beers are unfiltered and unpasteurized.

From the get-go Ale Asylum was a hit and growth came rapidly. Hopalicious and Madtown Nutbrown have become near staples at area bars. In August 2012 they completed construction of this 45,000 square-foot production brewery, and their annual production capacity jumped from their current 11,000 barrels/year to a maximum capacity of 50,000 barrels/year. To ensure they wouldn't have to move again, the brewery is designed to expand an additional 85,000 square feet. Expect more seasonals with longer run times. Their previous digs in an old industrial office space was too cramped for their growing business and had to be manipulated to be a brewery; this place is specifically designed for it, straight out of the brain of Dean Coffey.

Stumbling Distance: Just north on Packers Ave is *Smoky Jon's Championship BBQ* (smokyjons.com, 2310 Packers Ave, 608-249-7427), an award-winning carry-out or casual sit-down joint. The other direction out on East Washington will take you to *The Malt House* (2609 E Washington Ave, 608-204-6258, malthousetavern.com). One of Madison's finest beer bars, it is owned by a beer judge. A great place to catch a live band is *The Crystal Corner* (www.thecrystalcornerbar.com, 1302 Williamson St, 608-256-2953). They also run 19 beers on tap including such Wisconsin greats as Capital, New Glarus, Point, Leinie's and… Old Style? They still make that??

BREW & VIEW

Beer pairs well with a lot of things, not the least of which is film. **The Majestic Theatre** in Madison (around the corner from *The Great Dane Pub and Brewery*) is typically a live music venue but also hosts DJs and theme parties. The theme here (besides beer) is cinematic gems. The Brew and View tradition started with the classic *The Big Lebowski*, which makes a return from time to time. Other classics? *Office Space, Dazed and Confused, This is Spinaltap*-you get the idea. Watch for these events! (115 King Street, majesticmadison.com, 608-255-0901)

Granite City Food and Brewery

Founded: 2006
Brewmaster: Cory O'Neel in Iowa
Address: 72 West Towne Mall • Madison, WI 53719
Phone: 608-829-0700
Website: www.gcfb.net
Annual Production: 700 bbls in each location
Number of Beers: 5 regular styles + seasonal beers and brewer's choice selections

Staple Beers:
- » Broad Axe Stout
- » Brother Benedict's Bock
- » Duke of Wellington IPA
- » Northern Light Lager
- » Wag's Wheat

Most Popular Brew: Northern Light or Bock

Brewmaster's Fave: The IPA and specialty beers

Tours? Yes, by request.

Samples? A tray for about $4.95 for eight 3-oz. samples. Also try a "2-Pull," the Northern Light/Bock blend, invented by pub patrons.

Best Time to Go: Whenever you wanna be there. While someone else is hitting the mall hard. Happy hour is 3-6 and 9-close Monday-Friday. Cheap pints on Wednesday.

Where can you buy it? Growlers on site (or any of the other 28 Granite City locations)!

Got food? Yes, a wide range (90-100) of traditional and trendy dishes with large portions.

Special Offer: A free membership to their mug club, a $10 value!

Directions: To get here get off the "Beltline" (Hwy 12-18) at Gammon Rd exit and head north. The first traffic light marks the West Towne Mall entrance on the left and Granite City is right there.

The Beer Buzz: The first Granite City restaurant and brewpub was in St. Cloud, a city famous for its granite quarries, and the chain takes its name from the town's nickname. The interior is upscale casual and done up with stonework to honor the name. A display kitchen allows you to see the food prep just as the glass window shows the brewing facility. The menu pairs beers with particular items. There are a few TVs about the place, but it's not a sports bar per se. For anyone who has been dragged to the mall to shop, this is a perfect escape. The brewpub offers an excellent mug club as well as gift cards. Daily specials are a good reason to check the website and Tuesdays and Thursdays offer $6.50 refills on their growlers! (That's an absurdly great deal.) Granite City currently has 28 locations in 11 states.

Stumbling Distance: *Capital Brewery* is just north of here in Middleton and *Vintage Brewing Co.* is one exit east off the Beltline Highway. For a superb liquor store to take some Wisconsin beer home, go south on Gammon Road to *Woodman's* grocery store. You can find a ton of craft beers plus a section that allows you to build your own six-pack.

THE GREAT DANE PUB AND BREWERY

Founded: November 1994
Brewmaster: Eric Bruseweicz
Address: 123 E Doty Street • Madison, WI 53703
Phone: 608-284-0000
Website: www.greatdanepub.com
Annual Production: 2700 bbls
Number of Beers: 17 on tap

Staple Beers:
  » BLACK EARTH PORTER
  » CROP CIRCLE WHEAT ALE
  » DEVIL'S LAKE RED LAGER (on a nitro tap)
  » EMERALD ISLE STOUT
  » LANDMARK LITE
  » MR. NATURAL'S BROWN ALE (old comic-book character)
  » OLD GLORY APA
  » PECK'S PILSNER
  » STONE OF SCONE SCOTCH ALE
  » TEXAS SPEED BUMP IPA
  » VERRÜCKTE STADT GERMAN PILS

Rotating Beers:
  » BARLEYWINE
  » A couple BELGIAN BREWS throughout the year
  » FRUIT BEERS in summer (Watermelon is one!)
  » Always two GRAVITY CASKS
  » JOHN JACOB JINGLE HEIMER SCHMIDT DUNKEL-DOPPEL-HEFE-WEIZENBOCK (ask them to say it for you really fast)
  » IRISH ALE around St. Patty's
  » OKTOBERFEST
  » SPICED Holiday Ale
  » ... *and loads of others*

Most Popular Brew: Crop Circle Wheat

Brewmaster's Fave: Verrückte Stadt German Pils

Tours? By appointment only.

Samples? Yes, a couple 2-ounce tasters, side by each, dontcha know, or sampler platters of as many 4-ounce tasters as you want for $1.50 each.

Best Time to Go: Happy hour 4-6 PM Mon-Fri plus free popcorn. When the university is in session, the place hops on weekends (and even when it's not). Sunday brunch is nice too.

Where can you buy it? On-site growlers, pub kegs, and half barrels (with 24-hour notice), but see their other locations at Hilldale and in Fitchburg (also brewpubs), at the airport, and the latest Great Dane East Side location. The Duck Blind at Madison Mallards Northwoods-League baseball games is fueled by four specially brewed Great Dane beers. In 2012 the Dane did its first limited bottles with Imperial Red Ale, available in house. And for something farther afield, find the Dane in Wausau, WI. 100+ tap accounts around the state.

Got food? Yes, and it's very popular for lunch and dinner. Full menu of soups, salads, burgers, entrees and more. The bratburger (created on a dare) is an original with bacon on a pretzel bun. Beer, brat and cheese soup is Wisconsin in a bowl. Beer bread is standard, fish and chips available, and a load of other great dishes. Friday night pilsner-battered fish fry!

Special Offer: A 10 oz. beer and all the coasters you can eat.

Directions: Head for the Capitol and follow the Capitol Loop (two streets out from the Capitol) along Doty Street where it meets King and Webster St. The Dane is on the corner. Street parking is metered until 6 PM or park in the ramp on the opposite end of the same block.

The Beer Buzz: The Great Dane has been around long enough to be a landmark in itself just off the Capitol Square in Madison, but its home is also the former Fess Hotel, built in the 1850s with an addition in 1883 and remodeled in 1901. The opening of the Dane by college buddies Rob LoBreglio and Eliot Butler saw some more remodeling in 1994 and it is now a lively joint with music, a pool hall and three bars. You'll spot the big neon Brewpub sign as you come up the hill. The Rathskeller (the basement bar) was once a stable for horses and keeps the original stone walls. Outside dining is a seasonal bonus in the beer garden where hops climb the bricks

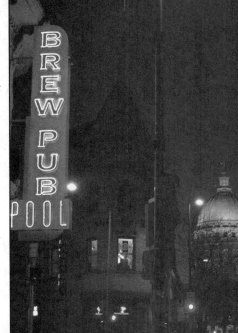

on the backside of the building. There are also some tales of spirits of the nonalcohol kind, perhaps former guests of the Fess.

But all the character of the historic building and the awesome menu aside, the beer is the crowning centerpiece of this place. On the way to the restrooms downstairs, you can pass the tanks where this magical stuff works its way up to the bars through a tangling system of tap lines Brewer Eric refers to as The Matrix. Eric has brewed at Water Street in Milwaukee and Titletown up in Green Bay. He got into the kitchen at the Dane and met Rob through a friend. He headed to Siebel Institute in Chicago, and the rest is history. The Red Lager is run through a Guinness tap (under nitrogen) which gives it that cascading foam head which can hypnotize you to drink more beer. This is brewmaster Rob LoBreglio's pride and joy and a rare beer to find on a nitro system. Expect innovative ideas from this bunch, always with an insistence on quality. The Dane now also sells Eliot Butler's Scotch Ale jerky as well as beer soap. "It'll get you clean but not necessarily sober."

Trivia note: Right across the street is a sign marking the site of Madison's first public house: Peck's Cabin.

Stumbling Distance: The *Wisconsin State Capitol* (www.wisconsin.gov, 608-266-0382) is one block from here and a definite must-see with daily free tours and a 6th floor observation deck and museum. The square itself hosts a variety of events throughout the year, but especially a Saturday morning *Farmers' Market* (exclusively local produce, cheese, meats, and other products) and Wednesday evening *Concerts on the Square* or *Jazz at 5* in summer. Based on a design by Frank Lloyd Wright, the *Monona Terrace* (www.mononaterrace.com, 608-261-4000) is also just a short walk away. *The Old Fashioned* (www.theoldfashioned.com, 23 N Pinckney St, 608-310-4545) offers an all-Wisconsin menu and 52 taps of Wisconsin beers plus a truckload in bottles. **Recommended highly!** *Capital Tap Haus Tavern* (capitaltaphaus.com, 107 State St, 608-310-1010) is a tied house for Capital's beers and does a good fish fry. And the *Rathskeller* and outdoor *Terrace* at the *UW Memorial Union* are the very heart of the community and ideal in the summer. Watch the sunset and hear free live music while drinking an assortment of Wisconsin beers on the shores of Lake Mendota. In the past, you needed to have a Union membership to buy beer; now you just sign a slip for the day and you're good to go!

The Great Dane Pub and Brewery (Hilldale)

Founded: 2006
Brewmaster: Don Vasa
Address: 357 Price Place • Madison, WI
53705 (Hilldale Mall on Midvale Blvd.)
Phone: 608-661-9400
Website: www.greatdanepub.com
Annual Production: 2500 bbls
Number of Beers: 11-12

Staple Beers:
- » Crop Circle Wheat
- » Emerald Isle Stout
- » Imperial IPA
- » Landmark Lite Lager
- » Old Glory American Pale Ale
- » Peck's Pilsner
- » Stone of Scone Scotch Ale
- » Verruckte Stadt German Pils

Rotating Beers:
- » Amber Lager (summer)
- » Barleywine
- » Bock
- » Doppelbock (winter)
- » Maibock (spring)
- » Oktoberfest
- » Pine Marten Red Ale
- » Siam Strong Pale Ale
- » ... and cask ales from downtown.

Photographs courtesy of Kristin Abraham

Most Popular Brew: Imperial IPA and Verruckte Stadt German Pils

Brewmaster's Fave: Imperial IPA or anything hoppy

Tours? By chance or appointment but always welcomed.

Samples? Yes, a couple 2-ounce tasters, side by each, dontcha know, or sampler platters of as many 4-ounce tasters as you want for $1.50 each.

Best Time to Go: Happy hour is 4-6 and offers beer discounts

Where can you buy it? On-site growlers, pub kegs, and half barrels (with 24-hour notice), but see their other locations in Fitchburg (also a brewpub), at the airport, and the original downtown location. The Duck Blind at Madison Mallards Northwoods-League baseball games is fueled by 4 specially brewed Great Dane beers. In 2012 the Dane did its first limited bottles with Imperial Red Ale, available in house. And for something farther afield, find the Dane in Wausau, WI. 100+ tap accounts around the state.

Photograph courtesy of Kristin Abraham

Got food? Yes, a full menu of soups, salads, burgers, and entrees. The bratburger (created on a dare) is an original with bacon on a pretzel bun. Beer, brat and cheese soup is Wisconsin in a bowl. Beer bread is standard, fish and chips available, and a load of other great dishes. Friday night pilsner-battered fish fry!

Special Offer: A free 10 oz. beer!

Directions: From the Beltline Highway (12/14/18/151) go north on Midvale Blvd until just before University Avenue and turn left at Heather Crest (or come south one long block south of University Avenue and turn right). The Dane is on the left corner at the next cross street right before the Hilldale Mall building.

The Beer Buzz: This brewpub was a challenge to an outdated brewing law in Wisconsin that didn't allow a brewer producing over 4,000 barrels each year to have more than two brewing locations. When the Hilldale location opened its doors in 2006 it could not serve its own brews and for a while got by on featuring other Wisconsin beers. When the law finally changed in 2007, the expected varieties of Dane brews started flowing. Brewer Don used to help out downtown and then took the reins at this place when it opened. A modest sort, Don's a great guy making some really great beer.

Abundant table seating for diners is complemented by booths in the bar area as well as tall tables and a long narrow bar-table with stools down the middle of the room in front of the bar itself. The near west side location has been a huge success and an expansion in 2009 opened up more seating including a mezzanine section and added room for pool tables, shuffleboard and foosball. Lots of big TVs pipe in sports from around the world. The Dane equation for its multiple locations can be expressed thus: similar enough that you can count on all of them for good beer and good times, different enough that you want to visit them all. Parking is on the street or in a nearby free ramp.

Stumbling Distance: *Sundance Cinemas 608* (www.sundancecinemas. com, 430 N. Midvale Blvd, 608-316-6900) in the nearby Hilldale Mall was the first of its kind in the country and shows primarily independent films. Also really close are fabulous eateries *Café Porta Alba* (cafeportaalba. com, 608-441-0202) with some true Italian wood-fired oven pizza, some of Madison's best sushi at *Sushi Muramoto* (muramoto.biz, 608-441-1090), and the tequila bar and southwestern restaurant *Pasqual's* (pasquals.net, 608-663-8226). Right down the row in front of Hilldale Mall.

BASEBALL AND A BEEYAH HEEYAH! (A BEER HERE!)

It's our national pastime, the perfect way to enjoy a summer afternoon—nostalgic, exciting, and as American as apple pie and American Idol. Beer, I mean. And it goes great with baseball, too. Wisconsin's professional baseball team is of course the Milwaukee Brewers (brewers.mlb.com) and they play in Miller Park. That's as beery as it gets. Don't be surprised to see some of New Glarus Brewing's Spotted Cow on tap there as well.

Part of the Summer Collegiate Baseball's Northwoods League, the Madison Mallards (www.mallardsbaseball.com) have The Duck Blind, a great beer garden serviced by The Great Dane out at Warner Park on North Sherman Avenue. The games are a lot of fun but don't pinch the wallet so much as the majors do. It's all you can eat and drink in the Duck Blind and around 18 beers are on tap including some Great Dane, Tyranena, and New Glarus brews.

Up in Appleton, Stone Cellar is brewing Rattler Brau (their Scotch-style ale) for the Wisconsin Timber Rattlers, a Class A minor league team of the Midwest League affiliated with the Milwaukee Brewers.

Be careful as you pass the next cup down the bleacher row. Nobody likes a spiller.

House Of Brews

Founded: 2011
Brewmaster: Page Buchanan
Address: 4539 Helegesen Drive • Madison, WI 53718
Phone: 608-347-7243
Website: www.houseofbrewsmadison.com
Annual Production: up to 960 bbls
Number of Beers: 6 on tap

Staple Beers:
  » A-Frame Amber
  » Prairie Rye
  » Standing Stone Scotch Ale

Rotating Beers:
  » Bungalow Rye Esb
  » Snug Stout
  » A variety of barrel-aged brews and various test brews along the way of others...

Most Popular Brew: A-Frame Amber

Brewmaster's Fave: Prairie Rye

Tours? Yes, best on Saturdays and best by appointment. Check the website for a schedule.

Samples? Yes, always. Get a flight of six 4-oz. beers for $6–10.

Best Time to Go: The tap room is open from 3:30 pm Tuesday-Saturday, closing around 11ish during the week, but later on weekends.

Where can you buy it? On-site growlers, kegs, and around Madison at many of the good beer bars.

Got food? Packaged snacks only, but carry-in is encouraged and there are a few menus around to order delivery.

Special Offer: A free glass of Page's beer.

Directions: Take Stoughton Road (US 51) south from East Washington Ave (or north from the Beltline Hwy) and go east at Buckeye Road. The next right is a frontage version of Stoughton Road that takes a couple turns before running parallel to US 51. Turn left on Helgesen Dr and the brewery will be on your right halfway down the block.

The Beer Buzz: Page Buchanan is the owner/head brewer of this little brewery tucked into an industrial neighborhood. While he had been brewing at home for almost 18 years, he hadn't decided to go commercial until he lost his job as a labor rep in 2009. By mid-2010 he was building his facility, and selling from his first batch on September 1, 2011 (to the awesome Madison beer bar The Malt House).

His brewhouse has hand-me-down equipment from O'so Brewery in Plover, Lake Louie's of Arena, and Central Waters of Amherst. The tap room is small with just a few tables, most made out of old barrels, and the space feels like what it was – some office space at the front of the facility. There's a dartboard, a TV, and a jukebox, and a fridge for some sodas and wine. A couple board games are lying around, but really people come here for conversation and to relax with a few beers.

Page has a couple unusual things going on here, however. The first is nearly unheard of in the USA: a CSB, Community Supported Brewery. That's right, just like that investment you can make with a CSA farmer so you get a weekly basket of vegetables. Well, this is a weekly distribution of beer! Member numbers are limited, so hurry. He also hopes to offer a few smaller brew kettles for a "brew on premises" program for aspiring brewers. "I want to be inclusive, reaching out to the community in different ways, working with local chefs," says Buchanan. In cooperation with local restaurants, he will come up with specialty brews for their menus. Not a bad start!

Stumbling Distance: The drive to *The Great Dane's East Side* location isn't long from here (876 Jupiter Dr, 608-467-1231). The liquor store at *Woodman's* grocery just off of US 51/Stoughton Rd at Milwaukee St has a killer assortment of Wisconsin microbrews if you want to put together some chilled souvenirs from your trip to town.

KARBEN4 BREWING

Founded: September 2012
Brewmaster: Ryan Koga
Address: 3698 Kinsman Blvd • Madison, WI 53704
Phone:
Website: www.karben4.com
Annual Production: 1000 barrels
Number of Beers: 5 plus seasonals

Staple Beers:
» AMERICAN AMBER
» IRISH RED
» RYE PA
» SESSION ALE
» SMOKED PORTER

Rotating Beers:
» BLACK IPA and other seasonals

Brewmaster's Fave: "They are all my kids....but in hot weather it would be our RyePA and the Irish Red in the cool weather."

Tours? Yes, sometimes randomly or by appointment.

Samples: Yes.

Best Time to Go: Hours will likely be 11 AM–midnight on Monday-Thursday; 11 AM–2 AM on Friday and Saturday; Noon–10 PM on Sunday (unless the Packers play a late game—they will have a big screen for Packers and Badgers games). Live music twice a month, something light not loud.

Where can you buy it? Locally, for starters.

Got food? Yes, likely something from a partnering local restaurateur with a thought to beer pairings.

Special Offer: Buy one beer, get one free.

Directions: Take US Hwy 151 on Madison's east side (E Washington Ave) and turn north on Hwy 51/Stoughton Rd. At the cross street Kinsman where there's a McDonald's on the right, go left and it is the first driveway on the right.

The Beer Buzz: Nature abhors a vacuum, they say. As soon as Ale Asylum moved out of this place to their new big brewery, Karben4 moved right in, even keeping some of the previous brewers' equipment (but they lost the pool table). Ryan went to school for pre-med so has a background in biology, chemistry and psychology. But life took a malty turn when he moved to Montana for a grad program in sports medicine. Another guy in his program was a brewer and needed some bottling help. Ryan started bottling for rent money. He wasn't into beer, didn't homebrew, but when he popped open an oatmeal stout on the line, he had his A-ha! moment and was hooked. "All beer experiences should be like this," he says. He finished school and picked up more responsibilities at the brewery and was soon co-brewer. Then the other guy left.

What's the best part about brewing? "The people you meet in the tap room." He met his wife at the brewery in Montana, as well as his best friend, doctor, mechanic… "You get to meet a lot of cool people." Yes, beer brings us together. Originally from Appleton, he made the move back to Wisconsin at just the right time to take over the old Ale Asylum digs.

Geeks Brewing Co. was the original name idea. Ryan has the passion of a beer geek and believes the name ought to reflect that, thus the sci-fi sounding name. In terms of brewing style, he loves the varieties of malt out there. While he's fine with a hoppy brew, he really likes looking at beer from the malt angle. He also likes to do a lot of research into a beer style and reads the culinary and cultural history of a place to influence his recipes. He plans to do some oak curing as well—no bourbon, probably Sonoma Valley stuff.

The taproom keeps its lounge feel and there's still outside seating on the patio with hops creeping up the building. Karben4 is also on the #6 bus line!

Stumbling Distance: *Dexter's* (www.dexterspubmadison.com, 301 North St, 608-244-3535) is a stellar neighborhood bar and grill with superb burgers, unbelievable garlic-chile fries and loads more, plus a rotating menu of top-notch microbrews. Dexter's lies at one corner of the *Beermuda Triangle* (see One Barrel Brewing's Stumbling Distance).

One Barrel Brewing

Founded: July 2012
Brewmaster: Peter Gentry
Address: 2001 Atwood Ave.
               Madison, WI 53704
Phone: 608-630-9286
Website: www.onebarrelbrewing.com
Annual Production: 200 bbls
Number of Beers: 12 on tap

Staple Beers:
  » Commuter Kölsch
  » Penguin Belgian IPA
  » #2 Strong Ale

Rotating Beers:
  » Around 6 constantly changing brews, plus a couple guest taps from other Wisconsin brewers

Most Popular Brew: Commuter Kölsch

Brewmaster's Fave: #2 Strong Ale

Tours? Yes, randomly and if you ask politely, but the tour can be done from the bar stool.

Samples? Yes, of anything. They do beer flights too, starting at around $4.50 for three 4-ouncers.

Best Time to Go: Closed Mondays! Packers Sundays are great, Thursdays is Commuter Night when you can get a deal on Commuter Kölsch if you came on bike (just show your helmet). The local bike guru guest bartends! Open from 11 AM on Sat-Sun, otherwise 4 PM.

Where can you buy it? Only right here. They fill growlers. A few local tap accounts in town.

Got food? Some Wisconsin tavern classics here. Pickled eggs, Braunschweiger and crackers, Fraboni's pizzas, nuts, chips, hot pretzels, piragis (bacon buns!), and Landjager. Or just carry in—it's OK!

Special Offer: A hug or the best high five you'll ever get!

Directions: From East Washington Ave (US Highway 151) go south on S. 2nd Street and then go right on Winnebago Street a half block to where it intersects Atwood Avenue. It's right there at this intersection on the corner, known as Schenk's Corners.

The Beer Buzz: As might be apparent in the name, this is a nanobrewery, brewing one barrel (two half-barrels, 31 gallons, see the index if you're measure-curious) at a time. Peter Gentry was born and raised in this neighborhood, as was his father. This is as local as you get. Gentry thought he was buying his father a brewing kit back in 2004 when he picked one up from the Wine and Hop Shop in Madison. But it turned out he loved it more. He brewed for friends at first but won the Grumpy Troll brewing challenge in 2008. From there he went on to a national competition and in 2010 his #2 Strong Ale got honorable mention in the US Beer Tasting Championship. He quit his day job in 2011 to plan this brewery that opened not long after.

Set in an old brick building that was once a cooper's shop (barrel maker, how appropriate!) and then a grocer's in the early 1900s, the brewpub has hardwood floors and exposed brick walls. Track lighting is left over from its previous occupation as an art gallery. The brew system is glassed in at the back of the bar. They brew 3-4 one-barrel batches per week, so you can expect something new every time you stop in. Jukebox playing, and a large-screen TV only unveiled for special games. Free WiFi. A jackalope on the wall.

Stumbling Distance: This is Schenk's Corners, the heart of one of Madison's old neighborhoods, and there are a number of places to eat around here. But One Barrel also touches on the *Beermuda Triangle*, a combo of three *excellent* beer bars: *Alchemy Café* (across the intersection, 608-204-7644, alchemycafe.net), *Dexter's Pub & Grill* (301 North St, 608-244-3535, dexterspubmadison.com), and *The Malt House* (2609 E Washington Ave, 608-204-6258, malthousetavern.com). The *Barrymore Theatre* is also a stone's throw down Atwood Ave offering great live music of local, national, and international acclaim.

Vintage Brewing Co.

Founded: December 2009
Brewmaster: Scott Manning
Address: 674 S Whitney Way • Madison, WI 53719
Phone: 608-204-2739
Website: vintagebrewingco.com
Annual Production: 1000 bbls
Number of Beers: 12–20

Staple Beers:
- » Better Off Red Ale
- » Flyover Pale Ale
- » Lady of the Lakes Blonde Ale
- » Scaredy Cat Oatmeal Double Stout
- » State o' Jeff Oaked IPA
- » Weiss-Blau Weissbier

Photograph courtesy
of Kristin Abraham

Rotating Beers:
- » Dedication Abbey Ale
- » Elder Skelter Elderberry Brown Ale
- » Finnish Sahti
- » Sconie Common Amber Lager
- » Smoked Scottish Ale
- » Sprucifer Winter Warmer
- » Thirty-Point Bock
- » ... and on and on

Most Popular Brew: Only time will tell.

Brewmaster's Fave: Scaredy Cat or Dedication.

Tours? Free impromptu tours nearly anytime or by appointment.

Samples? Yes, $1 per 4-oz. sample singly, or five samples for $4.25.

Best Time to Go: "Thirsty Thursdays" offer pint specials or come for real ale firkin tapping parties. Watch for Beer Enthusiast dinners on select Tuesdays (call for info). The busiest times are Friday and Saturday nights.

Where can you buy it? Served here or at Vintage Spirits and Grill, 529 University Ave, Madison.

Got food? The menu offers made-to-order, from-scratch dishes and the chef favors local ingredients with modern twists. They offer their own fine beers but also an assortment of other great brews making this a great foodie and, um, beery? destination.

Special Offer: For each book previously unsigned, $1 taster set with up to seven 4-oz. tasters of VBC beers (number of tasters depends on availability of beers) OR a FREE taster set of their handcrafted sodas (sodas are available for all ages).

Directions: From Hwy 12-14 (the Beltline) take the Whitney Way exit heading north. Cross Odana Road (the traffic lights one block away from the highway overpass) and take the next left into the parking lot of the Whitney Square strip mall. Vintage is in a stand-alone building in the lot.

The Beer Buzz: Vintage Spirits and Grill had already had good success over on University Avenue with its retro style and convivial spirit. So when JT Whitney's Brewpub closed its doors in 2009 and this location remained vacant, the family-based partnership at Vintage decided it was time not just to serve great beer but to brew it as well. Vintage aims for some class without snobbery combining a plush lounge atmosphere with some old-school brewery décor.

Scott was born and raised in Wisconsin and graduated from the University of Wisconsin-Madison. From 1997 on, his professional brewing took him out west to places in AZ, CA and NV. His brother Bryan and cousin Trent had been secretly plotting a brewpub for years with the aim of luring Scott back to the Beer State. The nefarious plan worked and Scott has

happily become his own boss and brewmaster for their family business.

Stumbling Distance: Just south of Madison off Hwy 151 is *Bavaria Sausage* (www.bavariasausage.com, 6317 Nesbitt Rd, 800-733-6695) which sells a wide variety of German and other sausages (a lot of it made in house) and much more. Fresh cheese curds are delivered here on Thursday afternoons and Friday mornings. Do mini-golf, a year-round driving range, a par 3, a climbing wall, or batting cages interest you at all? Go across the highway from here to *Vitense Golfland* (www.vitense.com, 5501 Schroeder Road, 608-271-1411).

PHOTOGRAPH COURTESY OF KRISTIN ABRAHAM

CAPITAL BREWERY

Founded: April 17, 1986
Address: 7734 Terrace Ave • Middleton, WI 53562
Phone: 608-836-7100
Website: www.capital-brewery.com
Annual Production: 28,000 bbls and climbing
Number of Beers: Up to 16 annually

Staple Beers:
  » CAPITAL DARK
  » CAPITAL PILSNER
  » HOP CREAM
  » ISLAND WHEAT ALE
  » SUPPER CLUB
  » U.S. PALE ALE
  » WISCONSIN AMBER

Rotating Beers:
  » AUTUMNAL FIRE (Doppelbock assaults Märzen, Sept 1)
  » BLONDE DOPPELOCK
  » MAIBOCK (Spring)
  » OKTOBERFEST (Aug–Oct)
  » RADLER
  » WEIZEN (Summer)
  » WINTER SKÅL and MAIBOCK (Nov–Jan)
  » various CAPITAL SQUARE SERIES beers

Most Popular Brew: Wisconsin Amber (but Supper Club commands the beer garden).

Tours? Yes. Fridays, Saturdays and Sundays—check the website for the current schedule. Reservations recommended. $5 includes the tour, 3 samples of the beers, and a 3-oz. glass to take home.

Samples? On the tour, of course.

Best Time to Go: The Bier Garten is open from May to October (weather willing) seven days a week with live music on Fridays. Check online for shorter winter hours. *Bockfest*, the last Saturday of February. Bundle up for the Bier Garten and come see the brewmaster ride a green Sinclair dinosaur to the edge of the roof and throw chubs (small fish) into the crowd of over 2,000 below (microwaved so they blow up easier—the fish, I mean). I can't make this stuff up and you can't miss it. When the Bier Garten closes for winter, head inside for the Bier Stube to keep on drinking.

Where can you buy it? Bottles—four-packs, six-packs, and 22 oz. bombers—as well as in cans. Their distribution is all over Wisconsin with a growing presence in Minnesota, Iowa, Illinois, and Florida.

Got food? No, but what the heck, have something delivered.

Special Offer: A free tour for two!

Directions: Best way to get here is from the West Beltline (Hwy 12/14 on the west side of Madison metro area). Take Exit 252, go east on Greenway Blvd to a three-way stop and go left (north) on High Point Rd just three blocks to Terrace Ave and the brewery is there on the corner.

The Beer Buzz: "We were bankrupt before the first keg was filled. And on a first name basis with collection agencies." So said former Brewmaster Kirby Nelson about the early struggles of this tremendously successful operation. Capital is more of a lager specialist (though they do make some great ales as well) which is in line with the Wisconsin tradition. Island Wheat was a return to being more dependent on local suppliers. Most of the wheat comes from Washington Island off the tip of the Door County Peninsula. Hop Cream has a local angle as well, getting hops from Gorst Valley Hops. Keep an eye open for limited releases known as Capital Square Series. These come in four-pack bottles and include Dark Doppelbock, Eternal Flame, and

Eisphyre. Also, some beers such as Fest Beer or Weizen Doppelbock are in hibernation and may whimsically reappear over the years.

The brewhouse holds two 1955 Huppman copper kettles, and the tanks are all named after Zappa songs (Big Swifty, Heavy Duty Judy, etc.). Be sure to see the trophy case sagging from the wall near the gift shop to appreciate how many awards these brews have won. Check out their website for flavor profiles of their beers. In the summer, the Bier Garten is truly one of the best places to grab a beer in the Madison area. Longtime brewmaster Kirby Nelson departed to join Wisconsin Brewing Co. in fall of 2012, and Brian Destree, who once brewed for Miller and Leinenkugel's, took over as an interim brewer.

Stumbling Distance: Just a short walk away is *The Village Green* (7508 Hubbard Ave, 608-831-9962) a homey restaurant featuring one of Madison area's best Friday fish fries. Try the grilled summer sausage and Capital on tap. *The Club Tavern* (1915 Branch St, 608-836-3773) has been around over 100 years. Live music, volleyball, great food. The Moose Burger is my fave. Look for crazily cheap beer the first day in the year that the temperature goes over 70. Make a reservation with *Betty Lou Cruises* (www.bettyloucruises.com, 608-246-3138) to eat dinner and drink Capital on Lake Mendota or Monona. *Sprecher's Restaurant & Pub* (sprecherspub.com, 1262 John Q Hammons Dr, 608-203-6545) is an independent restaurant exclusively serving Sprecher's beer.

Brewery Creek Brewpub

Founded: June 1998
Brewmaster: Jeffrey Donaghue
Address: 23 Commerce Street • Mineral Point, WI 53565
Phone: 608-987-3298
Website: www.brewerycreek.com
Annual Production: 500 bbls
Number of Beers: At least 4 but up to 8 on tap at any one time

Staple Beers:
  » Altbier
  » Amber Ale
  » Cream Ale
  » Golden Ale
  » Hefeweizen
  » Schwarzbier
  » ...basically one light, one dark and a couple in between

Rotating Beers:
  » Dark Wheat Doppelbock
  » Porter
  » Stout

Most Popular Brew: Whatever's lightest

Brewmaster's Fave: The most recent. "Imagine you had gallons of beer in your home. It wouldn't take long for you to look forward to the next one."

Tours? By appointment or by chance if he is not busy.

Samples? Yes.

Best Time to Go: Hours are tricky: Jun–Oct 23 11:30–8 PM Tues–Thurs, until 8:30 Fri–Sat, and til 3 PM on Sun. Closed Mondays. In winter only open Thurs–Sat hours, but odds are you will have the place to yourself. This is not a late-night place because that would disturb the B&B guests upstairs. Come for a pleasant afternoon or early evening.

Where can you buy it? On-site growlers.

Got food? Definitely! Very homemade meals (the owners live on site). A veggie burger with a reputation all the way back to Madison. Belgian fries,

homemade sauces and desserts, and a Friday fish fry (cod). Burgers are made with hormone-free beef. Don't miss the Brewery burger!

Special Offer: Not participating.

The Beer Buzz: The first commercial brewery was built here by John Phillips in 1835 on Brewery Creek just behind the modern brewpub. Mineral Point had two more breweries thereafter: Garden City until Prohibition came, and Terrill's Brewery. The latter was renamed "Tornado Brewery" after it was destroyed by one in 1878. It changed names once again, and ended its brewing days as Mineral Springs Brewery in the 60s. You can still see the old building on Shake Rag Street. Brewmaster Jeffrey has been a homebrewer since 1967 and when he and his wife decided they needed a change, they moved here from Minneapolis and found an 1854 warehouse with no heating, wiring, insulation or even interior walls. It was no small feat to turn this place into the charming restaurant, brewery and guesthouse we see today. If you plan to stay the night in one of the brewpub's guest rooms (recommended), be sure to call for a reservation. But they don't take dinner reservations.

Stumbling Distance: Mineral Point (www.mineralpoint.com) is loaded with art galleries, and *"Gallery Nights,"* when the stores stay open a bit later, might be a good time to come to town. *Hook's Cheese Co.* (320 Commerce St, 608-987-3259) is only open on Fridays but is world famous. Get your bleu cheese, cheddar and curds on your way through. If they are closed try the convenience store across the street—they carry Hook's products. History buffs will enjoy *Pendarvis* (www.wisconsinhistory.org/pendarvis, 608-987-2122) a Cornish miners' colony with guides in costume. Not a history buff? Visit the brewpub for a few pints first. Also, see Biking for Beer in the back of the book.

THE GRUMPY TROLL BREW PUB

Founded: 1996
Brewmaster: Mark Knoebl
Address: 105 South Second Street • Mount Horeb, WI 53572
Phone: 608-437-2739
Website: www.thegrumpytroll.com
Annual Production: 600+ bbls
Number of Beers: up to 12 on tap

Staple Beers:
- » CAPTAIN FRED AMERICAN LAGER (named after Captain Pabst)
- » ERIK THE RED
- » MAGGIE IMPERIAL IPA
- » SPETSNAZ STOUT
- » TRAILSIDE WHEAT

Rotating Beers:
- » AMNESIA BALTIC PORTER
- » CURLY (a wee bit smoky)
- » DRAGON SHIP WIT
- » GRUMPY CRIK PALE ALE
- » HEY NOW BROWN COW ALE
- » HOPPA LOPPA IPA
- » KELLER BRAU
- » SMOKY TROLL
- » SUN FLOWER FARMHOUSE ALE
- » TROLLFEST
- » Occasional Cask-Conditioned Ales

Most Popular Brew: Captain Fred, Erik the Red, Maggie Imperial IPA, and the Stout

Brewmaster's Fave: Spetsnaz Stout

Tours? By chance or by appointment.

Samples: Four-ounce samplers are $1.25 each.

Best Time To Go: Happy hours run from 4–6 PM Sun-Thurs when pints are discounted. Packer games are always a blast. Friday fish fry! There's also a mug club.

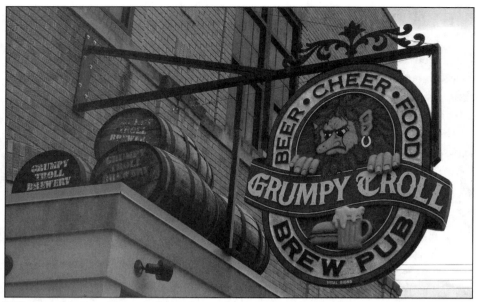

Where can you buy it? Strictly at the bar; but half-gallon growlers and 22 oz. bottles are available for carry out.

Got food? Yes, full lunch and dinner menus. Burgers with local beef, cheese curds and bar fare, but also plenty of great soups, sandwiches, salads, and dinner entrees. Check out the beer related items: beer-battered fish, beer cheese soup and stout cake! The pizzeria is a big hit and open Mon-Thurs 4 pm and Fri-Sun after 11 . They also brew their own root beer.

Special Offer: Bring your book for a signature and get a free 11 oz. glass of house beer.

Directions: Take Business Hwy 18/151 through downtown to 2nd Street. Go south and it is at the end of the first block on the left (east) side.

The Beer Buzz: Hard to imagine what makes this troll grumpy with such fine beer on hand. Originally a creamery when it was built in 1916, the building is said to be haunted. The pub name comes from this little town's Scandinavian-inherited obsession with trolls, and you will see plenty of troll-related stuff around town. Brewer Mark (who replaced Brewer Mark Duchow now at Sweet Mullets) has been brewing over 20 years and was already known around town for his great homebrewing (he won Midwest Homebrewer of the Year once) and commercial brewing at various area breweries (New Glarus, City Brewery and Sand Creek). He is a graduate of the Siebel Institute.

In 2007 at the Beverage Tasters Institute, Grumpy Troll won gold for their English Brown Ale, silver for Norwegian Frolic Wit, Curly Scotch Ale, and Trailside Wheat, and a bronze for Maggie Imperial IPA. Amnesia Baltic Porter nailed bronze at the GABF in 2007. At the United States Beer Tasting Championship in 2007 both Spetsnaz Stout and Trailside Wheat won "Best in the Midwest" in their respective categories. In 2008, Ratebeer.com listed The Grumpy Troll #40 out of the 50 Best Brewpubs in the World. Other awards include World Beer Cup gold in 2008 for Amnesia Baltic Porter, and silver for Rye Bob and bronze for Spetsnaz Stout in 2010.

Above the bar is an old copper whiskey still. Live music is hosted on occasion and a local competition among homebrewers yields a winner that will appear on tap. Upstairs you can enjoy shuffleboard, pool, and darts – the English kind with the metal tips, so pace yourself on those beers or wear Kevlar. The Grumpy Troll made the leap to serving some green beer. No, it's not a St Patty's thing. I mean solar panels on the roof generate the electricity for the brewpub. Free Wi-Fi on site and Grumpy Troll paraphernalia is for sale.

Stumbling Distance: *Tyrol Basin* (www.tyrolbasin.com, 608-437-4135) is a collection of short runs for skiers and snowboarders just down the road. Just a bit farther west on Highway 151 is *Blue Mound State Park* (4350 Mounds Park Rd., Blue Mounds, 608-437-5711) with a couple of scenic overlook towers, a swimming pool, and miles of hiking (or skiing) and mountain biking. Take a Grumpy Troll growler along for a picnic. Check out Mt. Horeb Summer Frolic in early June or the Art Fair in July.

PHOTOGRAPH COURTESY OF THE GRUMPY TROLL

Minhas Craft Brewery

Founded: 1845/2006
Brewmaster: Kristopher Kalav
Address: 1208 14th (Brewery) Ave • Monroe, WI 53566
Phone: 608-325-3191
Website: www.minhasbrewery.com
Annual Production: 300,000+ bbls
Number of Beers: 13 plus contract brews

Staple Beers:
- » 1845 Pilsner
- » Boxer Ice
- » Boxer Lager
- » Boxer Light
- » Clear Creek Ice
- » Huber Bock
- » Huber Premium
- » Lazy Mutt Farmhouse Ale
- » Minhas Light
- » Mountain Crest
- » Regal Brau
- » Swiss Amber
- » Tundra Ice
- » Malt liquors, flavored malt beverages, and many contract brews.

Most Popular Brew: Boxer Lager

Brewmaster's Fave: Huber Bock

Tours? Tours are offered Mon at 11 AM, Tues–Thurs at 1 PM, and Fri 1 PM and 3 PM, Sat–Sun at 11 AM, 1 PM and 3 PM. Make a reservation for large groups (12 or more) at 608-325-3191. The price is $10.00 for ages 13 and up and includes a Minhas Craft Brewery Gift Pack with several bottles of beer and Blumers Soda and other branded gifts.

Samples? Yes! (and Blumers sodas too. Blueberry Cream is my favorite!)

Best Time to Go: No time better than any other. Busier in summer.

Where can you buy it? Minhas products are in 16 states as far east as New York, as far west as Nevada, and north into Canada, with the core market being the Midwest.

Special Offer: A free pint glass.

Directions: If you are coming from the west on Hwy 11 take West 8th Street heading east (right) until 14th Ave then go right (south). From the east take Hwy 59 (6th Street) west to 15th Ave, turn left (south) to 12th St then hop a block right (west) to 14th Ave and take a left (south) to the brewery a block away. Coming in on 81 you will hit 8th Street and follow the rest of the

Hwy 11-from-west directions. Hwy 69 will hit 6th St—from there use the from-the-east directions. It's not as bad is it sounds; Monroe is a nice grid and streets are numbered: Streets run east-west, Avenues north-south. If lost, come on, men, the ladies won't mind if you stop for directions for a change.

The Beer Buzz: This is the oldest continuously running brewery in Wisconsin (older even than the state itself!) and the second oldest in the US. And recently it became the tenth largest brewery in the nation. That's impressive stuff. One of my first beer memories was a dusty case of Huber Beer empties which sat in our root cellar for much of the 1970s when I was a child. There's a fifty-cent deposit we can never get back! This is that case's birthplace. The brewery switched hands a few times and was known as The Blumer Brewery (now the name of the gourmet sodas produced here) when Bavarian-born Joseph Huber began working here in 1923. The company survived Prohibition with a non-alcoholic beer, Golden Glow, and in the end Huber organized an employee stock buyout which saved the brewery. In 1947, the brewery took his name. In 1960, it started producing Berghoff for a restaurant of the same name in Chicago. Former Pabst executives bought the company from Fred Huber in 1985, and some bad corporate shenanigans led to the near closing of the brewery and the Augsburger label being sold off to Stroh's (Stevens Point Brewery has since picked it up and we can drink it once again). Fred Huber bought the brewery back and with the help of the success of Berghoff beers and some other contract brewing the brewery stayed alive. In 2006, Huber was bought by Canadian entrepreneur Ravinder Minhas and took on its new name. The beer continues to flow and Lazy Mutt, Boxer, and Huber Bock are the flagship brews. They continue to brew Berghoff brands as well.

Stumbling Distance: Founded in 1931, *Baumgartner's Cheese Store & Tavern* (1023 16th Ave, 608-325-6157), on the historic central square, is Wisconsin's oldest cheese store and a must-see. They serve local beer with their sandwiches. You are definitely in Wisconsin. This is one of the only places you will ever find a limburger and onion sandwich. Feeling bold and invincible? Just ask for a sample of the stuff. There are those who love it. To see how cheese is made, call and make an appointment at *Franklin Cheese Factory* (7256 Franklin, 608-325-3725), one of the last remaining cooperatives in the state. Tours are personal and free; best between 8 and 11 AM, but not on Sunday or Wednesday. *Turner Hall* (www.turnerhallof-monroe.org, 1217 17th Ave, 608-325-3461) is a 1938 Swiss Emmental-style chalet, and represents the strong Swiss heritage of the town. Pop in for some local and traditional food in a real rathskeller.

New Glarus Brewing Co.

Founded: June 1993
Brewmaster: Dan Carey
Address: Hilltop Brewery, 2400 State Hwy 69 • New Glarus, WI 53574
Phone: 608-527-5850
Website: www.newglarusbrewing.com
Annual Production: 79,000 bbls
Number of Beers: 7 year round, 3-5 seasonals, 2-3 unplugged

Staple Beers:
- » Fat Squirrel
- » Moon Man
- » Raspberry Tart
- » Spotted Cow
- » Two Women
- » Wisconsin Belgian Red

Rotating Beers:
- » Back Forty Bock
- » Black Top
- » Cabin Fever Honey Bock
- » Crack'd Wheat
- » Dancing Man Wheat
- » Road Slush Oatmeal Stout
- » Staghorn Octoberfest
- » Stone Soup
- » Totally Naked

…but this list itself rotates each year! So many beers: Uff-da Bock, Hop Hearty Ale (IPA), Hometown Blonde Pilsner, Norsky (maibock), Solstice (hefeweizen), Coffee Stout, Snowshoe Ale (copper ale), Yokel (unfiltered lager), Copper Kettle (dunkelweiss), Apple Ale, the list can and does go on! Watch for R&D beers and the "Thumbprint" series (see below in The Beer Buzz). Check the website for current beers.

Most Popular Brew: Spotted Cow

Brewmaster's Fave: "I don't have a favorite beer. That's like asking a parent which is his favorite child! Secondly, beer is a food and I never limit myself to one food. I enjoy everything from an American Style Lager (like our Totally Naked) to a sour brown ale (like ours) and everything in between.

When I travel, I NEVER drink beer from the big brewers. Fresh, locally brewed beer is the way to go! One must be willing to experiment."

Tours? Yes, a free self-guided audio tour with handheld coded listening devices is available daily from 10–4 at the Hilltop Brewery. Tours have moved to the new facility meaning the Riverside facility is closed to the public. However, hard-hat tours of the older brewhouse are still available on Fridays at 1:00 PM for $20 and with prior arrangements. These are led by a brewer and end with a beer and cheese tasting. They book up long in advance!

Samples? Three 3-oz. samples and a souvenir glass for about $4. Pints are also available with the purchase of a pint glass designed by Deb (look for the little Wisconsin in the bottom). Some specialty beers are on draft here.

Best Time to Go: Open daily from 10–4.

Where can you buy it? 4-pack and 6-pack bottles, 750 ml bottles, and cases only in Wisconsin. On site including bottles, cases, and barrels. Spotted Cow is pretty popular on tap throughout the state as well. Single bottles of R&D (Randy and Dan) beers are available only at the brewery.

Got food? No.

Special Offer: A freebie on that sample deal above.

Directions: Head south of New Glarus on Highway 69 and watch for the entry on the left. You will see the brewhouse up on the hill but the road goes east first and then comes up the backside of the hill to give you that going-through-the-country-to-visit-a-farmhouse feel. (Intentional!) The Riverside facility is at the north end of town where Highway 69 meets County Highway W.

The Beer Buzz: There are, of course, brewers with multiple brewery locations, but this one has two in the same little Wisconsin town. Deborah Carey is the first woman to be the original founder of a brewery in the US. She is a native of our dear state of Wisconsin and an entrepreneur extraordinaire. Add her husband Dan, a superb brewmaster, and there really is no way they could have failed. Dan did his apprenticeship in Bavaria, studied at the Seibel Institute in Chicago, and earned the Master Brewer diploma from the Institute of Brewing in London. His beer and their brewery have awards all over the place. Dan used to install brewery equipment and several of the Wisconsin microbrewers have a story or two about him. His work at Anheuser-Busch pushed him to do his own thing, and we can all be thankful that Deborah made that possible. The original "Riverside" facility is a story itself with its 1962 vintage Huppmann brewery rescued from oblivion in Selb, Germany, purchased for a ridiculously low price, and hauled halfway round the world to find its new home in a Swiss town in a beer state.

In June 2009, the Careys opened their $20 million expanded brewing facility on a hilltop at the south end of town. This is now where the big work goes on but the Riverside brewery still does smaller specialty batches. Check out Dan's "Thumbprint" series of small, very limited (and typically one-off) batches of beers that he is let loose on. Smoked Rye Bock, Sour Brown Ale, Cherry Stout are some of the past creations. Look for the bottles with the red foil tops. These may never repeat, so if you miss one of these adventurous brews, you may be sorry! The R&D (Randy and Dan) beers are only available at the brewery. (Randy Thiel is the Laboratory Manager.) The hospitality center underwent more design upgrades in 2012 and a look of historic ruins graces the hilltop.

Stumbling Distance: New Glarus (www.swisstown.com) has a strong Swiss heritage and you can see it in the style of the buildings and the abundance of fondue. The *New Glarus Hotel Restaurant* (www.new-glarushotel.com, 100 6th Ave, 800-727-9477) is arguably the place for that melted cheesy (and also chocolatey) Swiss tradition. Eat other Swiss specialties in the balcony dining room of this landmark from 1853. *New Glarus Primrose Winery* (226 2nd St, 608-527-5053, daily May–Dec; Thurs–Mon Jan–Apr) offers free tastings. *Puempel's Olde Tavern* (www.puempels.com, 18 6th Ave, 608-527-2045) is one of the oldest taverns in New Glarus with folk art murals and the original back bar and ice box. New Glarus beer is on tap!

Potosi Brewing Company

Founded: First in 1852, again in 2008
Brewmaster: Steve Buszka
Address: 209 South Main St • Potosi, WI 53820
Phone: 608-763-4002
Website: www.potosibrewery.com
Annual Production:1200 bbls
Number of Beers: 8-10 on tap, 25 per year

Staple Beers:
- » Good Old Potosi Beer
- » Potosi Czech-Style Pilsener
- » Potosi Pure Malt Cave Ale
- » Snake Hollow IPA
- » (also Princess Potosa Root Beer)

Rotating Beers:
- » American Porter
- » Belgium Wit
- » Harvest Ale (uses on-site hops)
- » Holiday Lager Bock Beer
- » Oatmeal Stout
- » Pumpkin Beer
- » Scotch Ale
- » Steamboat Shandy
- » Tangerine IPA
- » Various barrel-aged beers

Brewmaster's Fave: The one he is drinking. He is partial to any of the IPAs.

Tours? Yes, by appointment. Remember the National Brewery Museum is here too: open 10–6 with a $5 entry fee.

Samples? Yes, a flight of six 5 oz. beers is $7.50.

Best Time to Go: The restaurant is open daily from 11 AM–9 PM. Look for live music on Saturdays in the beer garden in season.

Where can you buy it? Besides on-site growlers and bottles in the gift shop, it is distributed statewide and parts of IL.

Got food? Yes, a Wisconsin Supper Club menu—steaks, chicken, ribs, seafood—and the entrees come with two sides. Check out the beer cheese soup with Cave Ale, smoked Gouda, and roasted red peppers or the Cave Ale-boiled bratwurst.

Special Offer: A free pint of their beer.

Directions: Come into Potosi on Hwy 133 from the west or east. Coming from the east the brewery is on the right side of the road to the west side of Potosi across from the giant cone-top beer can. Hard to miss. If coming from Platteville consider taking County Rd O which is more direct but curvy and scenic.

The Beer Buzz: Potosi is home to the world's largest cone-top beer can. The town also has the longest Main Street in the world and it goes right past the old 1852 brewery building which is home to the National Brewery Museum. But what's a brewery museum without beer? Steve Zuidema of the former Front Street Brewery in Davenport, Iowa started the brewing again at Potosi, and then Steve Buszka took over. Steve (the new one) spent 13 years as brewmaster with Bells in Kalamazoo in Michigan and some time at Liquid Manufacturers in Brighton, Michigan, before joining Potosi. Other than the occasional lager, the brews are ales—faster to ferment—and are approximations of the traditional Potosi brews—Good Old Potosi and Holiday Bock. Potosi Brewery also makes its own root beer, so if beer is not your thing, there's something else to sample on a brewery tour. Besides being poured at the bar, Potosi beer is sold in 6-pack bottles, 22 oz. bottles, half-gallon "growlers," and kegs.

In making beer, the quality is, of course in the ingredients, and the first matter is the water. Many of the breweries of old were built around or on top of artesian wells and natural springs. Potosi is no exception. The water still rushes out of the ground into the old brewery pond behind the beer garden. The flow is so overwhelming that years ago it would get into the brewhouse and collect in puddles on the floor. Remodeling included an overflow pipe which diverts some of the spring water, and you can see it rushing beneath a piece of plate glass in the floor. Potosians Gary David, his son Tyler, and his father Marvin—three generations of woodworkers—created the beautiful handcrafted bar. The tables around the room are made with the cypress of the old fermentation tanks. As the brewery ad once asked, "Have you had your Good Old Potosi today?"

Stumbling Distance: Hardly much of a stumble, but right inside the same structure is the *National Brewery Museum* and the Great River Road Visitor Center. For a roadside attraction, check out the *Dickeyville Grotto* (www.dickeyvillegrotto.com, 305 W Main St, Dickeyville, 608-568-3119) a collection of shrines both religious and patriotic built by a priest in the 1920s using stone, mortar and all sorts of eye catching little objects. Watch Potosi for the annual Catfish Festival in August, the Potosi Brewfest at the end of August, and the Potosi Bicycle Tour in September.

THE NATIONAL BREWERY MUSEUM

Like any good Wisconsin boy, I collected beer cans when I was young. It was a veritable rite of passage to acquire all the Schmidt cans with their varying pictures, and a must for any collection was the Pabst Blue Ribbon beer can with the dawn-of-the-pull-tab message, "No Opener Needed." You were a hero in my neighborhood if you found one of the old bottle-can hybrids first introduced to the market by Milwaukee's Jos. Schlitz Brewing known as a cone-top. Potosi Wisconsin offers the opportunity to see the World's Largest Cone-top, in fact, but more importantly Potosi is also home to the National Brewery Museum.

The Potosi Brewery opened in 1852 and made a long run until 1972. The brewery that once produced Good Old Potosi lay in ruins and by the 1990s trees were growing through the roof, but locals had a plan to revive some of the town's heritage. What if they restored the old brewery and started brewing again. Better yet, what if that restored building was a tourist attraction?

Just so happens that the American Breweriana Association wanted a museum location to display the amazing collections of their members. Breweriana—collectible beer memorabilia and not a bad name for your first-born daughter I might add—ranges from cans and tap handles to beer signs and rare lithographs. Where would such a brewing tribute make its home? Milwaukee? Nope. St. Louis? No way. How about Potosi, Wisconsin, population 711?

How did that happen? Well, Potosi threw their bid in and the ABA made the rounds in 2004 to hear the proposals and see the sites. Remember the forest through the roof of the old brewery? It seemed as if their chances were slim indeed, but after the ABA members sneaked a peek at the building, the next day they said Yes. The reason for that was the brand-spanking new firehouse. They believed that if little Potosi could provide such a facility for their volunteer fire department and rescue squad, they could redo the brewery.

What's to see here? A vintage Pabst lithograph print worth $15,000. Rare character steins from the 1920s and 30s—even some of Mickey Mouse and Donald Duck—tap handles, serving trays, clocks, calendars, posters and even oil paintings fill the rooms. Watch vintage beer commercials and documentaries about the brewing process on a few video monitors. Another room holds a research library with information on nearly all of the American breweries that ever existed. On the ground floor is a transportation museum and an interactive interpretive center for Wisconsin's segment of the Great River Road Scenic Byway (a really lovely roadtrip all by itself with local beer both here and up in La Crosse). An old lagering cave is viewable behind a glass wall, and a gift shop offers all sorts of Wisconsin paraphernalia and a selection of locally produced cheeses, wines, syrup, honey, and beer.

I highly recommend a visit and when you are done, have a meal and a Good Old Potosi in the brewpub !

Entry to the Great River Road Interpretive Center and Transportation Museum is free. The brewery museum charges $5. (www.potosibrewery. com, 608-763-4002, 209 S. Main St., Potosi)

Directions: Potosi is located on the edge of the Mississippi River in the southwestern corner of Wisconsin on the Great River Road Scenic Byway (www.wigreatriverroad.org). Come into Potosi on Hwy 133 from the west or east. Coming from the east the museum is on the right side of the road to the west side of Potosi across from the giant cone-top beer can.

Double your fun and visit Potosi during its annual catfish festival, the second full weekend in August, when more than 2,300 pounds of fish are fried.

Corner Pub

Founded: 1996
Brewmaster: Pete Peterson
Address: 100 Main St, Reedsburg 53959
Phone: 608-524-8989
Email: cornerpb@mwt.net
Annual Production: up to 100 bbls
Number of Beers: 7 or 8 on tap at a time

Staple Beers:
» APA
» Cream Ale
» Dry Stout
» Milk Stout
» Old Gold Lager
» Porter
» Red Dot India Pale Ale
» Smoked Porter

Rotating Beers:
» Bock (winter)
» Dill Pickle (an APA with dill and garlic)
» Mint APA
» Oktoberfest (fall)
» Weiss (summer)
» and some bourbon-barrel beers (Scotch Ale)

Most Popular Brew: Porter or Red Dot IPA

Brewmaster's Fave: Red Dot IPA

Tours? By chance.

Samples? Nope.

Best Time to Go: Is there *ever* a bad time to go? Piano music on Friday nights during dinner, and piano luncheon on Tuesdays. Butter Festival in June recognizes Reedsburg as one of the world's largest producers.

Where can you buy it? Right here, or fill up a growler to go.

Got food? Good hearty pub fare. Blackened burgers are not something you see often and all burgers are fresh hand patties. Deep-fried local curds are in the house! Fish fry every Wednesday and Friday.

Special Offer: Not participating

Directions: Hwys 33 and 23 run right through town as Main St. Corner Pub is on the corner (oddly enough) at the first block of E Main St.

The Beer Buzz: This little two-barrel brewhouse is what microbrewing is all about—local beer, handcrafted, nothing glitzy or overdone. A small-town humility and a product worth some pride. Pete started homebrewing with a buddy of his in 1995 and moved it into his EndeHouse Brewery and Restaurant in 1996. In 2002, Pete brought his brewing into the current location. He enjoys the modest production and this is as unpretentious a place as you'll find. Local pastries and muffins are for sale by the door. Sports banners hang from the ceiling and four TVs pipe in the important games. Live music is hosted occasionally on a small stage. The popcorn at the bar is free and comes with the caveat: "Can't always guarantee fresh-ness." Food's good, people are friendly, and the beer is quite fine as well. In 2008 some regional flooding swamped the brewhouse and for a while the equipment was out on the sidewalk and beer was on hold. They got through it. Check out the mural on the side of the building dedicated to the history of hops growing in the area. If you like a little smokiness to your beer, do NOT miss Pete's Smoked Porter—one of my personal favorites.

Stumbling Distance: Just a couple blocks away is the start of the state's "400" bike trail which connects up to the Elroy-Sparta Trail. Check out the Beer, Boats and Bikes section for a pedaling-for-beer idea. Reedsburg is famous for its antiques shops, and there are several in town. Wisconsin Dells is not far down the road and *Devil's Lake State Park* is definitely not to be missed with its rocky outcroppings from where the glacier stopped in the last Ice Age. Fall colors are notable there. Over 60 varieties of cheese—including fresh curds—are waiting to be eaten twelve minutes northwest of Reedsburg at *Carr Valley Cheese Co.* in nearby LaValle (www. carrvalleycheese.com, S3797 Cty Hwy G, LaValle, 608-986-2781). Over 100 awards have been taken worldwide by this little cheesemaker.

1865   HOPS BOOM & BUST   1868

FURTHERMORE BEER

Founded: June 9 (*my* birthday too!), 2006
Brewmaster: Aran Madden
Address: P.O. Box 776 • Spring Green, WI 53588
Phone: 608-588-3300
Website: www.furthermorebeer.com
Annual Production: 1800 bbls
Number of Beers: 7 and more to come

Staple Beers:
>   » FATTY BOOMBALATTY (BIG DUMB BELGIAN or HOPPY BELGIAN BLONDE)
>   » FURTHERMORE PROPER (light-bodied English-style ale specially brewed for American Players Theatre)
>   » KNOT STOCK PALE ALE (with fresh black pepper)

Rotating Beers:
>   » FALLEN APPLE (a fermented mixture of fresh pressed cider and dairyland cream ale, made with milk sugar, not corn)
>   » MAKEWEIGHT (high-octane blend of 3 pale ales)
>   » OSCURA (Mexican lager with coffee)
>   » THERMO REFUR (made with… excuse me? Beets??)
>   » THREE FEET DEEP STOUT (with peat-smoked malt, reminds Aran of the smell of Ireland)

Most Popular Brew: Fatty Boombalatty

Brewmaster's Fave: "Knot Stock is the one-of-a-kind beer that gave me confidence to start my own brewing. Fallen Apple is a fun alternative to the usual harvest beers."

Tours? No place to go yet! (But see the Shitty Barn Sessions)

Samples? No place to serve them!

Best Time to Go: Whenever they finally get a location!

Where can you buy it? At American Players Theatre, bars and retail outlets in Spring Green, Madison, Milwaukee and really all throughout the state. Plus Twin Cities liquor stores, several Madison area bars and restaurants, and even some outlets in Pennsylvania. Could Chicago be next? (Check the website for an updated list).

The Beer Buzz: Aran started homebrewing in 1993, went to the American Brewers Guild, and then took his first job in 1997 at a microbrewery in Pittsburgh. Any new brewer sees the failure of another microbrewery as an opportunity: used equipment. But Aran saw it as a lesson. He didn't want to jump in so deep, so fast, and risk failure. So initially they have been brewing at Sand Creek in Black River Falls and evaluating site options in Spring Green. And as their production has grown they may start brewing at Milwaukee Brewing Co.'s 2nd Street Brewery. As for getting their own setup, it's simply a matter of time.

Aran's Knot Stock is a bit unusual perhaps, but he insists on being different. "For us to make just another amber it's like Who cares? There are a lot of beers out there—you may as well make it exciting. Don't give me the same old same old." The name Furthermore alludes to that, going beyond what's out there. If any of the recipe ingredients sound a little unusual, a taste will likely make you a believer. Check the website periodically to see if they found a home yet. Meanwhile, get thee to a liquor store or local pub. Also, watch their website because Furthermore is on the road a lot making appearances at a variety of tastings and special events.

Stumbling Distance: *American Players Theatre* (www.americanplayers.org, 5950 Golf Course Rd, 608-588-2361) is an open air theatre in the woods outside Spring Green. From June to early October each year they put on some of the best Shakespeare (and a few other select classics) you're likely to find anywhere. From Hwy 14 four miles west of Arena, head south on Cty Hwy C two miles until Golf Course Rd. Pack a picnic (don't worry about bug spray, APT provides that) and settle in with a bottle of Proper as the players strut and fret their hour upon the stage.

Music In A Shitty Barn: One great way to enjoy a Furthermore beer and some live music is to attend one of the many Shitty Barn Sessions. These live music events in an old barn remove the stage and put the performers up close and personal with the audience. Beer and wine are served, but despite the potty-mouth name, the events are totally family friendly. Tickets are required and popular acts sell out fast. Shows can occur multiple times per week and the season runs from June through October. (506 E. Madison St, Spring Green; shittybarnsessions.com) Also don't miss the annual Shitty Barn Party in October which is unticketed and maybe a little bit crazy.

Gray's Tied House

Founded: October 2006
Brewmaster: Fred Gray
Address: 950 Kimball Lane • Verona, WI 53593
Phone: 608-845-2337
Website: www.graystiedhouse.com
Number of Beers: 12

Staple Beers:
- » Bully Porter
- » Busted Knuckle Irish Ale
- » Gray's Light
- » Honey Ale
- » Oatmeal Stout
- » Rathskeller Amber
- » Rock Hard Red, a 'malternative'
- » Wisco Wheat

Rotating Beers:
- » Coffee Stout
- » Maibock
- » Pale Ale
- » ...and more

Most Popular Brew: Honey Ale or Rathskeller Amber

Brewmaster's Fave: Oatmeal Stout

Tours? Yes, on request and by appointment.

Samples? Yes, sample platters are on the menu.

Best Time to Go: After work or Sat/Sun during big games. Open daily 11 to close with happy hour from 3–6 Mon–Thurs.

Where can you buy it? , but check out Gray Brewing in Janesville as well.

Got food? Yes, a full menu with plates ranging from $8-22.

Special Offer: A free pint!

Directions: The brewpub/eatery is located just off of Hwy 151 at Verona. From Exit 79 take Old PB toward town and turn left onto Whalen Rd. It's behind the BP gas station.

The Beer Buzz: The Gray family has a long history of brewing, but it has only been recently that they have returned to beer after using soda to survive Prohibition. This restaurant and microbrewery was a new venture and has been very successful. The name is from a term used back when breweries had taverns that were obliged to sell only that brewery's beer. The 450-seat restaurant has a menu featuring a little bit of something from various regions of the U.S. including New England and New Orleans, and serves it up in a wood building with a Western touch to it. Two outdoor patios make up the beer garden which has portable heaters and a bonfire pit to extend the Wisconsin dine-outside season a bit. Expect acoustic guitar music inside and a fireplace lounge. Friday fish includes cod, walleye, and bluegill (beer battered and baked). The menu serves everyone from vegans to serious carnivores and includes beer cheese soup, a Reuben with amber ale sauce, hand-battered local cheese curds, and wood-fired oven pizzas. A private bar upstairs makes the Tied House a good place for parties, and the thirteen large-screen TVs bring in crowds on game days.

While the staple beers are shipped up here from the Janesville brewery, the specialty beers are brewed .

Stumbling Distance: Choco-holics won't want to skip *Candinas Chocolatier* (www.candinas.com, 2435 Old PB, Verona, 800-845-1554, Mon–Sat 10–5) where Swiss-trained Markus Candinas makes divine assortments that have been nationally recognized. *Edelweiss Cheese Shop* (edelweisscheeseshop.com, 202 W Verona Ave, 608-845-9005, open daily) sells the master work of the master cheesemaker from Monroe, Bruce Workman, plus other cheese, local beers, and wines. Just farther up the road toward Madison is *Bavaria Sausage Inc.* (www.bavariasausage.com, 6317 Nesbitt Rd, Fitchburg 53719, 608-271-1295, Mon–Fri 8–5, Sat 8–1) which makes a whole variety of outstanding sausages and sells over 100 different cheeses, including fresh cheese curds. From Hwy 151 just south of Madison turn west on Cty Hwy PD and a quick left onto Nesbitt Road heading south. See Gray's Tied House in the Biking for Beer section at the back of the book as well.

WISCONSIN BREWING CO.

Founded: June 2013
Brewmaster: Kirby Nelson
Address: 1079 American Way • Verona, WI
Phone:
Website: www.wisconsinbrewingcompany.com
Annual Production: Expecting to start with 50,000 bbls!
Number of Beers: Expect many styles, both staple beers and seasonals

Tours? Yes, but check the website for current times

Samples? Yes, of course!

Best Time to Go: Any time that beer garden is open. Watch for live music events.

Where can you buy it? Only in Wisconsin.

Got food? No, but it is food friendly and one can cater in for private events.

Special Offer: A free sample of their beer

Directions: From US-151 take exit 79 and go south on County Highway PB. American Way is the second left (east) and the brewery is on your left here in Verona Technology Park.

The Beer Buzz: News of this brewery came as a bit of a surprise. Kirby Nelson had been with Capital Brewery since day one back in 1986 and announced his departure in October 2012. He joins this endeavor with former Capital president and founder of this brewery, Carl Nolen. Unlike the typical startup brewery which usually gets rolling with a modest amount of beer, this $3.75 million project expects to have a capacity for beer that will rank it among the biggest craft breweries in the state. Phase 2 is already being talked about for 2016 and would bring the production capacity up over 150,000 barrels. This is some serious kind of big. The brewery is a 23,000 square-foot facility on five acres of land in an industrial park in Verona. Along with a tasting room, the brewery will have an outdoor beer garden. To one side is a scenic pond. Thirsty hikers are going to like this: the Ice Age National Scenic Trail passes right by the brewery.

Brewmaster Kirby is originally from Racine and made his reputation at Middleton's Capital Brewery over the years, generally leaning toward lagers in his style preferences. The plan here is to offer quite a diverse assortment of brews and one expects Kirby is going to quickly build a following for this place as he did in his previous position.

Stumbling Distance: The Verona Segment of the Ice Age Trail starts at the Ice Age Junction site off County Highway PD, heads south through Badger Prairie County Park, passes under East Verona Avenue and ends in Prairie Moraine County Park not far from the brewery. (Find this hike in detail in *60 Hikes Within 60 Miles of Madison*.) Also, the Military Ridge Trail isn't far away for bikers (See Biking for Beer in the back of the book). Choco-holics must visit *Candinas Chocolatier* (www.candinas.com, 2435 Old PB, Verona, 800-845-1554, Mon–Sat 10–5) where Swiss-trained Markus Candinas makes divine assortments that have been nationally recognized. *Edelweiss Cheese Shop* (edelweisscheeseshop.com, 202 W Verona Ave, 608-845-9005, open daily) sells the master work of the master cheesemaker from Monroe, Bruce Workman, plus other cheese, local beers, and wines.

Moosejaw Pizza & Dells Brewing Co.

Founded: 2002
Brewmaster: Jamie Martin
Address: 110 Wisconsin Dells Parkway South • Wisconsin Dells, WI 53965
Phone: 608-254-1122
Website: www.dellsmoosejaw.com
Annual Production: 1000 bbls
Number of Beers: 25 annually, 10 on tap

Staple Beers:
  » Dells Pilsner
  » Golden Lager
  » Honey Ale (brewed with pure Wisconsin honey)
  » Kilbourn Hop Ale (an APA with local hops!)
  » Raspberry Crème Ale
  » Rustic Red Ale

Rotating Beers:
  » Apple Ale
  » Apricot Ale
  » Betty's Breakfast Stout
  » Blonde Bock
  » Dunkel Lager
  » English Brown Ale
  » Milk Stout
  » Nitro Stout
  » Oak Aged Porter
  » Oaktoberfest
  » Pumpkin Spice Ale
  » Stand Rock Bock
  » Weiss Bier
  » Wisconsin Wheat Ale
  » Wyatt's Barleywine

Most Popular Brew: Rustic Red Ale

Brewmaster's Fave: Betty's Breakfast Stout and Wyatt's Barleywine

Tours? Yes, by appointment or by chance.

Samples: Yes, $8 for 6, $12 for 10 (5 oz. beers)

Best Time to Go: Any time you're thirsty or hungry. Autumn Harvest Fest in October is a family friendly festival with a craft fair, farmer's market, hayrides and the like. "Dells on Tap" is the microbrewfest portion of this event featuring around 25 Wisconsin brewers and over 100 microbrews along with live entertainment.

Where can you buy it? Growlers and some bottles , some Dells resorts/pubs on tap.

Got food? Oh yeah, their specialty is in their name! (Look for the giant moose sprawled on the roofs of their delivery cars.) They also have Beer Bread (Honey Ale) and Beer & Cheese soup (Amber Ale). Fantastic Friday Fish Fry. Check the website for printable coupons..

Special Offer: Not participating.

Directions: From I-90/94 take Exit 89 (Hwy 23) and go east and it will be in your right. Or from I-90/94 take Exit 92 (Wisconsin Dells Parkway) and head north and it will be on your left.

The Beer Buzz: This is not your typical tavern, and just walking in the front door ought to make you stop and simply take it in a bit. Designed like a giant backwoods lodge, the three-story, three-bar restaurant seats 500 and is laden with more game mounts than Hemingway could have shaken an elephant rifle at, including giant moose heads and chandeliers

fashioned out of antlers. The name comes from Moosejaw, Canada, where, during Prohibition, Al Capone and his gang of "hooch" runners used tunnels to bring booze into the US. If the decor isn't enough to please your eye, the gleaming 15-barrel copper-clad brewhouse upstairs should be.

Jamie Martin is one of only two female head brewers in the state (see Thirsty Pagan in Superior) and she's been around a good while now. It was her college professor in biotech who suggested she look into brewing beer. She is whipping out the suds and making a killer APA—actually a WPA, Wisconsin pale ale (Kilbourn) made with locally grown hops! This is a pretty large-scale operation for a brewpub, and Jamie keeps the copper tanks polished and purring. Her two favorite beers are named after her two favorite people (her kids).

Stumbling Distance: Wisconsin Dells is the center of Wisconsin tourism and combines resort town with natural wonder. *Noah's Ark America's Largest Waterpark* (www.noahsarkwaterpark.com, 608-254-6351) and a whole assortment of water park attractions are huge in summer, and many hotels have *indoor* water parks that rival the outdoor brethren. *Original Wisconsin Ducks* (www.wisconsinducktours.com, 608-254-8751) uses reborn WWII amphibious craft to run tours of the river and its awesome landscape. Odd museums, souvenir shops, shows, parks, restaurants, and casinos—the Dells can fill its own guidebook. Grab a beer at Moosejaw while you decide where to start stumbling.

Port Huron Brewing Co.

Founded: 2011
Brewmaster: Tanner Brethorst
Address: 805 Business Park Road • Wisconsin Dells, WI 53965
Phone: 608-253-0340
Website: www.porthuronbeer.com
Annual Production: 1,500 bbls
Number of Beers: 9–10

Staple Beers:
> » Alt Bier
> » Hefeweizen
> » Honey Blonde
> » Porter

Rotating Beers:
> » Bock
> » Kölsch
> » Oatmeal Stout
> » Oktoberfest
> » Pale Ale

Most Popular Brew: Honey Blonde

Brewmaster's Fave: "You can't ask me that! What day is it? All of them!"

Tours? Yes, by appointment.

Samples: Yes, 4–6 beers in a flight for about $4-6

Best Time to Go: Tap room is open Friday 3–9, Saturday 2–9, and watch for Wednesday–Thursday to be added.

Where can you buy it? Bottled six-packs and draft accounts can be found in an increasing circle around The Dells. Growlers and by the pint at the tap room.

Got food? Free popcorn and pretzels. You can order in too.

Special Offer: A free pint

Directions: From the center of the Dells take Broadway/Hwy 13 heading east. Where 13 heads north at a junction with Hwys 16 and 23, you continue straight east on Hwy 23 (still Broadway) and watch on your right for where Broadway breaks away from 23. Follow it and the next left is Business Park Road. The brewery is on your left.

The Beer Buzz: This is the first brewery in Columbia County since 1958! It starts with a running club. Tanner's father used to have a running and beer club. First the running, then drink a different Wisconsin beer every time. They eventually lost interest in the running part. Meanwhile, Tanner got a homebrew kit in college and it compelled him to get a summer job at Tyranena Brewing in Lake Mills. "I was a sponge that summer, soaking up knowledge." He finished an Ag Business Management degree at UW-Madison and six months later he was at the Siebel Institute for the full course which included some time hitting breweries in Germany and Belgium. A week after completion, he landed a job at Lake Louie. The guy that used to be chased down the highway in the Lake Louie truck by people looking for limited release beers? That was him.

He then spent 3 years at Capital Brewery when his family decided it was time for an intervention. They came to him and suggested he open his own brewery. "It had been a running joke before," he says. Something talked about after a few beers. But his father and uncles were dead serious and said if he drew up a solid plan, they would get behind it. Two years later he has turned an ink plant in a Wisconsin Dells industrial park into a spacious brewery. Sit in the tap room and you look right into the brewery. The woodwork at the bar was done by his uncle. In fact, the name itself is a reflection of a family ethic. His grandfather's 1917 Port Huron steam tractor still runs and is still in the family. As his grandfather once said, "There are two things you should never rush: a good story and quality built beer."

Stumbling Distance: *Showboat Saloon* (showboatsaloon.com, 24 Broadway, 608-253-2628) has food, drinks, live entertainment, and Tanner's beers on tap. In fact, Broadway is the main drag in the Dells, a place to find a lot shops and restaurants and some historical buildings. Try *Ravina Bay Bar & Grill* (ravinabay.com, 231 E Durkee St, Lake Delton, 608-253-0433) overlooking Lake Delton if you're looking for a good old Friday fish fry.

WOODMAN BREWERY (WHISTLE STOP RESTAURANT)

Founded: October 2011
Brewmaster: Dennis Erb
Address: 401 Main Street • Woodman, WI 53827
Phone: 608-533-2200
Website: www.woodmanwi.com
Annual Production: 250 barrels
Number of Beers: 6 on tap, endless styles throughout the year

Rotating Beers: (they all come and go)
» ARCTIC IPA (With Mint)
» BLACK IPA
» COCONUT WHEAT
» COLA INDIA BLACK ALE
» CRANBERRY CRÈME STOUT
» CUPCAKE ALE
» IRISH CRÈME STOUT
» JALAPEÑO BLONDE ALE
» MUSHROOM WHEAT (with Morels)
» RYE KÖLSCH BIER
» TIJUANA ALE
» VANILLA BOURBON ALE

Tours? No.

Samples: Yes

Best Time to Go: Open 7 days a week, from 9 AM to close. Get there early on euchre nights.

Where can you buy it? You can mix and match a few bottles here and refill a growler. A few Madison outlets sell it such as Jenifer Street Market and, naturally, Woodman's Grocery Store (unrelated).

Got food? Yes, including pizzas, sweet potato fries, chicken, burgers, and homemade soups. Friday night fish fry as well as Taco Tuesdays.

Special Offer: A free sample platter of 4 beers.

Directions: Highway 133 passes right through town as Main Street. Go 10 minutes west of Boscobel and you're here. Watch for the Whistle Stop/ Woodman Brewery/US Post Office on the river side of the road (north).

The Beer Buzz: This little brewery is really pushing the envelope – in more ways than one. Not only is Dennis coming up with a wide variety of adventuresome recipes, but the Whistle Stop Restaurant building is also the local US Post Office (53827)!

The family business is run by mom Leslie, and the brewing is the duty of her son Dennis. He likes to think of this as the smallest brewery in Wisconsin with the largest selection; he brews in the bar's kitchen. The Erb family came here from Milwaukee in 2008 buying the tavern-restaurant.

Dennis may be the only bootlegger you ever meet. Before the paperwork went through for his brewery, he was giving away beer to locals in the bar to see what they thought. Someone with a grudge reported it and he got a big fine and lost his equipment. The bar lost some liquor as well only because the paperwork proving its legal purchase wasn't on site. Lots of excitement for a little town, but luckily it ended up being a misdemeanor rather than a felony.

Dennis's father-in-law was a homebrewer and so Dennis took it up as well. He had thought of being a mixologist but has found a similar creativity in his brewing as you can see from many of the recipes. He loves to explore.

Pints are incredibly cheap so there is no best time to go get one. As they told me, "Every hour is happy hour." Whistle Stop has the look of your standard small town tavern, with darts and pool table, plenty of tables, a long looping bar and the token mounted buck. Plus you can mail a letter.

Stumbling Distance: The town is pretty small and this is about all that's going on here. The big attraction, however, is all around the place: the Great Outdoors. Hunting and fishing are popular, and hikers, bikers, and paddlers will find plenty to do. Boscobel is 10 minutes one way, *Wyalusing State Park* (608-996-2261) and the meeting of the Mississippi and Wisconsin Rivers are under a half hour the other. River fans should check *WI River Outings* (canoe-camping.com, 715 Wisconsin Ave, Boscobel, 608-375-5300) for paddling/camping options. No glass growlers allowed on the river though; find an alternative if you're thinking of packing beer!

ZONE 2

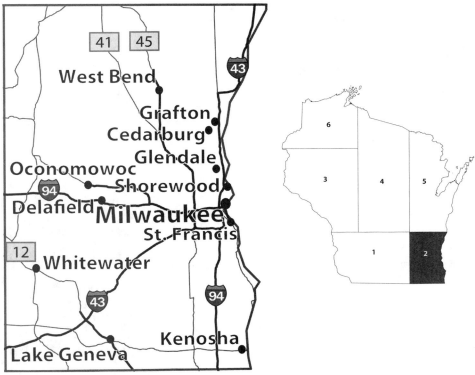

Cedarburg: Silver Creek Brewing
Delafield: Delafield Brewhaus
Delafield: Water Street Brewery: Lake Country
Grafton: Water Street Brewery: Grafton
Kenosha: Public Craft Brewery
Kenosha: Rustic Road Brewing Co.
Lake Geneva: Geneva Lake Brewing Co.
Milwaukee (Shorewood): Big Bay Brewing Co.
Milwaukee: Horny Goat Brewing Horny Hideaway
Milwaukee: Lakefront Brewery
Milwaukee: MillerCoors Brewing Co.
Milwaukee: Milwaukee Ale House
Milwaukee: Milwaukee Brewing Co./2nd Street Brewery
Milwaukee: Rock Bottom Restaurant and Brewery
Milwaukee (Glendale): Sprecher Brewery
Milwaukee: Stonefly Brewing Co.
Milwaukee: Tenth Street Brewery
Milwaukee: Water Street Brewery
Oconomowoc: Sweet Mullets Brewing
St. Francis: St. Francis Brewery and Restaurant
West Bend: Riverside Brewery and Restaurant
Whitewater: Randy's Fun Hunter Brewery and Restaurant

Silver Creek Brewing Co.

Founded: 1999
Brewmaster: Steve Venturini
Address: N57 W6172 Portland Road • Cedarburg, WI 53012
Phone: 262-375-4444
Website: www.silvercreekbrewing.com
Annual Production: 200 bbls
Number of Beers: 6-8 on tap of ours, 16 taps total

Staple Beers:
- » Hefe-Weiss
- » IPA
- » Pacific Coast Lager (light)
- » Porter (Baltic-style, more chocolate than coffee and 7.5% abv)

Staple Beers:
- » Imperial Mai-Bock (spring)
- » Oktoberfest (fall)
- » Session Ale
- » Vintage Ale (winter)

Most Popular Brew: Pacific Coast Lager (but Weiss is pretty popular in summer, Porter in cooler weather).

Brewmaster's Fave: Porter or IPA, depends on his mood

Tours? Not exactly. All the brewing facilities are visible, but if he's around, he'll chat about brewing.

Samples? Yes, four beers and a blonde root beer plus one of the several guest taps. $11.50 for six 4-oz. samplers.

Best Time to Go: Closed on Mondays. Opens at 5 PM Tuesday–Thursday; 3 PM Friday; and 2 PM Saturday. Open Sunday from 12–6 PM. In summer it is nice to sit alongside the river and watch the ducks. On Thursdays buy a Silver Creek pint glass with beer for $5 (normally $4 empty) and get refills on that or any Thursday for $1 off the regular price (while offer stands). Check the website for the live music schedule.

Where can you buy it? Originally only in growlers, but starting to distribute to local draft accounts.

Got food? Yes, snacks like cheese, bread rolls, and beef sticks. *Romano's Pizzeria* (262-375-9921) delivers here.

Special Offer: Buy a pint of their brew and get one free!

Directions: From I-43 take Exit 89 (Pioneer Rd). Go west to Washington Ave and take that north to Columbia Rd and go right (east). The first right before the bridge is Portland Rd and the Landmark Building.

The Beer Buzz: Cedarburg is only twenty minutes north of Milwaukee. Silver Creek is in the basement of the Landmark Building on the corner of Portland and Columbia Roads in the historic downtown. In the mid-1800s, German and Irish immigrants built five dams and mills on Cedar Creek, and this one, built in 1855, was a flour mill. The pub entrance is around back down along the river where you will find outside seating. Inside you will pass the remnants of the water-powered mill and enter through a large wooden door. This place has the air of an old lagering cellar with its wood ceiling and the brick and stone walls. Photos of the old town adorn the place and a few TVs pipe in the news or sporting events. The brewing equipment is there for all to see, cordoned off from the rest of the bar. Brewmaster Steve, originally a homebrewer calls it "A hobby that got way out of control." (A common theme among brewmasters.) Some other Wisconsin beers are also on tap here.

Stumbling Distance: As an alternative to the grains, try the grapes at *Cedar Creek Winery* (www.cedarcreekwinery.com, N70 W6340 Bridge Rd, 800-827-8020). Housed in an 1860s woolen mill, the winery offers a 45-minute tour for $3 at 11:30 AM, 1:30 PM, and 3:30 PM. See the brewery offerings in nearby Grafton as well: Water Street Brewery and a Grafton version of Milwaukee Ale House.

Delafield Brewhaus

Founded: May 1999
Brewmaster: John Harrison
Address: 3832 Hillside Drive • Delafield, WI 53018
Phone: 262-646-7821
Website: www.delafield-brewhaus.com
Annual Production: 900 bbls
Number of Beers: 8–10 on tap, 12–15 per year

Staple Beers:

- » Delafield Amber
- » Naga-Wicked Pale Ale
- » Pewaukee Porter
- » Sommerzeit Hefe Weizen

Rotating Beers:
- » County Cork Irish-style Stout
- » ESB
- » Fruhlingzeit Maibock
- » Hops and Glory APA
- » Imperial IPA
- » Millennium Belgian-style Tripel
- » Oktoberfest
- » Raspberry Weiss (100% juice, no extract)
- » Zagreb Pils (dry-hopped)

Most Popular Brew: Delafield Amber

Brewmaster's Fave: Oktoberfest, Oktoberfest, and Maibock! ("But they're like kids—you love 'em all, right?")

Tours? No, but the brewing system is in the center of the room in the open. You can still watch.

Samples? Yes, $6.50 for six 4-oz. samples (or you can sample them all!).

Best Time to Go: Happy hour is Monday, Wednesday, Friday 3–6 PM. Live music on Saturday nights and a great Sunday breakfast buffet. Oktoberfest is on tap in September.

Where can you buy it? Only : growlers, ¼ and ½ barrels.

Got food? Yes, a full menu! John makes his own Beer-B-Q sauce and

mustard, and you can buy bottles of it to take home. Fish fry on Fridays is Amber-battered, ribs come with the special Beer-B-Q sauce, and lunch and dinner have expansive menus. (If you have a party of 30 or more you can set up a beer dinner!)

Special Offer: A pint of John's beer or root beer.

Directions: If you take Exit 287 for Hwy 83 and go south there will be three traffic light-controlled intersections. The first is re-entry to 94, the second is Wal-Mart, and the third is Hillside Drive. Take it left (east) and follow it to the pub.

The Beer Buzz: Before brewing professionally, John was a homebrewer (he and friend Jim Olen of Milwaukee Ale House used to homebrew back in the day) and worked first in masonry and then as a branch manager for an outfit that sold fire safety equipment. "What's the best way to ruin a hobby?" he asks rhetorically. "If you don't love beer, how can you be in this business?" Originally, he founded Wisconsin Brewing Co. out of Wauwautosa in 1995, but when they were flooded out in '99—yet left high and dry by the insurance company—he opened this place overlooking I-94. He has total creative freedom and has put it to good use: he's made over 70 different beers since they opened! In 2000 Harrison won an award for Millennium Tripel at the WBC, for Barley Wine at the GABF, and a huge trophy with Rhinelander beer labels all over it from the Master Brewers Association.

The first thing you see as you walk in under the high ceiling is the brewhouse which rises up behind a low wall like some kind of pipe organ, and John can be seen composing his brews out here in the open. He designed the brewing facility first and then built the building around it. "Brewery in your face" he calls it and shuns the idea of tanks behind glass somewhere over behind the kitchen next to the bathroom. A private collector with some investment in the brewhaus displays his outstanding collection of breweriana along the walls. The basement is a banquet room that can hold up to 200 and a mezzanine has even more seating and another bar. The two front corners of the bar are closed off into private booths inside of giant wooden lagering barrels from Milwaukee's Dunck Tank Works from the late 1800s. Another old tank has been fashioned into a wood-fired oven for the pizzas. In addition to the variety of beers, he makes root beer and also does a malt beverage (a "malternative") called Bomb Pop, which is blue and tastes a lot like a Fla-Vor-Ice of the same color.

Stumbling Distance: If you are heading over to *Water Street Lake Country Brewpub* across the way, try this route: head east along the frontage road (Hillside Dr) to the first stop sign. Go left under I-94 overpass, take the first left on Golf Rd, and then follow that until the brewpub. Want some wine to go with your beer? Go see *Mason Creek Winery* (www.masoncreekwinery.com, N47 W28270 Lyndale Rd., Pewaukee, 866-511-WINE). They offer tastings and tours, and there's a courtyard for picnics and frequent live music. *Lapham Peak* (www.laphampeakfriends.org , W329N846 Hwy C), part of the Kettle Moraine State Forest, is a great place for hiking or mountain biking, and it also has lighted cross country ski trails. A 45-foot observation tower gives the highest view in the county of this unique topography left behind by the glaciers of the last Ice Age and the Ice Age National Scenic Trail actually passes through the park.

WATER STREET LAKE COUNTRY BREWERY

Founded: 2000
Brewmaster: George Bluvas III
Address: 3191 Golf Road • Delafield, WI 53018
Phone: 262-646-7878
Website: www.waterstreetbrewery.com
Annual Production: 800 bbls
Number of Beers: 8–9 on tap

Staple Beers:
» AMBER
» BAVARIAN WEISS
» HONEY LAGER LIGHT
» MUNICH LAGER
» OLD WORLD OKTOBERFEST
» PALE ALE
» RASPBERRY WEISS

Rotating Beers:
» BELGIAN WIT
» BLACK IPA
» BLACK LAGER (Schwarzbier)
» DOPPELBOCK
» IMPERIAL STOUT
» IRISH STOUT
» SAISON

Most Popular Brew: Honey Lager Light/Old World Oktoberfest

Brewmaster's Fave: Pale Ale

Tours? Yes, but by appointment.

Samples? Yes, $8 gets you seven to nine 4-oz. beers.

Best Time to Go: Summer offers outside seating next to a man-made pond in a strip mall parking lot. Lunch and dinner are busy! Best after 7 PM if you just want a beer.

Where can you buy it? Growlers and tap accounts at sister restaurants: Louise's, Trinity, Harp, Black Rose, Solo Pizza – all in Milwaukee, and at Water Street Grafton.

Got food? A full menu. Scotch eggs, beer-marinated Usinger bratwurst are total Wisconsin, the rest ranges from sandwiches to pasta, steak and seafood.

Special Offer: Not participating.

Directions: From I-94 take Exit 287 and go north on Hwy 83 to Golf Road. Take this to the right (east) and follow the gentle S-curve and you will see the brewpub on your left behind a small pond.

The Beer Buzz: Escape from the nearby shopping to a breweriana-laden brewpub. The copper brewhouse gleams behind glass and beer fans can marvel at a vast collection of cans and tap handles as well as signs from the regional breweries of the past. Wood beams rise overhead to a central skylight above the bar. Brewmaster George does triple duty here and in the downtown Milwaukee location and another up in Grafton.

The building, a bit like a German hunting lodge or beer hall, was previously a different restaurant that couldn't make a go of it. Water Street knew they would have better luck and so with little alteration to the structure crammed in a brew system. (Not a microbrewery, but a microscopic brewery, says George).

Stumbling Distance: Looking for something frosty? You're in a good neighborhood. *Le Duc Frozen Custard Drive* (240 Summit Ave, Wales, WI, 262-968-2894) does it up the old-fashioned way in a 70's style outlet in Wales two miles away. Or if you want it Italian, get over to Waukesha's *Divino Gelato Café* (www.divinogelatocafe.com, 227 W Main St, Waukesha, 262-446-9490) for authentic ice cream Italiano and specialty drinks and soups. Pewaukee Lake is popular for swimmers. *Delafield Brewhaus* is right across the freeway.

WATER STREET GRAFTON BREWERY

Founded: 2010
Brewmaster: George Bluvas III
Address: 2615 Washington Street • Grafton, WI 53024
Phone: 262-375-1402
Website: www.waterstreetbrewery.com
Annual Production: 800 bbls
Number of Beers: 8–9 on tap

Staple Beers:
  » AMBER
  » BAVARIAN WEISS
  » HONEY LAGER LIGHT
  » MUNICH LAGER
  » OLD WORLD OKTOBERFEST
  » PALE ALE
  » RASPBERRY WEISS

Rotating Beers:
  » BELGIAN WIT
  » BLACK IPA
  » BLACK LAGER (Schwarzbier)
  » DOPPELBOCK
  » IMPERIAL STOUT
  » IRISH STOUT
  » SAISON

Most Popular Brew: Honey Lager Light/Oktoberfest

Brewmaster's Fave: Pale Ale

Tours? Yes, but by appointment.

Samples? Yes, $8 gets you seven to nine 4-oz. beers.

Best Time to Go: Open daily at 11 AM and popular for weekend brunches 10 AM to 3 PM.

Where can you buy it? Growlers on site and tap accounts at sister restaurants: Louise's, Trinity, Harp, Black Rose, Solo Pizza—all in Milwaukee, and Water Street Lake Country in Delafield.

Got food? A full menu. Scotch eggs, beer-marinated Usinger bratwurst are total Wisconsin, the rest ranges from sandwiches to pasta, steak and seafood.

Special Offer: Not participating.

Directions: From the intersection of I-43 and Hwy 60 (Washington St), go east on Hwy 60 just a matter of feet and take the first street south which is still Washington St. The brewery will be on your right.

The Beer Buzz: Water Street, one of the oldest brewpubs in Milwaukee expanded first to Delafield and now north to Grafton with this third location. The beers remain the same as Brewmaster George does triple duty here and in the Delafield and downtown Milwaukee locations.

The restaurant, like the others, has breweriana on the walls. The main dining area is lined with booths and a high wood ceiling rises up past the surrounding mezzanine and its copper fermentation tanks. The large u-shaped bar sticks out from an impressive wood back bar. Like in Delafield this is a small brew system tucked inside. There is additional seating in another room. Outside you'll see wood siding that looks quite old school and the rising grain tank on the roof.

Stumbling Distance: *Milwaukee Ale-House* (ale-house.com, 1208 13th Ave, 262-375-2337) also has an outlet here in Grafton, and although they are not actually brewing there, you can get all the same Milwaukee Brewing Co. beers. If you are looking for some local foods and other products to take home, check out *Slow Pokes Local Food* (slowpokeslocalfood.com, 1229 12th Ave, 262-375-5522) for meats, cheeses, fermented foods, gluten-free items, and so much more.

PUBLIC CRAFT BREWING CO.

Founded: August 2012
Brewmaster: Matt Geary
Address: 716 58th Street • Kenosha, WI 53140
Phone: 262-652-2739
Website: www.publiccraftbrewing.com
Annual Production: 600 bbls
Number of Beers: 3 plus a seasonal, more in the tap room (8 in time)

Staple Beers:
>> HOP IN THE SACK IPA
>> K-TOWN BROWN ALE

Rotating Beers:
>> ESB, PORTER, STOUT, and such

Most Popular Brew: Too soon to tell, but we suspect the IPA.

Brewmaster's Fave: Hop in the Sack IPA

Tours? Yes, check the website for scheduled times.

Samples: Yes, flights available.

Best Time to Go: When the tap room is open—check the website.

Where can you buy it? Growlers out of the tap room, and draft accounts in the area.

Got food? Nope. Carry-in is OK.

Special Offer: A free pint of Matt's beer.

Directions: From I-94 take Exit 342 and head east on 52nd St/Hwy 158 until Hwy 32/Sheridan Rd. Go right (south) six blocks and take a left on 58th St. The brewery is on the left in the next block.

The Beer Buzz: Built in the 1910s, this bowstring truss-roofed brick building was an auto shop (they found the old pits when digging the drains for the brewery) and spent some time as a grocery store before it was divided in half intended to be two smaller businesses. Brewer Matt didn't aim for this to be a bar. This is really a brewery. While there is a tap room, it's really a production facility. No TVs, no food. Basically, it's a place to come in, sample, and chat a bit.

Matt Geary has been homebrewing since college. When he felt general discontent with his career, that hobby started looking tempting. Everyone says "We should open a bar!" So Matt went to Siebel in Chicago for a beer course. Then he did a feasibility study and decided it would work. "'Holy cow!' I thought, I'm really doing this." Matt plans to brew British styles tending toward the mild beers which he feels are a little underrepresented.

Matt likes the social aspect of beer, and finds it encourages good discourse. The idea behind Public was that it was for everyone. Get people a place to come together and talk and learn from each other and let the beer be at the hub of it, the common thread. The brewery also has what Matt calls The Public Library, a collection of resources on brewing that homebrewers are free to stop in and peruse.

Stumbling Distance: If you are looking for a Kenosha institution, don't miss *Frank's Diner* (franksdinerkenosha.com, 508 58th St, 262-657-1017) open for classic food from the wee hours to the wee hours. *Ashling on the Laugh* (ashlingonthelough.com, 125 56th St, 262-653-0500) is an Irish pub/restaurant with a good UK beer selection and some of Public's brews as well. The two most important attractions out on the interstate are *The Brat Stop* (bratstop.com, 262-857-2011) and *Mars Cheese Castle* (marscheese.com, 262-859-2244).

Rustic Road Brewing Co.

Founded: June 22, 2012
Brewmaster: Greg York
Address: 510 56th Street • Kenosha, WI 53140
Phone: 262-320-7623
Website: www.rusticbrewing.com
Annual Production: 180 bbls
Number of Beers: 4-5 at any time

Staple Beers:
- » Southport Wheat Bavarian Style
- » Simmons Island Imperial Blonde

Rotating Beers:
- » Accommodation Amber
- » Belgian Strawberry Blonde
- » Hazelnut Ale
- » KPA (Kenosha Pale Ale)
- » Rustic Farmhouse Ale
- » …a new beer each month!

Most Popular Brew: Simmons Island Imperial Blonde

Brewmaster's Fave: It depends on the day. All of them!

Tours? Yes, but you can see everything from the door. It's a nickel tour. (Actually it's free, so you've saved a nickel. Bonus!)

Samples: Yes. Sampler flight of 4-5 4-oz. $5

Best Time to Go: The tap room has a full bar with some other Wisconsin craft beers available as well. Hours are Wed-Thurs 5-10, Fri 4-1ish, Sat noon-1am, Sun noon-5pm. Different drink specials each day and Happy Hour is weekdays 5-7, Fri and Sat 4-7. Live music at least once a month.

Where can you buy it? Only here! Growlers available. Cans are likely coming soon.

Got food? Small appetizers, just some light fare like soft pretzels. The bakery next door makes a cheese bread with the wheat beer.

Special Offer: A free bumper sticker

The Beer Buzz: The idea started like many: one too many homebrews one night. Greg said, "One day when I retire, I will open a brewery." At that moment of beer talking the idea was a big thing. It'll have a movie theatre, pool tables, a bowling alley... But unlike most of our similarly big ideas, Greg's became reality. In 2009, he had heard "one too many stories of a 35-year old crossing a finish line and dying" and he began contemplating how life doesn't always wait around for you. While he had to scale down the Big Idea – sorry, no bowling alley, folks – it became the Serious Idea.

In 1999 during his last year of college, Greg went in for halfsies on a brew kit with of buddy of his and started homebrewing (dormbrewing?). The first batch was great. In the second, the thermometer shattered in the brew kettle and they had to dump it. At the end of the year, Greg bought out the other half of the kit. Then he began to read everything he could, and started going to conferences. The brew passion evolved and continued to grow. In 2010 he took Best In Category at the Wisconsin State Fair with a Summer Saison.

When he was ready, he put together a scaled down vision of something manageable, something small and more artisanal. "There was once a brewery on every block, providing for the locals, and they'd come down with their bucket each day." The brewery is a repurposed office building that had been empty. He worked with the landlord to take an eyesore and make it a fabulous little place in the heart of the south downtown, next to the performing arts center. It has a coffee house sort of vibe and free WiFi. The name Rustic Road comes from the legislated preservation program begun in 1973 to save Wisconsin's scenic country roads.

Trivia note: Kenosha's first brewery, Muntzenberger Brewing, opened in 1847, a year before Wisconsin's statehood.

Stumbling Distance: *Captain Mike's Beer and Burger Bar* (mikelikesbeer.com, 5118 6th Ave, 262-658-2278) shouldn't be missed, a crazy-big beer list. *Wine Knot Bar & Bistro* (wine-knot.com, 5611 6th Ave, 262-653-9580) is a great restaurant across the street. And do check out the Kenosha Harbor Park and the Market – great for walking around.

Geneva Lake Brewing Co.,

Founded: February 1, 2012
Brewmaster: Jonathan McIntosh
Address: 750 Veterans Parkway, Suite 107, Lake Geneva, WI 53147
Phone: 262-248-2539
Website: www.genevalakebrewingcompany.com
Annual Production: 400 bbls with hopes to double that
Number of Beers: 8–9 per year

Staple Beers:
- » Cedar Point Amber Ale
- » No Wake IPA
- » Narrows (Kölsch)
- » Weekender Wheat

Rotating Beers:
- » Coming soon!

Most Popular Brew: Cedar Point Amber

Brewmaster's Fave: Like father, like son—they both dig their No Wake IPA.

Tours? Tap room hours are 3–7 PM Thurs–Fri, 11–4 PM Sat–Sun.

Samples: Yes.

Best Time to Go: When the tap room is open.

Where can you buy it? Plenty of it on draft in the Lake Geneva area, a bit in Madison, Milwaukee, and even a few places as far west as Hudson. Some 22 oz. and 750 ml bottles locally; growlers in the tap room.

Got food? No.

Special Offer: A pint glass

Directions: From Hwy 120 outside Lake Geneva, take Exit 330A and head west toward town (still Hwy 120 South) and follow it again when it turns left on Edwards Blvd. Just over a half mile turn left onto E Townline Rd and left again onto the next street, Veteran's Parkway. It's in the two U-shaped buildings on your left.

The Beer Buzz: Pat McIntosh spent 28 years working the corporate end of the manufacturing industry, and when he retired early he was looking for a big change. His son Jonathan gave him a very good idea. You see, Lake Geneva is a tourist mecca (thus the Weekender Wheat name) and draws good traffic from Chicago. As Jonathan noted, most touristy areas have at least one microbrewery or brewpub, but Lake Geneva had none.

PHOTOGRAPH COURTESY OF
GENEVA LAKE BREWING CO.

Pat and Jonathan had started homebrewing back in 2005 or so, but it's a big leap from your basement to a production brewery. But they were up to the challenge. They both took some coursework, and Jonathan, as head brewer, enrolled in the Siebel Institute in Chicago. With guidance from brewing consultant Tim Lenahan of Brew to Win, they got their first two recipes perfected, and then developed two more as they opened their facility in an industrial condo in town.

What's their brewing philosophy? Pat says, "We almost named our wheat beer, No Fruitin' – don't put an orange or a lime in my beer. Just the four main ingredients." Not to say they won't some day branch away a bit from that, but right now the focus is just on straight-up good beer.

Geneva Lake is actually the second largest lake in Wisconsin, with 21 miles of shoreline and a widest point of 2.6 miles. They named their Kölsch after the half-mile narrowest point, and the IPA is an obvious reference to the lake life.

Stumbling Distance: The Lake is the main attraction, of course. *Champs Sports Bar & Grill* (747 West Main St, 262-248-6008) is the biggest beer seller in town (Geneva Lake is on tap) and a perfect place to gather for the big games. Anyone who comes to Lake Geneva pretty much eats at *Popeye's* sooner or later (popeyeslkg.com, 811 Wrigley Dr, 262-248-4381). A typical assortment of casual American foods, but the flaming chicken and the rotisserie meats are their signatures. *University of Chicago's Yerkes Observatory* (astro.uchicago.edu/yerkes, 373 W Geneva St, Williams Bay, 262-245-5555,) is open every Saturday for free tours. *Chuck's Tavern* (352 Lake St, Fontana, 262-275-3222) at the other end of the lake sits right on the water for some casual bar fare and good drinks.

MILWAUKEE

Wisconsin's largest city was once the nation's (and world's) largest manufacturing zone. It is the birthplace of Harley Davidson, the home of Happy Days, LaVerne & Shirley, and That 70s Show, and the site of Summerfest, the world's largest outdoor music festival. But a strong influx of German immigrants in the 19th century brought with them the one thing Milwaukee is most associated with: beer.

This is the original Brew City. Beer Town, U.S.A. By the late 1860s, Germans were associated with the 48 or so breweries already up and running. But the very first was Milwaukee Brewery—known locally as Owens' Brewery—which was built by three Welshmen in 1840 and brewed ales not lagers.

Many brewing giants emerged from the competition. What began as Best & Company in 1844, became Pabst Brewing Co. in 1889, going on to win the blue ribbon associated with its flagship beer. Valentine Blatz opened his brewery in 1851. Originally founded as a tavern brewery in 1849, the brewery of the beer that "made Milwaukee famous" would become Joseph Schlitz Brewery in 1858, two years after its former bookkeeper bought the works from the founder's widow and then married her. At one time Schlitz was the largest brewery in the world. Frederick Miller bought the Planck Road Brewery in 1855, and the massive operation that is there today still brews.

While Miller (MillerCoors) still produces millions of barrels each year, the non-brewery Pabst no longer has offices in Wisconsin but merely owns and contract-brews Schlitz, Blatz, and other classic brands. But thanks to the birth of microbreweries in the 1980s, Milwaukee's brewing tradition is alive and well, and growing every year. In addition to the many breweries beyond this page, you will also find beer-related attractions that you should consider on any *pilsgrimage* to the Great Brew City. Museums, restaurants, revived or repurposed old buildings, and more. Have a look; Milwaukee is going to take some time if you really want to explore it well.

Big Bay Brewing Co.

Founded: October 2010
Brewmaster: Jeff Garwood, Jim Lueders, Robert Morton
Address: 4517 North Oakland Avenue • Shorewood, WI 53211
Phone: 414-226-6611
Website: www.bigbaybrewing.com
Annual Production: 1000 bbls and growing
Number of Beers: 4 on tap, 6 styles per year, occasional guest taps

Staple Beers:
- » Boatilla Amber Ale
- » Long Weekend IPA
- » Wavehopper Kölsch-Style Ale

Rotating Beers:
- » Summer Tide Wheat Ale
- » Portside (mild porter)

Most Popular Brew: Long Weekend IPA.

Brewmaster's Fave: Long Weekend, though Summer Tide is quite tasty.

Tours? No.

Samples: Yes, flight of 4 styles for $5.

Best Time to Go: The tasting room is open Tues 4–7 PM, Wed 4–8 PM, Thurs Noon–8 PM, Fri Noon–9 PM, Sat Noon–9 PM, Sun Noon–4 PM. Late afternoon Thursday through Saturday see the biggest crowds.

Where can you buy it? Here on tap, in growlers, and in bottles. Wisconsin stores such as Pick & Save, Sendik's, Piggly Wiggly, Woodman's, and Festival, as well as a few draft accounts. Also available in Minnesota.

Got food? Pretzels. Come on, that's food. Menus to nearby places are available and it is food friendly.

Special Offer: 15% off of any purchase for anyone coming in to get the book signed at the establishment.

Directions: From I-43 on the north side of Milwaukee (toward Green Bay) go east on Capitol Drive/Hwy 190 to Oakland Avenue. Go left (north) about 8 and a half blocks and the tap room is on the left. Alternatively, if you are coming up North Lake Drive, go left (west) on Glendale Avenue to Oakland Avenue and go left (south) and it's on your right.

The Beer Buzz: The idea started over a couple of beers. Sound familiar? Jeff had 23 years in the business with Miller Brewing Co. (MillerCoors) and wanted to stay in Wisconsin. He had "enough background in beer to get in trouble but at least make some darn good beers." While we count this as Milwaukee in the book so you don't miss it on a visit to Brew City, this is technically Shorewood, and Big Bay is the village's first and only brewery.

At this time, the brewers head down to the south side of Milwaukee to brew their flagship beers at Milwaukee Brewing Co.'s 2nd Street Brewery. The Shorewood tap room is a nice modern place, with a fine looking bar, room to get together with friends and chat and enjoy the brews. There's a fireplace and a seating area near it. Free WiFi. Parking is on the street.

Stumbling Distance: This is a good foodie neighborhood. Check out *Village Pub* or *Oakcrest Tavern* for some good cheese curds. Nature lovers should continue up North Lake Drive to East Brown Deer Road and visit the *Schlitz Audubon Nature Center* (www.sanc.org, 1111 E Brown Deer Rd, 414-352-2880). Beer-related by name anyway!

MILWAUKEE NIGHTLIFE & DRINK CULTURE INFO

For an always changing nightlife guide and articles pertinent to the Milwaukee bar scene and drink culture in general, look for a copy of the free magazine Milwaukee Alcoholmanac (alcoholmanac.com). About 70 pages of articles, photos and ads about drink and food and drink in Brew City. A new issue comes out every two months.

BAR ON THE RUN

Way back in the day, **Potosi Brewery** (Zone 1) used to have a bar on wheels to take around to special events. Here in Milwaukee they've put a new twist on that idea. Get on board the Pedal Tavern for the most unusual pub crawl. The mobile tavern has room for 16 (10 seats have pedals) and is often booked for groups. Choose from some pre-made routes or put together your own. Individuals can join as well during specified times for about $25 for a 2 or 2.5-hour ride. The tavern does not actually serve alcohol but gets you Happy Hour prices at each of the many pubs and breweries you will hit. The **Historic Third Ward** (home to Milwaukee Ale House) is a popular touring area. (pedaltavern.com, 414-405-6682)

PHOTOGRAPH COURTESY OF POTOSI BREWING CO.

Horny Goat Hideaway (Horny Goat Brewing Co.)

Founded: 2009
Brewmaster: John "The Mad Scientist" Hannafan
Address: 2011 S. 1st Street • Milwaukee, WI 53207
Phone: 414-482-4628
Website: www.hghideaway.com or www.hornygoatbrewing.com
Number of beers: 10 on tap

Staple Beers:
» Belgian Wheat
» Exposed Cream Ale
» Hopped Up 'N Horny
» Horny Blonde
» Red Vixen

Rotating Beers:
» Apple Wheat
» Belgian IPA
» Berry Horny
» Brownie Porter
» Chocolate Cherry Stout
» El Hefe
» Horny Copia Pumpkin Ale
» Kiwi Saison
» Stacked Milk Stout
» Summer Ale
» Watermelon Wheat Ale

Most Popular Brew: Horny Blonde

Brewmaster'sFave: They're like children: I love them all the same.

Tours? On request.

Best Time to Go: Happy Hour is Mon–Fri from 11-6 with drink specials and buy one, get one appetizer menu.

Samples? Yes, $10 for six 3-ounce beers.

Where can you buy it? Growlers are only sold at the Horny Goat Hideaway but bottles are sold statewide.

Got food? Yes, a menu with sandwiches and burgers, chips & dip featuring Hopped Up 'n Horny beer cheese dip, Little Pig Wings, pork shank "wings" with Red Vixen BBQ Sauce and an endless variety of pizza. The all-day Friday Fish Fry was rated one of Milwaukee's best.

Special Offer: Free tap of Horny Goat with book signing.

Directions: Along I-43/94 just south from the center of Milwaukee, take Exit 312 for Becher Street heading east. Go just under a quarter mile east to First Street and go left (north). The pub is just before the river on the left.

The Beer Buzz: This building was once temporary living quarters for firemen and the pumping station which provided all the water pressure to fire hydrants in the Kinnickinnic area in the 1930s. Well, it's still a pumping station of sorts, pumping beer into your glass. Inside the bar you'll find nine big-screen TVs, a pool table, dart board, and some arcade games. The brew system is viewable. Outdoors is just as fun with four volleyball courts, seating for up to 500, and a bar with 75 places to hunker down with a pint. By land or by sea: the bar has boat slips for you, Cwwaptain, and plenty of parking for the rest of you. Watch for Big Band Brunches on Saturdays and Sundays from 9 to noon.

Stumbling Distance: You are close to the heart of Bay View here: See outstanding beer bars *Roman's Pub* (www.romanspub.com, 3475 S Kinnickinnic Ave, Milwaukee, 414-481-3396) and *Sugar Maple* (mysugarmaple.com, 441 E Lincoln Ave, Milwaukee, 414-481-2393). And the quirky and awesome sharable plates eatery, *Odd Duck Restaurant* (oddduckrestaurant.com, 2352 S Kinnickinnic Ave, 414-763-5881). Visit the *Mitchell Park Domes* (524 S. Layton Blvd, 414-649-9830). These three 85-foot-high glass beehive domes showcase a variety of plants from around the world as well as a lightshow in the evenings. See floral gardens, tropical jungle and even a bit of the desert. When that makes you thirsty, head back to the Hideaway.

PHOTOGRAPH COURTESY OF HORNY GOAT HIDEAWAY

LAKEFRONT BREWERY

Founded: 1987
Brewmaster: Marc "Luther" Paul
Address: 1872 N. Commerce St.
        Milwaukee, WI 53212
Phone: 414-372-8800
Website: www.lakefrontbrewery.com
Annual Production: 32,000 bbls
Number of Beers: 26

Staple Beers:
- BRIDGE BURNER STRONG ALE (Genius Series)
- CREAM CITY PALE ALE
- EAST SIDE DARK
- FIXED GEAR
- FUEL CAFÉ COFFEE STOUT
- IBA (GENIUS SERIES)
- IPA
- KILSCH PILSNER
- NEW GRIST (GLUTEN-FREE ALE)
- ORGANIC ESB
- RENDEZVOUS BIERE DE GARDE (Genius Series)
- RIVERWEST STEIN
- WHEAT MONKEY

Rotating Beers:
- BELGIAN WIT
- BIG EASY
- BOCK
- HOLIDAY SPICE
- LAKEFRONT CHERRY LAGER
- LOCAL ACRE (also a fresh-hop version)
- OKTOBERFEST
- PUMPKIN LAGER
- SNAKE CHASER IRISH STOUT
- WISCONSINITE SUMMER WEISS

Most Popular Brew: Riverwest Stein (in Milwaukee), Fixed Gear (out of state), New Grist (in Canada)

Brewmaster's Fave: Bridge Burner

Tours? Every day in summer (not on Sunday otherwise), but hours vary according to day and season. Check the website! You can buy tickets in advance online. Seriously, this is one of the best tours in the Midwest—Bob Freimuth was awarded best brewery guide in Milwaukee, and *Maxim* and *Tripadvisor* rate the tour as tops. Bob drinks with the guests. OK, they *all* drink with the guests. 'Nuff said. I'm partial to Brother Jim's tours. $7 includes a souvenir pint glass.

Samples? Before, during, and after the tour.

Best Time to Go: Fridays, but any old time is nice. There's a dock for boats in the summer and boat tours that include two other brewery tours on the river (see Booze Cruises in back).

Where can you buy it? Nationwide in 37 states and even a bit in Canada!

Got food? Only on Friday evenings from 4–9 PM. Fish fry!

Special Offer: A Lakefront Brewery bumper sticker

Directions: From I-43 take Hwy 145 East at 4th Street. Go east on Juneau Ave to Water St. Turn left on Water St to Pleasant St. Turn left, cross the bridge and go to Commerce St. Turn right. The brewery is on the river just before the Holton Street Bridge.

The Beer Buzz: Russ and Jim Klisch come from a long line of brewery history. Yes, their grandfather drove the street sweeper for Schlitz back in the 30s. This microbrewery, situated just under the Holton Street Viaduct, occupies the former coal-fire power plant that once gave the juice to Milwaukee's first light rail. Now the Klisch's make some juice of their own here in this historic neighborhood at the foot of Brewer's Hill. Lakefront was the first U.S. brewery brewing under its own label to be certified organic. Organic is a catchy title—and important quality—for modern times, but as Russ points out, old school brewing was organic already at a time when industrial farms and widespread chemical use didn't exist. New Grist is gaining notoriety as a gluten-free beer (no wheat or barley) using sorghum and rice for grains, and the Fuel Café Stout uses Milwaukee's roasted Alterra coffee from the cool and quirky local coffeehouse from which the beer takes its name. The high-octane Pure Milwaukee Genius Series beers in 22 oz. "bomber" bottles – such as Bridge Burner – shouldn't be missed. Watch for the My Turn series, a different brew every time. Everyone in the brewery is part of your beer. These are made from start to finish by someone other than Luther. Dan the Tax/Compliance Manager

made a Baltic Porter and won bronze in 2012 at the World Beer Cup.

Local Acre is brewed with Wisconsin ingredients from within 100 miles, but Wisconsinite takes it one step further. Not only are the malted barley, wheat, and hops from Wisconsin, but so is the yeast! Jeremy King of Northern Brewer Supply harvested an indigenous wild strain which was then refined for brewing. It's known as the Lakefront strain.

For the total Wisconsin experience, don't miss the Lakefront Palm Garden's Friday Fish Fry complete with live polka band. Here's another great idea: book your wedding reception at the brewery. The hall holds up to 400, and no matter how many alcoholics are in the family, you'll never run out of beer.

Awards for the beer here include a Great American Beer Festival bronze for Riverwest Stein; a 2011 GABF silver for New Grist as well as a Chesterfield award for excellence; silver for Oktoberfest in the category of Bavarian Style Marzen and silver for Klisch Pilsner at the 2009 European Beer Star Awards. Brad the Packaging Manager's My Turn Scotch Ale won gold at the 2012 L.A. International Beer Competition as did Wisconsinite.

Stumbling Distance: You can see the old breweries—Schlitz, Pabst and Blatz—from atop Brewer's Hill. Nearby *Café Brücke* (2101 N. Prospect Ave, 414-287-2053, Tues–Sat 5–9 PM) is a German-themed mom and pop restaurant with great beer and reasonably priced eats. You can also cross the river on the Holton St Marsupial Bridge—a walkway/bike path hung under the viaduct—and get to Brady Street where you will find a whole slew of great bars including *The Nomad Pub, The Hi Hat, The BBC, Hooligan's, The Palm* and *Roman Coin. Trocadero's* (1758 N Water St, 414-272-0205, open daily) is a Euro café with year-round outdoor seating. Weekend brunch is highly regarded. Check out *The Wicked Hop* (www.thewicked-hop.com, 345 N Broadway, 414-223-0345) in the Historic Third Ward—they exclusively serve Lakefront's Poison Arrow IPA. Lakefront also brews Motor Oil for the Motor Bar & Restaurant at the *Harley Davidson Museum* (harley-davidson.com, 400 W Canal St).

PABST MANSION: LIFE AS A BEER BARON

Frederick Pabst brought us a Blue Ribbon beer back in 19th century. Jacob Best opened a brewery in 1844 (four years before Wisconsin became a state) which his son Phillip took over. Pabst, a steamship captain, married Phillip's daughter Maria and invested in the brewery as well and became president of it in 1872 before changing the brewing company's name to his own in 1889. The blue ribbon was an award from competition but it wasn't until 1899 that the beer itself became known as Pabst Blue Ribbon Beer. Over a million barrels were being brewed before the turn of the century.

A beer baron of Pabst's caliber desired some serious digs and this Flemish Renaissance Revival mansion is a real beauty. Completed in 1892, the mansion was wired for electricity and had a state-of-the-art heating system. The good Captain filled it with great artwork and spared no expense on the interiors. Pabst died in 1904, however, and his wife two years later. From 1908 to 1975 the Archdiocese of Milwaukee occupied the home, but it was sold once again. This time someone had plans for something much more beautiful and magnificent, a true tribute to the times… er, a parking ramp? Seriously?

Fortunately for all of us, Milwaukee entrepreneur John Conlin stepped in and held the house until Wisconsin Heritages, Inc. could round up the dough to keep it from the wrecking ball. It has been no small expense to save this tremendous piece of Milwaukee's history, and restorations on the mansion continue. Much of it has been completed; however, this has been a painstaking process especially as some of the skills that went into making it are no longer readily available.

A tour of this mansion is a must on any brew visit to Milwaukee, and you can either guide yourself or join a guided tour on the hour. Reservations are required for the latter.

Open Mon–Sat 10 AM–4 PM and Sun 12–4 PM. Closed Mondays mid-January through February, and Easter. Special hours and prices during the Christmas season. Wheelchair accessible and parking .

Admission is $9 for adults ($10 from mid-Nov to mid-Jan)
2000 West Wisconsin Avenue • Milwaukee, WI 53233
www.pabstmansion.com
414-931-0808

MILLERCOORS

Founded: 1855
Brewmaster: David Ryder
Address: 4251 W State Street • Milwaukee, WI 53208
Phone: 414-931-2337
Website: www.millercoors.com or www.shopmillerbrewing.com
Annual Production: 9 million bbls!

Staple Beers:
» MILLER GENUINE DRAFT
» MILLER HIGH LIFE
» MILLER LITE
» MILLER 64
» MILWAUKEE'S BEST

Most Popular Brew: Miller Lite

Tours? Free hour-long tours of the historic Miller Caves, Miller Inn, and the plant floor typically Mon–Sat from 10:30–3:30 on the half hour. Open Sundays Memorial Day through Labor Day. Call 800-944-LITE for daily updates.

Samples? 2-3 samples at the end of the tour which vary by brand each day. (Remember they own Leinie's as well!)

Best Time to Go: Monday–Friday. Saturday can be busy and they don't take reservations.

Where can you buy it? Where *can't* you buy it? World famous!

Got food? Pretzels in the Miller Inn.

Special Offer: The girl in the Moon Gift Shop, located at 4251 W State Street will offer 10% off any one item of your choice. Offer excludes sale or clearance merchandise. Please mention promo code: 1855.

Directions: From I-94 West take Hwy 41 north to the State Street/Vliet Street exit. You are going to go east on State Street, and with this exit you will have to take a right on 46th Street to get you that half block to State. Another block east on State and the visitor center is on your right (south).

The Beer Buzz: Frederick J. Miller emigrated from Germany to Milwaukee in 1855 and bought Plank Road Brewery (built by Charles Best) and began to brew beer. The beer was immediately popular and he was soon selling well beyond Milwaukee. You can still see a brewhouse he built on State Street with "F. Miller" and "1886" visible at the top. He passed the brewery to his sons in 1888 and they built the Miller Inn, the Refrigeration building and the Stables. Prior to this Miller Caves were used for lagering. The brewery survived Prohibition making near beer, soda, and malt syrup, and modernized as soon as it was repealed. After World War II, Frederick C. Miller, a grandson of the founder, worked to make it the fifth largest American brewery. Miller died after a plane crash in 1954 (see the Caves photo), and the presidency of the brewery left the Miller family for the first time. Philip Morris bought it in 1970 and started the "It's Miller Time" ads. Miller Lite was introduced, starting a whole new trend toward light beers which helped make Miller the second largest brewer in the United States. Today, Miller is brewed in Ohio, North Carolina, Georgia, Texas, and California besides the original Milwaukee brewery. In 1988 Miller acquired Jacob Leinenkugel Brewing of Chippewa Falls, Wisconsin but has continued to run it as an independent operation. In 2002, Miller Brewing was bought by South African Breweries and became part of SAB Miller, one of the largest brewers in the world, brewing in 40 countries. In 2008, SAB Miller and Molson Coors entered into a joint venture to combine the U.S. and Puerto Rico operations of Miller Brewing Company and Coors Brewing Company and form a high-potential new brewing company with a unique foundation of great beer brands and 288 years of brewing experience and heritage. On July 1, 2008 MillerCoors began combined operations.

Stumbling Distance: Head over to *Miller Park* to watch the Milwaukee Brewers play some ball. During the Holidays, take a drive down to the Plank Road Brewery to see the awesome light show set to music. You may have seen something similar in one of their commercials. For a killer bar burger, you can't miss *Sobelman's Pub & Grill* (milwaukeesbestburgers.com, 1900 W Saint Paul Ave, 414-931-1919).

CRUIZIN' FOR SOME BOOZIN'

Check out listings in the back of the book for a couple ways to float your way around to some breweries here in Milwaukee!

MILLER CAVES

Built by Charles Best, these caves are all that remains of the original Plank Road Brewery. The 44-inch thick walls are made of brick and limestone, and the caves made a great cool place for fermentation, aging, and storing beer. Ice blocks cut from frozen lakes and hauled by horses kept them cool in winter and sawdust and hay insulated them in summer. The caves went back 600 feet and could hold as many as 12,000 barrels. Brewery president Frederick C. Miller created a tour program in 1952 and made a caves museum. The gas lighting was replaced by electricity and the displays were added. The museum officially opened in October 1953, and Milwaukee's famous pianist Liberace was part of the dedication ceremony.

The photo, taken on December 17, 1954, is of one of the famous "Cave Dinners" and shows Miller President Fred Miller having lunch with other members of the Wisconsin State Brewers Association. Later that same day Miller was fatally injured in a plane crash at Mitchell Field in Milwaukee. Also killed were his son Frederick C. Miller, Jr. and the two pilots, Joseph and Paul Laird. That was the last cave dinner until a fundraiser for the Museum of Beer and Brewing revived the tradition.

PHOTOGRAPH COURTESY OF MILLERCOORS

MILWAUKEE ALE HOUSE

Founded: 1997
Brewmaster: Robert Morton
Address: 233 N Water Street • Milwaukee 53202
Phone: 414-276-2337
Website: www.ale-house.com
Annual Production: 1400 bbls
Number of Beers: 12 on tap: 9 regular, at least 3 rotating styles all the time

Staple Beers:
- » DOWNTOWN LITES HONEY ALE
- » HOP HAPPY IPA
- » LOUIE'S DEMISE ALE (amber ale)
- » LOVE ROCK
- » OUTBOARD CREAM ALE
- » POLISH MOON MILK STOUT
- » PULL CHAIN PAIL ALE (APA)
- » SHEEPSHEAD STOUT
- » SOLOMON JUNEAU ALE (golden)
- » ULAO BELGIAN WIT
- » VIENNA LAGER
- » WEISS

Rotating Beers:
- » CELTIC RED
- » DEVIL'S ADVOCATE (Belgian)
- » DUNKEL-WEIZEN
- » IPA
- » LOUIE'S RESSURRECTION
- » SASQUASH PUMPKIN PORTER
- » WEEKEND AT LOUIE'S (with Rishi's Organic Blueberry Rooibus and Hibiscus teas)

"Session Beer" is Bert trying new brews; check with the bartender to see what the latest is. Some past creations were Penny Pickart Porter, J.P. McCabe's Irish Red Ale, Orange Blossom Cream Ale, Belgian Wit, Punt Pass & Pour Honey Pale Ale, Rye I Oughta and cask-conditioned ales.

Most Popular Brew: Louie's Demise Ale

Brewmaster's Fave: Louie's Demise Ale

Tours? Yes, on request. This is also one of three stops on the Brew City Queen (see Booze Cruises).

Samples? Yes, six 5-oz. samples for $8.

Best Time to Go: Happy hour is 3-6 Mon–Thurs (and another on Thurs night from 10-close!), live music after 7 PM Wed–Sat.

Where can you buy it? Growlers at the bar plus six-packs in cans and bottles throughout southeastern Wisconsin and in the Chicago area. Plus various draft accounts.

Got food? Yes, a great assortment of pizzas, pastas, and sandwiches. Stout pot roast, Friday fish fry, and the biggest pot pie in the world (think of a basketball). Beer cheese soup on Thursdays.

Special Offer: Half-price pints 4–7 PM

The Beer Buzz: Welcome to the Historic Third Ward of downtown Milwaukee. Once a warehouse and manufacturing district, the Third Ward is now a thriving arts and entertainment neighborhood of renovated brick and timber buildings. This particular structure dates from the late 1880s when it was a saddlery; the old beer wagons used to come here to service horses and repair wagons. Jak Pak Co. bought the building in the 1940s, and it became the first manufacturer to mass-produce hula hoops. By the mid-70s, the building was empty, and so it sat until someone had an idea.

Jim McCabe, an electrical engineer by trade, saw the potential of the old district and felt the city needed a local brew and entertainment venue. The Milwaukee Ale House became one of the first to move into the neighborhood just as the idea of reviving it took off. The City's Riverwalk runs directly behind the brewpub, so there's outside seating and a few boat slips as well. Schooners actually used to dock here to get fitted for sails before sailing back into Lake Michigan. The beer names have good stories—ask your bartender. The beer here has been so successful that the same group of beer nuts running the show at this location opened a second larger brewery over on 2nd Street: Milwaukee Brewing Co. (see separate listing). Up in Grafton you can find another *Ale House* (1208 13th Ave, Grafton, 262-375-2337) serving the beers brewed here in Milwaukee. Live music is common, and the bar has a couple of pours coming from beer engines.

Stumbling Distance: Six blocks from here on the shore of Lake Michigan Santiago Calatrava's architectural masterpiece, the *Quadracci Pavilion* at the *Milwaukee Art Museum* (www.mam.org, 414-224-3200). The museum has a sizeable collection including many works by Wisconsin-born Georgia O'Keeffe. But even if art doesn't do it for you, do not miss the Quadracci opening and closing its "sails" at 10, 12, and closing time. The world's largest music festival is the 11-day *Summerfest* also on the water's edge right next to the museum. The event features eleven stages with the best music in a variety of genres—just a 5-block walk from here. The pub sponsors several charitable events throughout the year including *Louie's Last Regatta* for Children's Hospital of Wisconsin and *Mid-Winter Brew Fest* for the MACC Fund usually in February. Check out *The Wicked Hop* (www.thewickedhop.com, 345 N Broadway, 414-223-0345) for some fine beer selections and the *Milwaukee Public Market* (milwaukeepublicmarket.org, 400 N Water St) for an assortment of local vendors selling eats, deli items and cheese, candies, wines, beers, even fresh seafood.

GATEWAY TO WISCONSIN I

From late April/early May through October, the *Lake Express* (www.lake-express.com, 866-914-1010), a comfortable, high-speed passenger and car ferry, makes two (three from July to September) round-trip crossings of Lake Michigan between Muskegon, Michigan and Milwaukee. The trip takes 2.5 hours and comes into Milwaukee just south of where the Summerfest grounds are. Take the I-794 overpass heading south and the first exit (Exit 3) takes you down to the port area.

HISTORICAL ATTRACTION:
BEST PLACE IN MILWAUKEE!

It's not just bragging. "Best" is a big beer name in Milwaukee. Before Pabst Brewing became Pabst Brewing, it was actually the brewery of Jacob Best Sr. who founded it in 1844 (before Wisconsin became a state). Best's son Phillip and Phillip's son-in-law, the venerable Captain Frederick Pabst, made a huge success of it, and Pabst eventually took it over and gave the brewery his name. The brewery closed in 1996 but you can still find Pabst Blue Ribbon (PBR) in bars as far away as Nepal (seriously). It is the beer of choice of hipsters everywhere. And you can have one at the end of this tour in the brewery's Blue Ribbon Hall. Be sure to get your picture taken with Captain Pabst in the courtyard.

Several Wisconsin beers are on tap in the beer hall. Tours are offered for about $8 (cheaper depending on how old you are) and generally scheduled for Fridays through Sundays at 1, 2 and 3 PM – no reservations required. Group tours can be scheduled any day. Be aware that weddings here are becoming increasingly popular (over 100 per year!) and can occasionally affect the tour schedule.

Best Place's gift shop doesn't just sell t-shirt, caps, and other Best Place paraphernalia; it also has an assortment of rare and collectible Pabst items from the old brewery itself as well as a number of others. This is super for collectors of breweriana. Best Place at the Historic Pabst Brewery, the former Pabst Corporate Offices and Visitor's Center is a Certified Historic Structure on the National Register of Historic Places. And there is much more going on out here as you shall see…

Directions: To get there from I-43 (if heading north) take the exit for WI-145. Keep right at the fork following signs for WI-145/McKinley Ave and merge onto WI-145. At N 6th Street go right and take the first right onto W Juneau Ave. Turn slightly right onto Winnebago for a half a block. Turn left at N 8th Street. Take the first right onto W Juneau Ave. If you're coming from the north though, take exit 72E for Highland Ave/11th St. Turn left at W Highland Ave. Turn left on N 8th St and take the first left onto W Juneau Ave. Or just type the address into your GPS maybe. Whew.

Best Place at the Historic Pabst Brewery
901 W. Juneau Avenue • Milwaukee, WI 53233
www.bestplacemilwaukee.com 414-630-1609

MILWAUKEE BREWING COMPANY
2ND STREET BREWERY

Founded: 2007
Brewmaster: Robert Morton
Address: 613 South 2nd Street • Milwaukee, WI 53204
Phone: 414-226-2337
Website: www.mkebrewing.com
Annual Production: 6000 bbls and growing
Number of Beers: : 3 familiar beers from the Ale House, 6 bottled seasonals, 4 releases in Attitude (ABV) series

Staple Beers:
- » BOOYAH FARMHOUSE SAISON
- » HOP HAPPY IPA
- » LOUIE'S DEMISE ALE
- » LOVE ROCK VIENNA-STYLE LAGER
- » POLISH MOON MILK STOUT
- » PULL CHAIN PAIL ALE (APA)

Rotating Beers:

Seasonal "Timed Release" series:
- » "ADMIRAL" STASH
- » BLACK IRON
- » OUTBOARD CREAM ALE
- » WEEKEND @ LOUIE'S (with Rishi's Organic Blueberry Rooibus and Hibiscus teas)

Attitude by Volume Series (examples):
- » ABBEY NORMAL ABBEY-STYLE
- » DEVIL'S ADVOCATE BELGIAN DOUBLE
- » O-GII SPICED IMPERIAL WHEAT
- » MONKEY PAW IPA

Most Popular Brew: Louie's Demise Ale

Brewmaster's Fave: Booyah

Tours? Yes, $7 on Fridays and Saturdays. Check the website for schedule and make reservations!

Samples? Yes, can't have a tour without samples.

Best Time to Go: See tour schedule.

Where can you buy it? Anywhere in southeastern Wisconsin, as far north as Eagle River, as west as Madison, and now south into the Chicago area.

Got food? Eventually, but plans for a small café are on hold.

Special Offer: A highly prized trinket.

The Beer Buzz: Just a few blocks south of sister brewhouse Milwaukee Ale House, this brewing facility opened in 2007 to meet a higher demand for the three staple beers heading to market in cans and bottles. Equipment includes an in-house lab from Pabst, grain handling equipment from a caffeine plant in Milwaukee, and water tanks from Texas. Ain't it funny how beer just brings things together? Housed in what used to be a produce company, the facility offers the brewers an opportunity to bottle a boatload of beer and go far beyond Metro Milwaukee.

The beer names typically have some kind of story. For Booyah, you'd need to head to the Green Bay area where Walloon immigrant culture brought this throw-everything-in sort of soup. Polish Moon, however, is right down the block at the former Allen-Bradley building: a lighted, four-face clocktower that's bigger than Big Ben. Overlooking what was once the Polish neighborhood, the clock shone down on workers on their way to their jobs in the wee hours. Love Rock was a bunker of concrete just off shore from Bradford beach, meant to protect an intake for the water

treatment plant. Folks would head out there to sit on it or even party on it. Someone spray painted "Love" on it and the name took. The Army Corps of Engineers blew it up as it was considered a danger to boaters. (Remember Flaming Damsel Lager? It's Love Rock now.)

The brewers are concerned about being environmentally friendly. The cans are actually more efficient and less wasteful than glass bottles. They have a grant for some solar panels for water-heating purposes, and they make their own biodiesel from used fryer oil which sometimes runs the boilers.

Stumbling Distance: Go here first, get the tour, and then stumble back to *Milwaukee Ale House* to lean over a pint and further contemplate what you've learned today. *Hinterland Erie Street Gastropub* (222 East Erie Street, 414-727-9300) offers some very nice dining of the gourmet type and gets its beer from its own brewery up in Green Bay. For an incredible locally-sourced dinner, make reservations for *Braise* (braiselocalfood.com, 1101 S. 2nd St, 414-212-8843) which practices Restaurant Supported Agriculture, and serves gourmet dishes from a menu that constantly changes based on what's available. Arguably the best eco-foodie experience in Milwaukee. Get fresh cheese curds across the street at *Clock Shadow Creamery* (clockshadowcreamery.com, 138 W Bruce, 414-273-9711) and fresh ice cream at *Purple Door* (purpledooricecream.com, 138 W Bruce, 414-231-3979) in the same room!

PABST REPURPOSED:
BREWHOUSE INN & SUITES

What could be a better beer experience than to go to Milwaukee for all the brewery visits and then spend the night in an historic brewery?? For years the massive brick buildings of the old Pabst Brewery have stood vacant, a sad reminder of the decline of Milwaukee's brewing in the late 20th century. But forget that – we are in the new Golden Age of Beer here in the Brew City with so many fine brewers and more breweries in planning. Development projects amid the old Pabst site have brought us the very cool Best Place in the former hospitality center and offices. But now up the block from there, where the big Pabst sign still crosses high over the street, you can stay the night in the former brew house.

The $19 million redevelopment of the late 1800s buildings has brought Milwaukee a uniquely beerstoric hotel property. Called the Brewhouse Inn & Suites, the 90-room hotel offers studios as well as one- and two-bedroom accommodations for extended stays. You can still see the original copper brew kettles all polished up like they were still in operation. A large, stained-glass window featuring a picture of the legendary beer icon King Gambrinus has also been preserved. Winding staircases, a mezzanine-area skylight, and some beer themes in six of the suites create an atmosphere one wouldn't have imagined. Three of the suites have balcony views of downtown. An outdoor patio offers gas grills and terrace seating. In the old mill house is a pub-style restaurant which will soon also have its own outdoor beer garden.

The **Pabst Brewery** has been given a second life. Book a stay here for your next pilsgrimage to Milwaukee!

1215 N. 10th Street, Milwaukee
414-810-0146
www.facebook.com/BrewhouseInnSuites

THE MUSEUM OF BEER AND BREWING

Really how is it that Milwaukee does not have a museum dedicated to beer yet? These things take time but rest assured some people are on it. The Museum of Beer and Brewing is dedicated to preserving and displaying the proud history of beer and brewing throughout the world and especially North America. At present this museum is mostly virtual, but that does not mean you have no place to go. The museum may one day have a permanent site, but in the meantime this society organizes events (even beer and cheese pairings) and exhibits in the Milwaukee area. Check their website for what's coming up, virtual exhibits, a gift store, and some really interesting articles related to brewing history (www.brewingmuseum.org).

Rock Bottom Restaurant & Brewery

Founded: March 1997
Brewmaster: David Bass
Address: 740 N Plankinton Avenue • Milwaukee, WI 53203
Phone: 414-276-3030
Website: www.rockbottom.com/milwaukee
Annual Production: 1100 bbls
Number of Beers: 11 on tap, 40 per year

Staple Beers:
» IPA
» Kölsch
» Naughty Scot Scotch Ale
» Red Ale
» Wit Ale

Rotating Beers:
» Alt
» Baltic Porter
» Belgian Dubbel and Tripel
» Bock
» Dark Lager
» Dunkelweizen
» Imperial Stout
» MaiBock
» Octoberfest
» Pilsner
» Porter
» and cask-conditioned ales and many more

Most Popular Brew: Wit Ale

Brewmaster's Fave: Pilsner, Octoberfest, and Naughty Scot

Tours? Yes, ask your server. Groups should make appointments. Saturdays are best, especially in summer. See brewery boat tour in the Beer, Boats and Bikes section of the book.

Samples? Yes, four 4-oz. beers for $4.

Best Time to Go: Open from 11 AM. Summer opens the great patio on the river with an outdoor bar. Happy hour runs Mon–Fri 3-6 and is great for mug club members (membership is free).

Where can you buy it? Growlers .

Got food? Yes, and some menu items are paired with particular beers. The BBQ ribs have stout in the sauce, the chili has beer in it, and the ballpark pretzel is brushed with ale.

Special Offer: Free sampler with signature visit.

The Beer Buzz: Rock Bottom originated in Denver, Colorado, and in twenty years has come to open 34 other locations including this one in an old bank building on the river in downtown Milwaukee. Despite being part of a larger chain, the brewpub does brew on premises and mills its own grain. The main floor offers a full menu restaurant and a bar that backs up against the brewhouse under glass. You can still see the old vault downstairs where there is another bar with a more casual bar atmosphere. But the best place to hang—at least in nice weather—is outside on the terrace. An outside bar serves you as you watch the river go by.

Listen for the hostess answering the phone: "Hello, you've hit Rock Bottom." The name comes from the original brewpub which was on the ground floor of the Prudential building in Denver. Remember the insurance ads? "Get a piece of the rock." Am I dating myself here?

David started like many as a homebrewer. It's one thing to brew in your basement, but quite another to nail a gold medal at the Great American Beer Festival as he did with 106 Pilsner in 2009. Rock Bottom is one of three stops on a popular brewery boat tour and is also one block from the Milwaukee Trolley route.

Stumbling Distance: This is close to the *Bradley Center* (where the Bucks play). You are also a block or two from *Riverside* and *Pabst* theaters. This is a good place to head after a concert or performance. Actually, you're really not far from anything here. *Water Street Brewery* is close, as is *Milwaukee Ale House*. Or *Grand Avenue Mall*. Or the *Milwaukee Public Museum* or *Milwaukee Performing Arts Center* or... well, you get the picture. In summer, check out the live music of *River Rhythms* on Wednesdays in Pierre Marquette Park three blocks north. *Cathedral Square Jazz in the Park* is every Thursday and three blocks east. And don't forget the boat tour!

RIDE THE TROLLEY!

Milwaukee has a $1 trolley that takes about 40 minutes to make a full loop of some of the best places in downtown. Milwaukee Ale House and Water Street Brewery are on the route, while Rock Bottom and some great beer bars—The Wicked Hop, for example—are just a block off. Other stops include the Milwaukee Art Museum, the Historic Third Ward, Old World Third Street, Discovery World and the Amtrak station. The trolley passes every 20 minutes and runs from late May or early June to early September, Wed–Sat 11 AM–9 PM. A downloadable map is online. Check the Milwaukee Downtown web site at www.milwaukeedowntown.com or call 414-562-RIDE.

Sprecher Brewing Co.

Founded: 1985
Brewmaster: Randy Sprecher
Address: 701 W Glendale Ave • Glendale, WI 53209
Phone: 414-964-2739
Website: www.sprecherbrewery.com
Annual Production: 22,000 bbls
Number of Beers: 20+ (plus 4 Chameleon beers)

Staple Beers:
  » Abbey Triple (Belgian-style)
  » Black Bavarian
  » Hefe Weiss
  » Pub Ale (non-bitter, English-style, deep brown)
  » Special Amber (lager)
  » Stout

Rotating Beers:
  » Barley Wine
  » Dopple Bock (Premium Reserve)
  » Generation Porter (with Dutch cocoa and raspberry)
  » Imperial Stout (Premium Reserve)
  » IPA^2 (Premium Reserve)
  » Mai Bock (dry hopped)
  » Oktoberfest
  » Pipers Scotch Ale (Premium Reserve)
  » Summer Pils
  » Winter Brew (Munich bock)
  » … watch for Barrel-aged brews and Limited Releases as well

Most Popular Brew: Special Amber, Black Bavarian

Brewmaster's Fave: Mai Bock

Tours? Yes, but reservations are highly recommended (414-964-2739) as some tours fill up fast. The tour is kid friendly (they make sodas too) and prices are adults $5, seniors $4, minors $3, and military free. Tours start weekdays at 3; Sat and Sun from noon to 4:20. Friday, Saturdays and Sundays host Reserve Tastings for $15 which bring out the premier and limited edition brews and pair them with Wisconsin artisanal cheeses. Check the website for tour additions and updates.

Samples? Yes, four 7-oz. beers, unlimited soda, and a commemorative tasting glass.

Best Time to Go: Anytime is good. Watch for special events.

Where can you buy it? , of course, and area taverns, stores, and restaurants. Distribution is heaviest regionally. The beer sells as far east as Massachusetts, as far west as California and south to Florida. Much of the Midwest especially around Wisconsin has it too.

Got food? Yes, pizza, large soft pretzels, Nueske's landjaeger sausage (locally made since 1933!), and cheese curds.

Special Offer: A Sprecher trinket of some sort.

Directions: Just off of I-43 heading north from Milwaukee, one street south of the 77A exit.

The Beer Buzz: Randy Sprecher was working for Pabst in the early 1980s when the company downsized. He was able to open his own brewery using only $40,000 in capital and relying on used equipment (is there a resale shop for fermenting tanks?). With breweries and other companies eliminating jobs, he felt it was important to have a positive effect on the local economy and so he has been dedicated to using locally produced ingredients as much as possible—cherries from Door County, cranberries from the area, ginseng from around Wausau, honey from Germantown. He spent time in Germany during his military service and modeled his opera-

tion after the neighborhood brewers in Augsburg. Sprecher was the first microbrewery in Wisconsin since Prohibition and they got Small Brewery of the Year award in 2004 at the Great American Beer Festival. Randy has been brewing that Black Bavarian since 1969 after his trip to Bavaria, and I must say it's my personal favorite. In fact, Black Bavarian has gotten high national praises from *Men's Journal, Beer Advocate Magazine* and the *Washington Times*. Even the root beer here was named best in the country in a *New York Times* article.

The tour reveals some Bavarian murals in the bottling room and the tasting room might have a bit of polka music going on. Up to 20 beers and 9 sodas are on tap to sample. Stop in the gift shop on your way out. Sprecher is active on Facebook and Twitter – follow them and you'll know about upcoming events and beer releases. Don't forget about their whole other line up with **Chameleon** beers (which are also on tap in the tasting room).

Stumbling Distance: Just a block away is the best butter burger you will ever have at *Solly's* (414-332-8808, 4629 N Port Washington Rd), a family-run joint since 1936. Homemade pie and a fish fry. (Say, that rhymes.) Celebs know about it too, and there is a plate for regular customer and long-time voice of Milwaukee Brewers baseball, Bob Uecker. Sprecher sodas are on tap. Also nearby, *Silver Spring House* (414-352-3920, 6655 N Green Bay Ave) has Sprecher beer on tap. An old-fashioned pub, it's family-friendly, with good eats and a beer garden.

CHAMELEON BREWING

If you're searching for this new Wisconsin brewery, the trail will lead you right to the front doors of Sprecher. Brewed by the same folks who do your Black Bavarian, Chameleon is sort of set apart from the other Sprecher products, intended to appeal to another market, a younger one and drinkers who prefer lighter session beers. These are less traditionally European than the Sprecher line, and aiming to stand out as simply Wisconsin craft beer. It's still technically Sprecher-made and it's still high-quality stuff (note a couple awards at Los Angeles International Commercial Beer Competition – Gold for Hop on Top, Bronze for Ryediculous IPA – and a Gold for Witty from the Beverage Tasting Institute), but it also stands on its own. Chameleon has its own thing going on, including events. Follow them on Facebook and Twitter. (chameleonbrewing.com)

Stonefly Brewing Co.

Founded: 2006
Brewmaster: Jacob Sutrick
Address: 735 E Center Street • Milwaukee, WI 53212
Phone: 414-212-8910
Website: www.stoneflybrewery.com
Annual Production: 170 bbls
Number of Beers: up to 11 on tap

Staple Beers:
> » Amber Lager
> » Brewtown Brown
> » Four Wolves English Ale
> » Lager Lager
> » Moustache Ride Pale Ale
> » Oatmeal Stout
> » Ol'Sealaway (Scotch Ale)
> » Pierce Street Porter
> » Simon Bagley Stout (dry stout)

Rotating Beers:
> » Bock
> » Imperial Stout
> » Oktoberfest
> » ... and others

Most Popular Brew: Moustache Ride Pale Ale

Brewmaster's Fave: Right now? Probably pale ale.

Tours? Yes, by appointment or chance.

Samples? Yes, casual tasters to help you choose or $2 for each 5-oz glass.

Best Time to Go: Open seven days a week from 4 pm on weekdays, 10 am on weekends. Really relaxed from 4–8 pm, usually music at night.

Where can you buy it? only. No growler fills at this time.

Got food? The menu, served 5–10 daily (and brunch on Sat–Sun from 10 am), mixes Wisconsin, pub, and healthy. Hot pretzels, wings, bratwurst, burgers, bangers and mash, but also soups, pastas, sandwiches, salads, and some vegetarian and vegan options such as tofu and homemade veggie burgers. Little beer touches are nice such as stout mustard, beer battered deep-fried Usinger's bacon, and ale cheese sauce, and bless 'em, there's a fish fry on Fridays.

Special Offer: Buy one Stonefly beer, get one free.

The Beer Buzz: Formerly Onopa Brewing Co., the pub is now run by owner Julia LaLoggia who closed it for a month's remodeling and re-opened in April 2006. When Paul Onopa decided to leave brewing, his friend Julia stepped in. Julia is passionate about clean water—Wisconsin is a regular water paradise with so many lakes and rivers—and she chose the name for her brewery accordingly. The stonefly is a good indicator of a healthy body of water. It is also a good lure for fly fishing and she is a big fan of that as well. Brewmaster Jacob has a slightly different story from the "I was into homebrewing for many years." He was working the door at the bar in 2002 and started lending the brewmaster a hand until finally taking over the position. A real American success story, no?

Expect a funky mix of urbanites, old hippies, young professionals, and beer enthusiasts. This is a popular live music venue and pulls in a lot of great bands, mostly weekends. The bar has a good neighborhood feel to it and the tap handles are minor works of art. Kate Sanerib made them. She has a Masters in metal art. (In fact, most employees here are artists or musicians looking to pay the bills!) Enjoy the patio in season. Free WiFi. Parking is on the street.

Stumbling Distance: *Fuel Café* (www.fuelcafe.com, 818 E Center St, 414-374-3835) is a popular coffeehouse with sandwiches just down the street in this funky eclectic neighborhood. They also contribute one of their brews to one of Lakefront Brewery's brews. *Nessun Dorma* (2778 N Weil St, 414-264-8466) is one of Julia's faves (and mine), serving gourmet sandwiches and wine, with a nice beer selection of Belgians and microbrews. *Centro Café* (centrocaferiverwest.com, 808 E Center St, 414-455-3751) serves some really nice and reasonably priced Italian right across the street.

10TH STREET BREWERY

Founded: 1996
Brewmaster: Greg Walter
Address: 1515 North 10th Street • Milwaukee, WI 53205
Website: www.leinie.com
Annual Production: 45,000 barrels
Number of Beers: varies

Staple Beers:
» BIG EDDY'S BALTIC PORTER
» BIG EDDY'S IMPERIAL IPA
» BIG EDDY'S RUSSIAN IMPERIAL STOUT
» BIG EDDY'S WEE HEAVY SCOTCH ALE
» LEINENKUGEL'S HONEY WEISS

Tours? Not open to the public!

Special Offer: Not participating.

The Beer Buzz: Not everyone knows this brewery is even here. Passing by on Interstate 43 one could easily mistake the big Leinie's banner as a mere billboard. But this is the 10th Street Brewery, or the "Tiny Leinie" if you prefer. It's not actually so tiny when you consider the 45,000 barrels it produces each year. Leinenkugel's Chippewa Falls brewery needed help keeping up with demand, so in 1996 they started brewing here as well. While supplementing production of Leinenkugel's year-round and seasonal beers, 10th Street is also home to Big Eddy. No, that's not the hefty security guard at the gate, it's their own line of craft brews. New beers in 2012 included Big Eddy Imperial IPA, Big Eddy Wee Heavy Scotch Ale and Big Eddy Baltic Porter. Veteran brewer Greg Walter is 10th Street's brewmaster.

WATER STREET BREWERY

Founded: 1987
Brewmaster: George Bluvas III
Address: 1101 N Water Street • Milwaukee, WI 53202
Phone: 414-272-1195
Website: www.waterstreetbrewery.com
Annual Production: 600 bbls
Number of Beers: 8-9 on tap

Staple Beers:
>> AMBER
>> BAVARIAN WEISS
>> HONEY LAGER LIGHT
>> MUNICH LAGER
>> OLD WORLD OKTOBERFEST
>> PALE ALE
>> RASPBERRY WEISS

Rotating Beers:
>> BELGIAN WIT
>> BLACK IPA
>> BLACK LAGER (Schwarzbier)
>> DOPPELBOCK
>> DUNKEL WEISS
>> IMPERIAL STOUT
>> IRISH STOUT
>> SAISON

Most Popular Brew: Honey Lager Light/Oktoberfest

Brewmaster's Fave: Pale Ale

Tours? Yes, but by appointment.

Samples? Yes, $8 gets you seven to nine 4-oz. beers.

Best Time to Go: This place hops a bit more at night and is popular with the twenty-something and university crowd. It gets busy around lunch and dinner.

Where can you buy it? Growlers and tap accounts at sister restaurants: Louise's, Trinity, Harp, Black Rose, Solo Pizza—all in Milwaukee, plus the Water Street locations in Delafield and Grafton.

Got food? A full menu. Scotch eggs, beer-marinated Usinger bratwurst are total Wisconsin, the rest ranges from sandwiches to pasta, steak and seafood. A little upscale.

Special Offer: Not participating.

The Beer Buzz: Owner R.C. Schmidt wanted to start something that paid a little homage to his German heritage. That'd be beer, of course, and when he opened Water Street there weren't any brewpubs in the state and less than 100 in the whole country. The building itself dates to 1890 and is one of the first commercial structures in the city to have electricity. It had served various purposes over the years—grocery store, floral warehouse, apartments. When it was renovated, efforts were made to keep the stamped tin ceiling and Cream City brick. The project was one of the first in a renaissance of a rundown neighborhood that is now quite trendy. The dining is great and the ambience classy but social—don't expect pool tables or live music. The breweriana collection here is amazing and the Schlitz reverse-glass corner sign is a true rarity. The collection includes 6,000 cans on display, tap handles, coasters, serving trays and neon signs and can be seen at all three brewpub locations.

George started brewing when he was 17 years old because "the government wouldn't let me buy it, but I could get ingredients." A friend first showed him how to make wine out of apple juice. Later he worked under great brewmasters at Lakefront and Water Street (where he started working in 1999). Now he does triple duty here and at Water Street Lake Country out in Delafield as well as Water Street in Grafton.

Stumbling Distance: *Milwaukee Public Museum* (www.mpm.edu, 800 W Wells St, 414-278 2728) is walking distance from here and home to an IMAX theatre. *The Pabst Theater* (www.pabsttheater.org, 144 E Wells St, 800-511-1552) is just a great place to see a concert and also just down the street. After a show, the crowd often comes to Water Street. The 1883 *Historic Turner Restaurant* (1034 N. 4th St, 414-276-4844) offers more great dining in an historical setting. This is one of the best Friday fish fries in town and Water Street beer is on tap. Looking for other brewpubs nearby? Check out the Milwaukee Trolley.

SWEET MULLETS BREWING CO.

Founded: March 2012
Brewmaster: Mark Duchow
Address: N58W39800 Industrial Road, Suite D
         Oconomowoc, WI 53066
Phone: 608-669-0259
Website: www.sweetmulletsbrewing.com
Annual Production: 600 bbls
Number of Beers: 14 on tap, 30 throughout the year

Staple Beers:
- » 505 EXPORT STOUT
- » RYE BOB

Rotating Beers:
- » THE CAPTAIN PILSNER
- » 501 RED ALE
- » JORGE JALAPEÑO ALE
- » MECO HEFEWEIZEN (with ginger)
- » WILD-HOPPED BUCKWHEAT

Most Popular Brew: Jorge Jalapeño Ale

Brewmaster's Fave: Wild-hopped Buckwheat

Tours? Yes, by appointment.

Samples: Yes, a flight of 8 three-ounce beers for $7

Best Time to Go: Wed–Thurs 4–10ish, Fri 4–11ish, Sat 12–11ish, Sun 12–10ish. Packer games feature indoor brewery tailgating.

Where can you buy it? Mostly here and in growlers to go, but a few draft accounts are shown on their website.

Got food? Heck yeah. Charcuterie and cheese (including fresh curds), small plates and snacks such as gourmet tacos, housemade dips, meatloaf. Fish tacos on Fridays, Bloody Marys on Sundays.

Special Offer: A free pint of house beer

Directions: Coming into Oconomowoc from the west side on Highway 16, take a right (south) on Division Street into an industrial park. Go left on Industrial Road and the brewery is on your left.

The Beer Buzz: Like many famous brewers, Mark got his start in Milwaukee. He was washing kegs in 1992 at Water Street Brewery and worked his way up to head brewer. George, who's brewmaster there now, was his assistant. He put some time in at Gray's in Janesville, then opened a brewery called Flatlanders in Illinois. Then Oconomowoc Brewery. Then on to Mount Horeb Brewery. When that became The Grumpy Troll, he went to Iowa City, then quit for a while before he got the itch again and did some work in Texas and North Carolina. In 2006, Mark went back to The Grumpy Troll until he and his partner Barbara Jones (a former engineer for NASA!) finally found that timing was right to move back to Oconomowoc, where Mark grew up, and open their own brewpub.

Mark has won many prestigious awards including a bronze at the World Beer Cup in 2010 for his stout, and that same year, a silver for Rye Bob—a beer dedicated to his late father. The brewery hosts Beer Appreciation Night, a ticketed personal tasting event held typically once a month. And don't miss it when Mark does a traditional stein beer with hot rocks. Using a Bronze-Age method of heating water, he throws 1500-degree stones into a dairy tank to heat the wort. Must be seen to be believed.

Stumbling Distance: Many people talk up what a great community theater Oconomowoc has. Check out *Theatre on Main's* website for a schedule of events and get some tickets for before/after a brewpub visit. (www.theatreonmain.org, 25 S Main St, 262-560-0564)

St. Francis Brewpub

Founded: 2009
Brewmaster: Scott Hettig
Address: 3825 South Kinnickinnic Avenue • St Francis, WI 53235
Phone: 414-744-4448
Website: www.stfrancisbrewery.com
Annual Production: 450 bbls
Number of Beers: 5+ seasonal

Staple Beers:
- » Archbishop Amber
- » Kitzinger Kölsch
- » KK Weiss
- » Mariner Nut Brown Ale
- » South Shore Stout (dry Irish-style oatmeal stout)
- » (also 49 Maples Root Beer)

Rotating Beers:
- » Bohemian Pilsner
- » Doppelbock
- » Double Red
- » Maibock
- » Oktoberfest

Tours? By appointment, $5 includes two samples.

Samples? Yes, a sample platter goes for $8.

Best Time to Go: Open daily at 11 AM. Wednesdays are Pint Nights with beer discounts. Sunday brunch is 10 AM–2 PM.

Where can you buy it? At the bar and growler refills are available. Planning to bottle soon.

Got food? Yes, a full pub menu with sandwiches, soups, and salads. Fridays host fish fries. Beer is worked into a couple of dishes including the ale-braised beef, stout BBQ sauce on some ribs, a Kölsch-marinated bratwurst and the classic beer cheese soup.

Special Offer: A free can koozie while supplies last.

Directions: Take I-794 to Howard Ave and go east toward the lake just a short distance to Kinnickinnic Ave and you can see the pub on your left.

The Beer Buzz: You can't miss this place at the corner of a busy intersection: a grain silo stands in the middle of its outdoor seating area. The newly built 7200 sq-foot-building has a long bar, plenty of dining (and banquet) space and that breezy terrace in the sun. Parking is off street and easy. Regulars can join a mug club for discounts and special offers. St. Francis is a nice little community just south of Milwaukee and this is its first brewery.

Scott is a native Wisconsinite—born in Milwaukee, raised in Slinger—who started by homebrewing for 10 years or so, before he grew unhappy with his day job. The classic turn-a-hobby-into-a-career. He interned at Rock Bottom Restaurant and Brewery in Milwaukee, and then was a full-time assistant brewer for nine months at two of Rock Bottom's locations out in Cleveland. When this position opened, he headed back to Wisconsin. In December 2011 he had the opportunity to take a sabbatical and spent about 7 months helping out a brewer in southwestern Germany.

Stumbling Distance: Just north of here on Kinnickinnic (or K K as locals call it) are two of the best beer bars in the Milwaukee area: *Roman's Pub* (www.romanspub.com, 3475 S Kinnickinnic Ave, Milwaukee, 414-481-3396) and *Sugar Maple* (mysugarmaple.com, 441 E Lincoln Ave, Milwaukee, 414-481-2393). Also, St Francis is the closest brewpub to Milwaukee's Mitchell Airport!

RIVERSIDE BREWERY & RESTAURANT

Founded: October 2005
Brewmaster: Chris George
Address: 255 S Main Street • West Bend, WI 53095
Phone: 262-334-2739
Website: www.riversidebreweryandrestaurant.com
Annual Production: 350 bbls
Number of Beers: 8 on tap, 12 or so per year

Staple Beers:
- » BEE HOME SOON HONEY ALE
- » BENT RIVER BERRY WEISS
- » DIZZY BLONDE WEISS
- » FEELIN' LUCKY IRISH STOUT
- » MAIN STREET AMBER ALE

Rotating Beers: *(2 or 3 Brewer's Choices)*
- » BROKEN OAK ABBEY DUBBEL ALE
- » CHERRY TWIST ALE
- » CLEV'S AGED OLD WORLD OKTOBERFEST
- » IMPERIAL PALE ALE
- » RASPBERRY FRUIT WEISS
- » WEST BEND LEGACY LAGER

Most Popular Brew: Main Street Amber Ale

Brewmaster's Fave: "I will not pick a favorite from among my children."

Tours? Yes, available some Fridays, best by appointment. Call the brewery!

Samples? Yes, seven 4-oz. mugs for $8.95.

Best Time to Go: Happy hour is 3–5 ($1 off microbeers), Friday night fish fry. In warm weather, go for the outside seating. Live music in the bar on Saturday nights. Be sure to join the Mug Club for some good deals.

Where can you buy it? Only , growlers.

Got food? Yes, a wide selection in fact. Beer-battered cheese curds and mushrooms, beer cheese soup, excellent ribs, steaks, seafood, top-notch sandwiches, and the fish fry offers cod, walleye, lake perch, and shrimp.

Special Offer: A free pint.

Directions: Follow Hwy 33 through town to the west side of the river and take Main St south through a traffic circle. Riverside will be down the street on your left past the Walnut St intersection.

The Beer Buzz: The brewpub is just south of the quaint downtown and its collection of historic buildings and shops in a Cream City brick building on the river. This used to be a vacuum cleaner store but has since been totally remodeled in a sort of 1920s décor with breweriana and photos of pre-Prohibition scenes on the walls. (The place received a local award for interior design.) Outdoor dining has two options: the sidewalk along the street and the terrace along the river. Owner Wayne Kainz was the manager of another restaurant and when he and his wife, Dana, decided to open their own place, the downtown association brought him the brewpub idea. Riverside Brewery and Restaurant has that hometown restaurant appeal, and quality food served with great beer is never a bad thing. It's a good place to meet up with friends or family and has a touch of class.

Stumbling Distance: The downtown is a nice collection of little shops in historic buildings and walking distance from the pub. And if walking's your thing, the path along the river is nice enough and features a series of sculptures. The *West Bend Art Museum* (www.wbartmuseum.com, 300 S 6th St, 262-334-9638) showcases early Wisconsin art from 1800 to 1960 and seventeen temporary exhibitions from contemporary Wisconsin artists and some national and international ones as well. Admission and tours are free and it's open Wed–Sat 10–4:30 PM and Sun 1–4:30 PM. Are you ready for a Wisconsin-style safari? *Shalom Wildlife Sanctuary* (shalomwildlife.com, 1901 Shalom Drive, 262-338-1310, $8/person) gives a two-hour guided wagon ride through 100 acres full of bison, elk and deer. Shalom Dr is five miles north of town off Hwy 144. Be sure to call for a reservation and bring a growler or two from the brewpub.

Randy's Fun Hunters Brewery & Restaurant

Founded: 1994
Brewmaster: Randy Cruse
Address: 841 E Milwaukee Street • Whitewater, WI 53190
Phone: 262-473-8000
Website: www.funhunters.net
Annual Production: 160 bbls
Number of Beers: 6 on tap

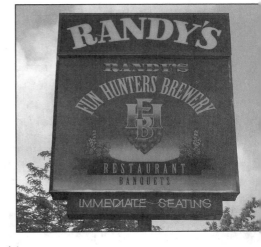

Staple Beers:
>> Amber Lager
>> Oatmeal Stout
>> Minnieska Maibock
>> Lawnmower Light
>> Warhawk Wheat Ale

Rotating Beers:
>> Oktoberfest

Most Popular Brew: Warhawk Wheat Ale

Brewmaster's Fave: Amber Lager or Pale Ale

Tours? No.

Samples? Yes, $6 for six 5-oz. glasses.

Best Time to Go: When you're thirsty. Funhunters gets a good lunch crowd. Dining room closes at 9 PM. Closed Mondays!

Where can you buy it? Only . Growlers available.

Got food? Yes, look for Prime and a Pint on Wednesdays (they are famous for steaks), beer-battered fish fry on Fridays. Here's something unusual: hand-dipped, battered *Colby* cheese curds (not cheddar).

Special Offer: A $2 10-oz. beer.

Directions: Business Hwy 12 is Milwaukee St. If you come in on Hwy 59 from the north or south, it passes the pub on Milwaukee as well.

The Beer Buzz: On the east side of town, this supper club draws 'em in for the food as well as the microbrews. Since 1972, there has been a restaurant on this site. An arsonist did his dirty work back in 1989, however, and it had to be rebuilt. The story of that is in articles on the walls in the entryway. Randy Cruse received a brew kit for Christmas one year and set out to master the skill. He got serious, worked with brewer Carl Strauss, and did coursework at the Siebel Institute before deciding to go public with his own beer here in the restaurant.

Expect a supper club atmosphere, total Wisconsin. A banquet facility seats 325. The bar is dim and features three flat-screen TVs. Vintage beer serving trays from various old breweries decorate the walls. Above the bar hangs a row boat which in the 1820s belonged to a young gentlemen's social club called the Funhunters. No one seems to be sure what kind of fun they were hunting for in 19th century Whitewater, but apparently there was some fishing involved. There are pics of the group in the bar.

Stumbling Distance: Nightlife in Whitewater is downtown where the college-aged patrons hang out. The town is also the southern end of the Kettle Moraine Scenic Drive. Starting at Cty H/Hwy 12, a 115-mile

stretch meanders north through the natural beauty left behind by the glaciers of the last Ice Age. Whitewater Lake is popular with boaters. *Frosty's Frozen Custard* (535 E Milwaukee St, 262-473-2320) is just down the road and offers some great frozen delights. *The Fireside Dinner Theatre* (www.firesidetheatre.com, 1131 Janesville Ave, Fort Atkinson, WI, 800-477-9505) puts on high-quality shows and plays in a 700-seat theatre in the round. Eat first, watch later.

ZONE 3

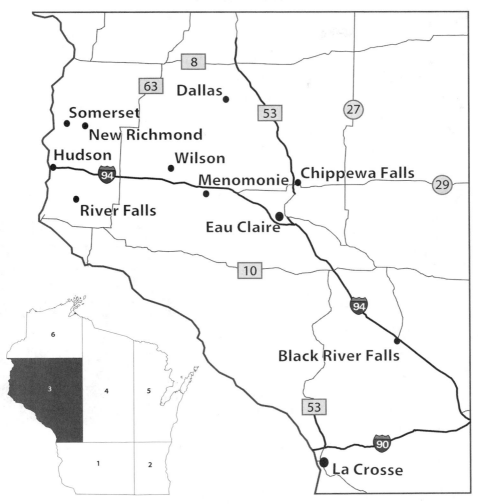

Black River Falls: Sand Creek Brewing Co.
Chippewa Falls: Jacob Leinenkugel Brewing Co.
Dallas: Valkyrie Brewery (formerly Viking Brewing Co.)
Eau Claire: Lazy Monk Brewery
Eau Claire: Norsky Northwoods Brewpub
Hudson: Hudson Brewing Co.
La Crosse: City Brewery
La Crosse: Pearl Street Brewery
Menomonie: Das Bierhaus
Menomonie: Lucette Brewing Co.
New Richmond: Brady's Brewhouse
River Falls: Rush River Brewing Co.
Somerset: Oliphant Brewing Co.
Wilson: Dave's BrewFarm

SAND CREEK BREWING CO.

Founded: 1999
Brewmaster: Todd Krueger
Address: 320 Pierce Street • Black River Falls, WI 54615
Phone: 715-284-7553
Website: www.sandcreekbrewing.com
Annual Production: 10,000+ bbls
Number of Beers: 12 or so

Staple Beers:

- » BADGER PORTER
- » ENGLISH-STYLE SPECIAL ALE
- » GOLDEN ALE
- » ONE PLANET ALE
- » OSCAR'S CHOCOLATE OATMEAL STOUT
- » SAND CREEK HARD LEMONADE
- » WILD RIDE IPA
- » WOODY'S WHEAT

Rotating Beers:

- » CRANBERRY SPECIAL ALE (fall)
- » GROOVY BREW (Kölsch, summer)
- » ODERBOLZ BOCK
- » PIONEER BLACK RIVER RED - OKTOBERFEST
- » SAND CREEK IMPERIAL PORTER

Most Popular Brew: Oscar's Chocolate Oatmeal Stout

Brewmaster's Fave: Depends on season/mood/hangover.

Tours? Yes, Fridays at 3 PM. From May–Sept also Saturdays noon–4 PM.

Samples? Yes, freebies and sample trays for $5 with eight 5-ounce beers.

Best Time to Go: Karner Blue Butterfly Festival in July, when 500 people tour the brewery that day or Sand Creek Brewery Oktoberfest, the first Saturday in October right in a huge tent with crafts and music all day and night.

Where can you buy it? Growlers, bottles, cases, pub kegs, ¼ and ½ barrels . Throughout Wisconsin, parts of Minnesota, Iowa and Illinois (mostly Chicago area).

Got food? No, but on Friday nights you can bring in something to pass—they always seem to find something.

Special Offer: A free pint and a hearty handshake and/or pat on the back

The Beer Buzz: The brewing force is strong in this one! Beer has been happening here since 1856 when Ulrich Oderbolz opened his brewery on this very same site. It was sold and renamed Badgerland Brewery but went beer belly up in 1920 (yep, Prohibition!). Then all hell broke loose here: turkeys, land mines, Coca Cola, and finally just storage, until 1996 when Jim and Dave Hellman remodeled the brick building and started Pioneer Brewing Co. In 1998, they acquired Wisconsin Brewing Co. from Wauwatosa and moved those brews to Black River Falls. Meanwhile, out on a farm near Downing, WI, Cory Schroeder and Jim Wiesender turned a farm shed into a brewery (talk about retro) and a semi-trailer into a beer cooler. Pudding tanks for mash kettles? If the tank fits… Thus was born Sand Creek Brewing Co., and in 2004 they bought Pioneer and left the farm. Original Pioneer Brewmaster Todd stayed on with the new owners and the lagers and ales keep flowing. They also contract brew another 30 beers. In 2000, Sand Creek took two golds at the World Beer Cup (Oscar's and Black River Red)—the first microbrewery to do it and followed up with another gold in 2002 for Oderbolz Bock. The tasting room feels like you are hanging with the neighbor guy at a bar he put in his basement—except this neighbor also happens to have a half dozen or so great homemade beers on tap. Very cool.

Stumbling Distance: *Rozario's* (42 N 1st St, 715-284-0006) near Main St is the best pizza in town and has beer on tap. Get your fresh cheese curds at *Del Bean Coffee & Cheese* (delbean@centurytel.net, 715-284-9840, 500 Oasis Rd, Hwy 54 exit 116 by the orange moose) and sample any of the cheeses or just have a cup of Joe or some ice cream. Visit the *Black River Chamber of Commerce* (blackrivercountry.net, 800-404-4008) for current ATV- and snowmobile-trail conditions along with scuba diving (no, seriously) and biking info. *Laura's Brickhouse Grill & Saloon* (44 Main St, 715-284-2888) will get you a Friday fish fry, a Saturday prime rib, and several Sand Creek taps.

Jacob Leinenkugel Brewing

Founded: 1867
Brewmaster: John Buhrow
Address: 1 Jefferson Avenue • Chippewa Falls, WI 54729
Phone: 715-723-5557
Website: www.leinies.com
Annual Production: 350,000 bbls
Number of Beers: 10 (7 year round, 3 seasonal)

Staple Beers:

- » Berry Weiss Bier
- » Classic Amber
- » Creamy Dark
- » Honey Weiss Bier
- » Leinie's Light
- » Leinie's Original Lager
- » Red Lager
- » Sunset Wheat

Seasonal Beers:

- » 1888 Bock
- » Fireside Nut Brown
- » Oktoberfest
- » Summer Shandy

Most Popular Brew: Honey Weiss

Brewmaster's Fave: Year round: Original Lager, Seasonal: Oktoberfest

Tours? Yes.

Samples? Two freebies every day you visit.

Best Time to Go: Oktoberfest is nice.

Where can you buy it? In 49 states, but most widely distributed in the upper Midwest.

Got food? Maybe some pretzels.

Special Offer: A free pint glass with any $10 purchase.

Directions: Follow Hwy 124 to the Elm St intersection. Turn onto East Elm Street and you'll see the Leinie Lodge on your left.

The Beer Buzz: This is a bit of a shrine for those of you who grew up knowing Leinie's as a local brewery. It's the seventh-oldest brewery in the US and a *pils*-grimage here is indeed a must. In the 1840s, Matthias Leinenkugel brought his family from Prussia (now part of Germany) to settle in Sauk City where he started brewing. Is brewing genetic? Could be. His sons opened two more: one in Eau Claire (where an uncle already had one) and another in Baraboo. Another son Jacob wasn't about to be left out and moved north eventually finding the lumber center of Chippewa Falls. Apparently lumber workers like beer. Lots of it, in fact. And so it was. It becomes huge local beer legend, yadda yadda yadda, fast forward to 1988: Miller (now MillerCoors), second largest brewer in the world, buys Leinie's. Purists clutch their chests, breaths are held, there is much gnashing of teeth. Somewhere in the distance a dog barks. But the brewery was not dismantled or swallowed up, and the old classic Leinie's has emerged bigger and better than before, producing some rather exceptional large market beers in a microbrew style. At the 2006 World Beer Cup, Sunset Wheat got bronze and Honey Weiss silver while Red Lager took gold in 2002. To keep up with sales, Leinie's operates 10th Street Brewery in Milwaukee which is also where they brew Big Eddy, their own line of craft beers

Stumbling Distance: Talk is the Friday fish fry is tops at *High Shores Supper Club* (17985 Cty Hwy X, 715-723-9854). *Fill-Inn Station* (104 W Columbia St, 715-723-8282) has deep-fried cheese curds, 6 Leinie's beers on tap, 10 different burgers, and a Friday fish fry, prime rib Saturday. Leinie's hosts or gets involved with a lot of little fests and such, but one of the most unusual is the *Family Reunion*. On the Saturday of Father's Day weekend head out to meet Leinenkugel brothers Jake, Dick and John as they host

a free get together featuring some live music, tours, and plenty of brats, beer, chips, beer, pickles, cookies, and of course beer. All free to 3000 participants. The event lasts from noon to sunset and the first 100 guests get a little extra gift.

VALKYRIE BREWING CO. (FORMERLY VIKING BREWING CO.)

Founded: 1994
Brewmaster: Randy and Ann Lee
Address: 234 Dallas St. West, Dallas, WI 54733
Phone: 715-837-1824
Website: www.valkyriebrewery.com
Annual Production: 400 barrels
Number of Beers: 22+

Staple Beers:
» BIG SWEDE (Swedish-style Imperial Stout
» DRAGON BLADE (American retro lager)
» RUBEE RED (a Marzen style lager)
» WAR HAMMER (coffee, oatmeal, milk porter)

Rotating Beers: (Most are seasonal batches and new ones come up once or twice a month.)
» ABBY NORMAL (Belgian tripel – Aug)
» BLAZE ORANGE EXOTICALLY SPICED BEER
» CRIMSON WONDER (Scotch Ale – Dec)
» GOLDEN HORN (Weizenbock)
» HOT CHOCOLATE (Fair Trade organic cocoa & cayenne pepper)
» INVADER DOPPELBOCK
» LIME TWIST (wheat beer)
» NIGHT WOLF (German-style Schwarzbier)
» RAVEN QUEEN (Black IPA)
» SUPERNOVA (Royal Australian India Pale Ale)
» VELVET GREEN (Dry Irish stout)
» WHISPERING EMBERS (Oktoberfest with beechwood-smoked malt – Sept)

Most Popular Brew: Rubee Red

Samples: Yes.

Brewmaster's Fave: Randy: Invader Doppelbock, Ann: Big Swede

Best Time to Go: The tap room is open Fridays 4–8 and Saturdays noon–8. Don't miss Oktoberfest.

Where can you buy it? In six-pack bottles, mostly in Western, Northwestern, and Central WI.

Got food? In a brewery? Be serious.

Tours? Yes, free tours most Saturdays at 1 PM (check website for when they are gone for Beer Shows) or by appointment.

Special Offer: A bottle of beer, sure, why not?

The Beer Buzz: Tiny Dallas makes a not-so-tiny mark on the beer map with this husband-and-wife operation. Housed in the basement of an old brick building on the main street, this was originally a Ford dealership selling Models T and A. (Was Ford a perv?) In the 30s it became a creamery and a handful of other things thereafter. Why did Randy open a brewery? "We were out of work at the time." Unemployment is the mother of invention. Or is it Randy's wife and co-brewer Ann? She comes up with a lot of the brew ideas and Randy makes the recipes. A stout with cocoa and cayenne? You better believe it. Dallas was dry until the early 60s, so heads turned when the brewery opened under its original name Viking Brewing and became one of the pioneers of microbrewing in the 90s in western Wisconsin. Randy sold the Viking name to an Icelandic brewery that wanted it worse than he did, and began brewing again as Valkyrie, a mythical Norse female who determines who lives and dies in battle. The tour lasts an hour and a half and is comprehensive, not just a show of what he's doing but also explanations of the different kinds of beers.

They now have a tap room at the front entrance with a walk-in beer cave and 16 beers on tap. It has an old castle look to it all, as befits the name. Be aware that Valkyrie brews unpasteurized beer. If you pick some up, take good care to keep it cool and out of the sun until you're ready to drink it!

Trivia note: Randy ran for state governor in 2002 as the BEER Party candidate. Hard to believe, but he didn't win. And now we are facing beer taxes. See where not voting gets you??

Stumbling Distance: This isn't far from lake country and nearby Chetek, and the surrounding area draws a lot of fishermen and outdoors types. Since Prohibition, Chicago travelers have come here for cabins. There's a Class A trout stream near Dallas and the town itself has a growing **Oktoberfest** the first Saturday of that month. Beer, brats, polkas, and if you're lucky, a traveling band of Vikings who set up a camp in town (seriously). *Clicker's Restaurant and Bar* (210 W Dallas St, 715-837-1416) has the best eats in town and a Friday night fish fry. If you're into antiques, hit up *Old Farmer's Mercantile* (115 W Dallas St, 715-837-1919). Eyeball some local pottery at *Losse Clay Studio* (201 W Dallas St, 715-837-1109).

ALTERNATIVE USES FOR BEER CANS

So perhaps you are now coming to see that beer really is supposed to have flavor and you love it that way. So what to do with all that other stuff in the fridge? Worry not, there are plenty of ways to put it to use. Consider these:

Party wear. Not sure what to wear to the next beer fest? How about a hat made out of cans and yarn? This will surely be hitting the runways in Paris (Paris, Wisconsin, population 1,473).

Davis Thuecks is sporting his grandpa's hat and shirt here. His friend, Robin Reese, apparently left his at home.

My great uncle John Lajcak had a knack for making furniture out of beer cans. A bit on the smallish size, but stylish.

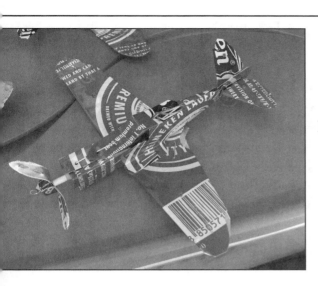

If beer could fly...

Remember Body on Tap shampoo? Me neither, but it was back in the 70s when it was believed beer would give your hair body. Back when the big curl was all the rage for the ladies, the steel cans made great rollers and the beer helped set the hair. A big thanks to Pat Breister and Sara Napiwocki down at Madison College for the re-enactment and Kristin Abraham, the brave volunteer. There was no permanent damage—other than possible emotional scarring.

Lazy Monk Brewery

Founded: May 2011
Brewmaster: Leos Frank
Address: 320 Putnam Street • Eau Claire, WI 54703
Phone: 715-271-5887
Website: www.lazymonkbrewing.com
Annual Production: 240 barrels
Number of Beers: 4 on tap

Staple Beers:
» Bohemian Pilsner
» Bohemian Dark Lager

Rotating Beers:
» Baltic Porter
» Bock
» Mai Bock
» Marzen
» Oktoberfest
» Summer Lager
» Vienna-Style Lager
» Winter Lager

Most Popular Brew: Bohemian Pilsner.

Brewmaster's Fave: It depends, which child do you like more?

Tours? Yes.

Samples: Yes, a paddle of 4 beers for $4

Best Time to Go: Wednesdays, Thursdays, and Fridays from 5 – 8 PM.

Where can you buy it? Growlers in area grocery and liquor stores.

Got food? No.

Special Offer: Not participating.

Directions: From Business Hwy 53 take Birch Street west into Eau Claire. At about 14 blocks watch for Putnam and go left (south) and find the brewery in the 320 Putnam Street Building. Park in the lot next to the railroad tracks and enter at the side door where there is a business directory. The tap room is suite 123.

The Beer Buzz: Brewer/owner Leos Frank was born and raised in what was then Czechoslovakia (now central Slovakia). We didn't have enough room or consonants to spell his hometown. When he moved here he couldn't find a beer he enjoyed and missed the brews of his culture. "It is a beer culture, it is part of life. Not too many people think they could make it, but they expect to have it." There were just a few microbreweries at that time, just starting up. "I stopped drinking beer at one point. Until someone told me, 'Do you know you can make it at home?'" It all started as a hobby and became an obsession.

"I started with a 40 gallon kettle, the biggest I could find. Then 55. Not enough." Then he had a guy from Menomonie make him a 5.5 barrel kettle. That's how it all got started. "Then I got a stainless steel fermenter and really started feeling like a pro." The name makes reference to the tradition of the monks while adding a kick-back-and-relax attitude to it. In deciding how to package he realized the bottled six-pack is rather pricey. So he decided to go with returnable packaging, namely the growler. Customers pay a deposit. The tap room, known as the Monk Cellar, has some barrels converted to tables and a monk mural on the wall, giving the place a really cool beer hall feel.

Stumbling Distance:
Definitely check out *The Coffee Grounds* (thecoffeegrounds.com, 3460 Mall Dr, 715-834-1733) which is much more than a cool coffee shop with a nice menu of food – it is also a stellar beer cellar with over 450 brews. If you like wood-smoked BBQ, then the award-winning *Mike's Smokehouse* (mikessmokehouse.co, 2235 N Clairemont Ave, 715-834-8153) should satisfy. Gyros anyone? *Olympic Flame* (2920 London Rd, 715-835-7771) gets raves. Unassuming place in a strip mall. Great food, friendly people.

Northwoods Brewpub and Grill

Founded: 1997
Brewmaster: Tim Kelly
Address: 3560 Oakwood Mall Drive • Eau Claire, WI 54701
Phone: 715-552-0510
Website: www.northwoodsbrewpub.com
Annual Production: 1000 bbls
Number of Beers: 13

Staple Beers:
- » Birchwood Pale Ale (low levels of bitterness)
- » Bumbl'n Bubba's Buzz'n Brew (honey golden ale)
- » Floppin' Crappie (light caramel-colored ale with honey)
- » Half Moon Gold
- » Kelly's Stout
- » Lil' Bandit Brown Ale
- » Mouthy Muskie Light Ale
- » Poplar Porter
- » Prickly Pike's Pilsner (Kölsch-style)
- » Red Cedar Red Ale
- » Walters Premium Pilsner
- » White Weasel(golden ale with barley, corn and rice)
- » Whitetail Wheat (unfiltered golden ale)

Rotating Beers:
- » Bumbl'n Bubba's Lingonberry Light (an actual berry)
- » Irish Red Ale
- » Oktoberfest Lager
- » Ripplin' Red Raspberry Wheat

Most Popular Brew: Floppin' Crappie

Brewmaster's Fave: Lil' Bandit Brown

Tours? Yes.

Samples? Yes, a sampler with eight 4-oz. beers for $5.00 and a free 8-oz. beer with a brew tour.

Best Time to Go: Happy hour is 11–6 Mon–Fri. Popular with the college crowd on Friday and Saturday nights. They are open from 7 AM to close, and serve breakfast, lunch and dinner.

Where can you buy it? Six-packs, growlers, kegs, party pigs. Grocery stores in Eau Claire, Hayward, Chetek and some regional taverns.

Got food? Yes, they have a full menu, are big on burgers, open for breakfast and the typical Friday fish fry, deep-fry cheese curds.

Special Offer: A free house beer or soda

Directions: The brewpub is on the frontage road on 53 just north of the I-94 interchange. Exit US-53 at Golf Rd and go west a short block to Oakwood Hills Parkway. Turn right (north) here and Oakwood Mall Drive is on your left.

The Beer Buzz: Where once were 800 acres of farmland is now a major shopping area. In the middle of all this is a pond saved from the surrounding development, and next to that is a brewpub. Founder/owner Jerry Bechard, a Wisconsin native, actually started homebrewing when he lived in Colorado. His co-workers (fans and test subjects of his beers) named Bumbl'n Bubba's Buzz'n Brew upon the arrival of Jerry's newborn son. When Jerry bought the Norske Nook in 1990 he was making the move into some of the best pies around and bread (which isn't too far off from beer (liquid bread), or so the monks of Europe would have said). But the call of beer is strong and in 1995 he decided he needed to make beer commercially and began Northwoods Brewing Co. Brewmaster Tim grew up with Jerry, and Jerry wanted him to brew. So Tim went off to Siebel Institute to study, already knowing where he'd be working when he was done.

The interior aims at rustic for the Northwoods theme, and the pond-side beer garden and patio are great in the summer. Their Lil' Bandit Brown Ale won silver at the Great American Beer Festival in 2000 while Floppin' Crappie wowed the crowd and took a best beer title at Sturgis in 2004. The restaurant menu shows some Norwegian items as well as about 25 specialty pies from the on-site bakery.

Stumbling Distance: If you are ready to shop till you drop, the surrounding area is chock full of places to do so. If you are not so inclined but with someone who is, the brewpub can be your refuge! *Carson Park* has the Paul Bunyan Camp (a recreation of a 19th century logging camp), a working quarter-scale railroad, and the baseball stadium where former Milwaukee Brave and Brewer Hank Aaron first played as a pro. The *Chippewa Valley Museum* (www.cvmuseum.com, 715-834-7871, free on Tues, closed Monday during school year, $4 adult) is also with exhibits about local history and the native Ojibwe (Chippewa), as well as some historic buildings. And the turn of the century ice cream parlor is serving ice cream sodas. Apple fans should come sometime from August to mid-November to visit *Eau Claire Orchards* (715-839-8370, 6470 Balsam Rd, 9–6 PM, closed Tuesday, pick your own on weekends) They also sell wholesale year-round. Check in at *The Coffee Grounds* (www.thecoffeegrounds.com, 3460 Mall Dr Hwy 93, 715-834-1733) for beer of the month and occasional beer, wine and coffee tastings. See Clearwater Beer Festival and Biking for Beer in the back of the book.

HUDSON BREWING (AMERICAN SKY BEER)

Founded: 2012
Brewmaster: Rick Sauer
Address: 1510 Swasey Street • Hudson, WI 54016
Phone: 651-503-3165
Website: www.americanskybeer.com
Annual Production: 2500 barrels capacity
Number of Beers: 3

Staple Beers:
  » AMERICA SKY BEERS:
  » AMBER SALUTE
  » TAILGUNNER GOLD
  » USA IPA

Rotating Beers:
  » Seasonals every three months

Most Popular Brew: Tailgunner Gold

Brewmaster's Fave: Amber Salute

Tours? Yes, every other Saturday for starters. Check the website.

Samples: Yes.

Best Time to Go: During tour times!

Where can you buy it? Draft accounts and bottles in Western Wisconsin with eyes on Minnesota.

Got food? No. Carry in is OK.

Special Offer: A free beer

Directions: Take Exit 2 from I-94 and head south on Carmichael Road. Go right (west) on Hanley Road and take it to the end to turn right on Heggen Street. Next right is Livingstone Road and Swasey Street is the next left.

The Beer Buzz: Founded by a husband and wife team, the 6000 square-foot brewery is Hudson's first in a long time. (Artesian Brewery and City Brewery were here in the 1890s but were both gone soon after the turn of the century.) Brewer/founder Greg Harris learned the art from his wife Molly's late stepfather back in 2002 when he was an engineer for Boston Scientific. That same job took him to Ireland for three years where he tried his brews on the locals. The reception was quite positive and it encouraged him to follow through on their dream of opening a brewery. Amber Salute, the first in their line-up was ten years in the making as he perfected the recipe.

Brewmaster Rick Sauer came to the brewery in August 2012. Rick got into brewing professionally at the Marinette Brewery in 1995, doing double duty for three years there and at the Choo Choo Bar in Superior, WI. In 1999 he opened Twin Ports Brewery (now Thirsty Pagan) until he sold it and ended up at Brady's Brewhouse for a couple years before this latest gig. He is a yeast farmer ("People don't create beer; yeast does. I create the conditions for yeast to do its work.")

The taproom has a World War II aviation theme going, and the bar is built to look like a plane's wing. Total Americana. Expect five beers on tap and with one of them always being a small batch of something new. The brewery is planning to offer a shuttle up the hill from Lakefront Park to the brewery. Watch the website.

Stumbling Distance: Rustic Road 13 is a hilly, wooded scenic drive through the St. Croix Valley. *Knoke's Chocolates* (knokeschocolates.com, 220 Locust St, 715-381-9866) are the handcrafted variety and delicious. For a good dinner, try *Pier 500 Restaurant* (pierfivehundred.com, 500 First St, 715-386-5504) with a menu that includes burgers to steaks, but also a lot of seafood options. Also, brie cheese curds? Nice!

CITY BREWERY

Founded: November 1999 (1858)
Brewmaster: Randy Hughes
Address: 925 S. Third Street • La Crosse, WI 54601
Phone: 608-785-4200
Website: www.citybrewery.com
Annual Production: 2,000,000 bbls (100% contract brewing)
Number of Beers: 40+

Brewmaster's Fave: "The one in my hand, but La Crosse Lager is my table beer."

Tours? No public access, though there are some historical markers outside.

Samples? No.

Best Time to Go: La Crosse Oktoberfest (see Festivals in back of book).

Got food? No.

Special Offer: Not participating.

Directions: Highways 14/61 go right through the city and the brewery is on it where it meets 3rd Street.

The Beer Buzz: Look for the world's largest six-pack and you've come to the right place. On Third and Mississippi St, this is the former G. Heileman Brewery, founded as a partnership in 1858 and officially G. Heileman's in 1890. Remember Old Style and Special Export? "Pure brewed from God's country; you can travel the world over and never find a better beer." In the late 19th century, after the death of her husband, Johanna Heileman was one of the first women presidents of a US corporation. In 1959, G. Heileman began buying up other breweries and became a bit of a giant producing 17 million barrels altogether. Bond Corporation of Australia bought G. Heileman in 1987 and then the brewery was passed about until it was sold to Pabst in 1999. All the breweries shut down and found different purposes except this facility which became City Brewery, owned partly by employees of the former company. The 1870 home of Gottlieb and Johanna Heileman is right across the street and holds the offices. The brewery sits on an artesian well from which it takes its water for brewing. Many travelers will stop for the photo op with the giant six pack.

Brewmaster Randy was here 22 years with G. Heileman and all of City Brewery's years. He studied biology at UW-La Crosse and went straight to the brewery to do lab work, ie. beer analysis. He's been brewmaster since 1995. Several beers have taken home awards including 2000 World Beer Cup Silver for City Lager/Light, La Crosse Lager/Light, silver for City Lager, La Crosse Lager, and Festbier at the 2004 World Beer Championships, and more silver for Winter Porter and Pale Ale at 2005 World Beer Championships. For a while City Brewery maintained ownership of the La Crosse brands, but since the sale of those, the brewery is doing contracted brews exclusively, and now has brewing facilities also in Latrobe, PA and Memphis, TN.

Stumbling Distance: *Kramers Bar & Grill* (1123 3rd St, 608-784-8541) next door is a good place to get a bite and it serves City brews. Menu is mostly burgers and the like, plus deep-fried white cheddar cheese curds and beer-battered shrimp. If you are already road-tripping here, don't miss the Great River Road from Prescott to Prairie du Chien (by way of La Crosse). Signage is clear (a green pilot's wheel) and Hwy 133 goes all the way to Potosi, home of Potosi Brewery and the National Brewery Museum. The bluffs are beautiful and the drive is recommended by several national publications. Granddad Bluff is most popular for a view of the river valley and the city.

PEARL STREET BREWERY

Founded: 1999
Brewmaster: Joe Katchever
Address: 1401 S Andrew Street
       La Crosse, WI 54603
Phone: 608-784-4832
Website: www.pearlstreetbrewery.com
Annual Production: 1000 bbls
Number of Beers: 4 for sure plus others coming and going

Staple Beers:
- » D.T.B (brown ale)
- » EL HEFE (Bavarian-style hefeweizen)
- » PEARL STREET PALE ALE (APA)
- » THAT'S WHAT I'M TALKIN''BOUT ORGANIC ROLLED OAT STOUT!

Rotating Beers: Watch for regular seasonal bottled and draft choices and limited releases such as DANKENSTEIN IMPERIAL INDIA PALE ALE, EVIL DOPPLEGANGER DOPPLEBOCK and FRUITBAT TAMBOIS.

Most Popular Brew: In La Crosse, it's the D.T.B.

Brewmaster's Fave: "I tend to drink the hoppier beers, but a good bock is a great thing!"

Tours? Yes, Saturdays from Noon-5 PM with tastings, or call with your group or for a special event.

Samples? Sure! They do samples individually or you can get a flight of eight different beers!

Best Time to Go: La Crosse is in the Guinness Book for having the most bars per capita. It's an exciting town with festivals and ongoing events year round. The city is particularly jovial during Oktoberfest or Great River Jazz Fest in August, but the Tasting Room at the brewery is open all year from 4-8 PM Tues–Fri and from noon–5 PM on Saturdays. Watch for their Annual Winter Ball in February.

Where can you buy it? Everywhere in La Crosse and throughout Western Wisconsin and Madison.

Got food? La Crosse has lots of great restaurants who deliver right to the brewery.

Special Offer: A free pint!

Directions: From I-90 take the Hwy 35/53 exit south to the first traffic light and go left on to George Street. After you've gone over the bridge over the train tracks, take a left at the 2nd set of traffic lights (Saint Andrew St) and go half a block down on the left to the four-story La Crosse Footwear building.

The Beer Buzz: Brewmaster Joe lived in Colorado and worked at several breweries there before journeying to La Crosse to found Pearl Street, which takes its name from its original location on Pearl Street down town. Things were going well and he was putting out 12 different beers annually, but growth was inevitable. The new facility was up and running before renovations were even complete. They have much more space in this renovated boot factory from the early 1900s. It was once home to La Crosse Footwear which moved its operations to China in 2001 and left the factory empty. And as with most emptiness, beer just seems like the best solution. The Tasting Room offers a hand-crafted bar to go with the hand-crafted beers, and there is always something on tap that you cannot get anywhere else. They have a nice little gift shop here as well. Past awards include a gold for D.T.B. and a silver for Pale Ale at the World Beer Cup in 2003.

Stumbling Distance: For a taste from the other end of the Mississippi, check out Cajun eatery *Buzzard Billy's Flying Carp* (www.buzzardbillys. com, 222 Pearl St, 608-796-2277). Right across the street from there is *T.J. Cheddarheads*, the original home of those foam cheesehead hats and a bunch of other Wisconsin souvenirs. The Mississippi is king here and to take in a view of it and have some great eats, head down to *La Crosse Pettibone Boat Club* (2615 Schubert Pl, 608-784-7743, under the big blue bridge to Minnesota). Boaters can use the marina and outside seating features a tiki bar. Famous for hand-dipped cheese curds, Pettibone serves anything from nice dinners to casual burgers. Open from May–Oct. And of course the biggest beer event in town is also one of the biggest in the state: *La Crosse Oktoberfest*.

NOTE: There are a couple of pubs in town that call themselves "brew-pubs" but at the moment of printing the only two brewers in La Crosse are included here.

DAS BIERHAUS

Founded: September 1, 2006
Brewmaster: Robert Wilber
Address: 120 6th Ave West • Menomonie, WI 54751
Phone: 715-231-3230
Website: www.dasbierhaus-wi.com
Annual Production: 1000 bbls
Number of Beers: 6 on tap

Staple Beers:
» ALTBIER
» DOPPELBOCK
» HEFEWEIZEN
» OKTOBERFEST or MÄRZEN
» PILSNER
» PILSNER LIGHT

Rotating Beers:
» HEFEWEIZEN DUNKEL
» MAIBOCK

Brewmaster's Fave: Pilsner

Tours? Yes, just walk in, but not while brewing is going on.

Samples? Yes, about $6 for a rack of six samplers.

Best Time to Go: Oktoberfest (end of September). Mug club for the regulars. Open 11 AM daily. Three-liter beer towers on Tuesdays, two-liter boots on Wednesdays. Lady's Day is Thursday (or men dressed in drag). Closed Mondays.

Where can you buy it? ½ liters and liters and a smaller mug, one-liter and two-liter Grolsch-style snap-top growlers on site.

Got food? Yes, some bar food but also a lot of German fare, such as hearty sausages, spiced camembert cheese, currywurst (a Berlin specialty), and

pork schnitzel sandwiches. Perch, flounder, walleye and salmon for the Friday Night Fish Fry.

Special Offer: A free half liter!

Directions: Sixth St actually intersects Hwys 12, 25 and 29. Just go west on it when you get there and the brewpub is just off Broadway.

The Beer Buzz: "Import the brewmaster, not the beer!" Talk about Wisconsin's German heritage. Brewmaster Robert was born in Germany. He did his apprenticeship at Würzburger Hofbrau in Bavaria (making pilsners since 1643). Apprentices "do all the bullshit work" like cleaning and mopping, and only upon graduation do they get to do the more serious tasks. Robert moved to the US and is married to a Wisconsinite. He was brewing with 'Sconnie Ales up in Clear Lake, and when that project just didn't come together, many were disappointed—including the farmer who had been using the spent grains. He and Robert came up with the idea of setting up an authentic beer hall in Menomonie. Robert did not want to open a restaurant with a brewpub attached—he wanted a place where the emphasis was the beer, a true beer hall like those in Munich. When they found a former meat packing facility just a block from the University of Wisconsin-Stout (say, was it named after a beer??), they knew they had a winner. Décor and atmosphere aimed to be strictly German. But the market dictated a switch and now the bar has more of a college vibe, and owners Lee and Marge Quale keep a very active Facebook page with many special events. Beer is not served in pints but rather liters and half-liters and is brewed in strict accordance with the Bavarian Reinheitsgebot of 1516.

Stumbling Distance: At the other corner of the block is *The Raw Deal,* an impressive raw food, organic juice, coffee house that also serves regional craft beer (rawdeal-wi.com, 603 S Broadway, 715-231-3255). The *Historic Mabel Tainter Theater* (www.mabeltainter.com, 205 Main St, 715-235-9726) is a Victorian Era venue that still puts on a variety of performing arts shows from October through May each year. See the still-operational Steere and Turner tracker pipe organ with 1597 pipes. Five miles north of town on Tainter Lake is *Jake's Supper Club* (jakessupperclub.com, E5690 Cty Rd D, 715-235-2465) a great option for a Friday fish fry (walleye) and highly recommended for prime rib. You can get deep-fried cheese curds here or get them fresh over at *Cady Cheese Factory* (www.cadycheese.com, 126 Hwy 128, Wilson, WI, 715-772-4218). Take a tour or sample over 100 different cheeses and sausages. Just 3 1/2 miles south on Hwy 128, off I-94, or right off Hwy. 29 at Cty Rd T and Hwy 128.

LUCETTE BREWING CO.

Founded: 2011
Brewmaster: Jon Christiansen
Address: 901 Hudson Road • Menomonie, WI 54751
Phone: 715-233-2055
Website: www.lucettebrewing.com
Annual Production: 1200 barrels
Number of Beers: 4

Staple Beers:
  » EASY RIDER PALE ALE
  » FARMER'S DAUGHTER SPICED BLONDE ALE (coriander and grains of paradise)
  » SHINING DAWN GOLDEN BELGIAN STYLE ALE
  » SLOW HAND STOUT

Most Popular Brew: Farmer's Daughter.

Brewmaster's Fave: Shining Dawn

Tours? Free tours first and third Sat at 2 PM. Right next to Red Cedar State Trail

Samples: Only on the tours.

Best Time to Go: Only during scheduled tour times!

Where can you buy it? Only sold via distributors, mostly western Wisconsin and Twin Cities metro area.

Got food? No.

Special Offer: 10% off the purchase of Lucette Brewing merchandise during visit.

Directions: From I-94 take Exit 41 for Hwy 25 and head south through downtown on Hwy 25. Go west on Hwy 29, across from the university, and follow it ¾ mile and you'll see Lucette in a white building on your left (south side).

The Beer Buzz: From the road this place could be mistaken for a farmhouse, painted white, a porch out front. So don't expect a big industrial brewery. They wanted to fit in with their surroundings. Co-founder

Michael Wilson is very serious about the local aspect of beer and part of his business philosophy is making a difference not just for himself, but for the businesses that support him. Thus, all beer is sold via distribution and retail outlets, not on site.

Mike is originally from Minnesota and while studying at University of North Dakota he determined that he wanted to be involved with the craft brewing industry. He dabbled in homebrewing and learned he wasn't good at it. But that wouldn't deter him. He moved to Menomonie and got experience in distribution. He met his business partner Tim Schletty who had a retail background. The two had experience in two of the three aspects of a brewery; now they only needed the all-important brewer. They hired Jon Christiansen who has been brewing with them since day one. Jon got his start at Water Street Lake Country in Delafield and spent some time at Joseph James Brewery in Vegas before being hired by Lucette Brewing.

Stumbling Distance: *Red Cedar State Trail* runs right past the brewery. If you're a biker, this is a nice ride. See Biking for Beer in the back of the book.

Brady's Brewhouse

Founded: October 10, 2010
Brewmaster: Luke Nirmaier
Address: 230 South Knowles Avenue • New Richmond, WI 54017
Phone: 715-246-9960
Website: www.bradysbrewhouse.com
Annual Production: 250 barrels
Number of Beers: 8–9 on tap

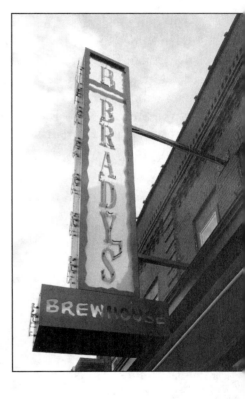

Staple Beers:
- » Derailed Pale Ale
- » Harvester Oatmeal Stout
- » Hop Tornado IPA
- » Sunny Golden Wheat
- » Vagadond Irish Red

Rotating Beers:
- » Drag Buster Brown Ale
- » Hefweizen
- » Oktoberfest
- » Smoked Rye Porter

(Basically, a strong ale, a weekly special, and two seasonals are always on tap)

Most Popular Brew: Hop Tornado IPA

Brewmaster's Fave: Oktoberfest

Tours? Yes, by chance from 9–5; see if Luke is around.

Samples: Yes, a flight is $12 for eight 5-oz. pours.

Best Time to Go: Open for lunch and dinner, from 11 AM. Happy Hour Sun-Thurs 2–6 PM and 10 PM–close. Discount growler refills on Mondays.

Where can you buy it? Only at the bar or take-away in growlers.

Got food? Full menu with good burgers and pizza, including deep-fried cheese curds, beer cheese soup, and so much more.

Special Offer: $1 off a house beer

Directions: Highway 65 comes right into New Richmond and become Knowles Avenue. If you are coming from the south, watch for Brady's on the right between 2nd and 3rd Streets.

The Beer Buzz: There's a lot going on here. Great food, house-brewed beer, TVs, and plenty of space to kick back and relax with friends or family. The kitchen has a wood-fired oven, and the bar also offers a wide assortment of wines and cocktails. Head brewer Rick Sauer (now of Hudson Brewing) started the ball rolling and was then joined by Luke Nirmaier who took over when Rick left. Luke started in college and jumped in at Brady's via the kitchen. When he applied for a job, he recalls, "I brought in a six-pack—here's my portfolio." It got him in the door and after doing most of the brewing with Rick supervising, it wasn't a big deal when he found himself taking the reins alone.

A 10-gallon batch of R&D beer is typically on tap, so there's always something new to try. Brady's is family friendly and one of the finest places to eat in town. A room upstairs in back overlooks the brewhouse.

Stumbling Distance: Get a tour and tasting over at *45th Parallel Distillery* (45thparallelspirits.com, 1570 Madison Ave, 715-246-0565)—be sure to call for an appointment. *Star Prairie Trout Farm* (starprairietrout.com, 400 Hill Ave, Star Prairie, 715-248-3633) just north of town lets you catch 'em or just take home already caught and cleaned.

Rush River Brewing Co.

Founded: May 2004
Brewmasters: Dan Chang and Nick Anderson
Address: 990 Antler Court • River Falls, WI 54022
Phone: 715-426-2054
Website: www.rushriverbeer.com
Annual Production: undetermined
Number of Beers: 9

Staple Beers:
- » Bubblejack IPA
- » Double Bubble Imperial IPA
- » Lost Arrow Porter
- » Small Axe Golden Ale (Wisconsin-style Hefeweizen with local wheat)
- » The Unforgiven Amber Ale (dry-hopped)

Rotating Beers:
- » Lyndale Brown Ale (Aug–Nov)
- » Nevermore Chocolate Oatmeal Stout (winter)
- » Über Alt (April–July)
- » Winter Warmer (Oct–Jan; based on Scotch Ale with a malty emphasis)

Most Popular Brew: The Unforgiven Amber Ale

Brewmaster's Fave: Bubblejack IPA

Tours? Free tours with samples the second Saturday of each month at 1 PM. Numbers are limited and you must reserve a spot (use the website).

Samples? Yes.

Where can you buy it? In six-pack and twelve-pack bottles. Their website shows their distribution in western Wisconsin, the Madison area, and eastern Minnesota (especially the Twin Cities).

Got food? Nope.

Special Offer:
Not Participating.

The Beer Buzz: Dan and Nick were co-workers at a brewery in Seattle when they met. Nick's from Minneapolis and Dan hails from Milwaukee, so the logical place to set up shop was right in the middle, just inside the border of Wisconsin, as it turns out, in Maiden Rock. Dan put in some time at Summit Brewing Co. in St. Paul to perfect his art while Nick worked in retail to gain experience in that all-important aspect of the microbrewing world. Robbie Stair, a third partner, brought a site to the table—his farm on Lake Pepin. The twenty-barrel brewhouse, designed and built by the three owners, was a showcase of ingenuity. Then in March 2007, they packed up the farm, as it were, and moved into a new facility in River Falls. This change means more beer is a-flowing and bottles became available, but also we, the public, can now stop in for a tour.

Stumbling Distance: Fill your belly with some highly regarded local home-style cooking at *River Falls Family Restaurant* (702 North Main Street, 715-425-9440).

ARE YOU A WISCONSIN BEER LOVER?

I mean, like *officially*? The Wisconsin Brewer's Guild brings together many of the state's great craft brewers and the businesses that support them to promote the art and educate the public about good beer. You may not be a brewer, but you can still join the club as a Wisconsin Beer Lover. Annual fees are about $30 and benefits include quarterly newsletters, VIP benefits at events sponsored by the guild, and discounts at some of the member breweries... and, of course, a lovely t-shirt. Go to their website to get an application or to find more information: www.wibrewersguild.com.

OLIPHANT BREWING

Founded: Spring 2013
Brewmaster: Matt Wallace and Trevor Wirtanen
Address: 350 Main Street • Somerset, WI 54025
Website: www.oliphantbrewing.com
Annual Production: nano-sized
Number of Beers: 8 on tap

Staple Beers:
» Nothing permanent – always rotating!

Tours? By appointment.

Samples: Most definitely.

Best Time to Go: Anytime they're open.

Where can you buy it? At the brewery or at Liquor Depot.

Got food? Bring your own if you want.

Special Offer: Bring this book in and receive a pretty good high-five (maybe even a great one?) and a beer or whiskey on us. Also, if you get a permanent face tattoo of our logo, we'll give you free beer for life!

Directions: Take Hwy 64 west from New Richmond and take the Business 64 exit into Somerset. This becomes Main Street.

The Beer Buzz: I suspect some of their story is a bit suspect, but trouble is I can't figure out which parts. Best to quote them: Trevor and Matt "met in Nepal at the secret caves underneath Mt. Everest fighting the Secret Ninja of the would-be American Communists group "El Luchadores." Trevor was mortally wounded until he saw a toucan, smelled Froot Loops, and was reborn. At that very instant, Matt fell asleep and dreamed of the Oliphant. The Oliphant approached Matt with his hot pink sucker-fins and commanded him to open a brewery and distillery in Somerset, Wisconsin, to spread the liquid consciousness of the Oliphant to the people."

Fortunately, Trevor and Matt had been brewing for a while prior to their mindnumbing experience with the Oliphant. Trevor started homebrewing on a whim with the help of a friend's equipment and instantly became a fervent supporter of fermentation in all aspects. Next thing Matt knew, Trevor was forcing him to participate in weekly brewing sessions at times in the morning when no one should be brewing. Although not the career path they originally planned on, (Trevor has a Master's Degree in Music Composition and Matt double majored in English and Anthropology) they felt like it was in everyone's best interest not to get on the wrong side of the Oliphant and to do what it told them to do. You know… for the children.

The brewery is also a distillery and will feature an ever-rotating tap list of beers as well as new whiskies to try every month or so. "We believe in having constant variety, and we feel that having only a few beers that we brew over and over is more akin to manufacturing than crafting. We are brewers, not manufacturers, and we strive to create something that will keep our patrons excited and surprised."

Stumbling Distance: *Liquor Depot* (820 Rivard St # 200, 715-247-5336) has a good assortment of Wisconsin products. Go tubing down the Apple River with *Float Rite* (floatrite.com, 715-247-3453) but be sure not to take glass out on the water. Find an alternative growler for Oliphant beer or a metal flask for their whisky.

Dave's BrewFarm – A Farmhouse Brewery

Founded: March 2008
Chief Yeast Wrangler: Dave Anderson
Address: 2470 Wilson St., Wilson, WI 54027
Phone: 612-432-8130
Website: www.davesbrewfarm.blogspot.com
Annual Production: 200 bbls
Number of Beers: 8 taps at the farm, too many styles to list!

Rotating Beers:
  » BrewFarm Select
  » Matacabras
  » Mocha Diablo
  » AuBEXXX
  » Anything goes here! You never know what to expect!

Most Popular Brew: Mocha Diablo

Brewmaster's Fave: "You want me to pick my favorite child?!? Depends on the mood. I usually say the beer in my right hand."

Tours? Yes, they do free tours and have open tap room hours in the LaBrewatory but they vary. Make an appointment or watch the website/blog.

Samples? "Oh yes, the best way to sell my beers!"

Best Time to Go: Whenever you made your appointment.

Where can you buy it? Kegs as well as 22-oz. and 750 ml bottles in Western Wisconsin and the Twin Cites area, plus major metro areas of Wisconsin such as Milwaukee, Madison, Eau Claire, and maybe Green Bay.

Got food? No but peanuts in the shell are usually on hand. There's a few restaurants nearby.

Special Offer: A 15% discount on a BrewFarm T-shirt.

Directions: Take Exit 28 off I-94, head north about 2.5 miles to 80th Ave. Take a right onto 80th to the "T" intersection. You can't miss the red barn board building with the wind generator on the 120-ft. tower making power!

The Beer Buzz: Like many, Dave's brewing problem started with home-brewing in 1992, and progressed with him going to the Siebel Institute in

1996. By then he was too far gone and wanted to open his own brewery. He conceived of the "BrewFarm" in 1995. Dave wanted to brew beer and be out in the country in a farmhouse setting. He brewed for the short-lived Ambleside Brewery in Minneapolis and Paper City Brewery in Holyoke, MA, worked for a variety of beer distributors, worked both import and export of craft beer and consulted with start-up breweries in places around the world, including Vietnam, Italy, and Israel. In the end he landed in Wilson, WI to finally make the BrewFarm a reality. Dave started brewing here and an immediate demand compelled him to do some contract brewing offsite, producing cans and bottles. In the end, he decided that wasn't for him, so he has cut the contract and now just brews at the farm. He's a one man show, and this is quality not quantity.

Dave's beer is looking pretty green. You can see Jake, the 120-foot-tall 20kW wind generator that provides nearly all the power for Dave's brewery and home. (One blog entry shows his electric bill was 81-cents one month!) The beer name Matacabras comes from a Spanish term for a wind that "kills goats." But Wisconsin wind is a bit nicer; here on the wind-powered farm, it brews beer! Throw in some recycled dairy equipment repurposed for beer plus a solar thermal system in the works and this is about as eco-friendly as a brewery can get. Drink some beer to protect the environment.

Stumbling Distance: There's not much out here, but if you are looking for a good place to eat, try *Peg's Pleasant View Inn* (3015 US Highway 12, Wilson, 715-772-4610). *Das Bierhaus* and *Lucette Brewing* are in Menomonie another 20 minutes east on I-94.

PHOTOGRAPH COURTESY OF DAVE ANDERSON

ZONE 4

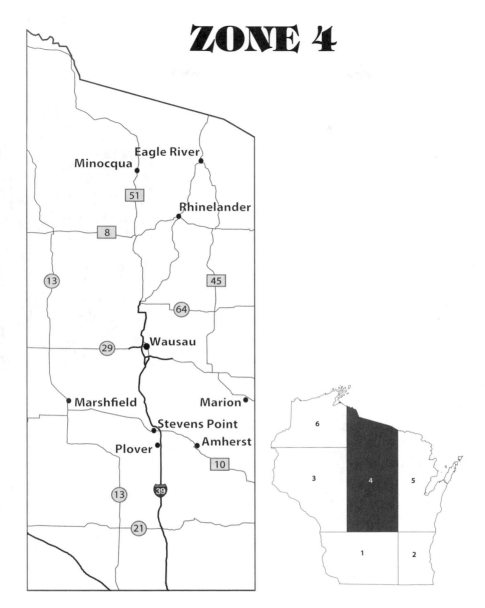

Amherst: Central Waters Brewery
Eagle River: Tribute Brewing Co.
Marion: Pigeon River Brewing Co.
Marshfield: Blue Heron BrewPub
Minocqua: Minocqua Brewing Co.
Plover: O'so Brewing Co.
Rhinelander: Rhinelander Brewing Co.
Stevens Point: Stevens Point Brewery
Wausau: Bull Falls Brewery
Wausau: Great Dane Pub and Brewery
Wausau: Red Eye Brewery

Central Waters Brewing Co.

Founded: January 1998
Brewmaster: Paul Graham
Address: 351 Allen Street • Amherst, WI 54406
Phone: 715-824-2739
Website: www.centralwaters.com
Annual Production: 11,000 bbls
Number of Beers: 20+

Staple Beers:
- » Glacial Trail IPA
- » Honey Blonde
- » Happy Heron Pale Ale
- » Mud Puppy Porter
- » Ouisconsing Red Ale
- » Satin Solstice Imperial Stout
- » Shine On Red Ale

Rotating Beers:
- » Belgian Blonde
- » Brewhouse Coffee Stout
- » Hop Harvest
- » Hopsessional
- » Kosmyk Charlie's Y2K Catastrophe Ale (Barleywine!)
- » Octoberfest
- » Slainte Scotch Ale
- » and several bourbon barrel-aged beers (Barleywine, Stout, Cherry Stout, and Peruvian Morning, an Imperial Stout with coffee).

Most Popular Brew: Glacial Trail IPA

Brewmaster's Fave: The one in his hand.

Tours? Yes, call or check the website for tour times.

Samples? Yes. Flights offer 5 samples for $3.50.

Best Time to Go: The Tap Room is open Fridays and Saturdays 3–9 PM.

Where can you buy it? Bottles and kegs around Wisconsin, Minnesota, Illinois. Local taverns should have it.

Got food? No.

Special Offer: A Central Waters bumper sticker.

Directions: From US Hwy 10 take the Cty Rd A exit north onto Old US Hwy 10 into Amherst. The first right is Main St. Take this to the next right on Washington St, and follow that to the next right which is Allen St. Be aware that this area is developing and other streets may be popping up to throw off my "first right" directions. Rely on street signs or use the Force.

The Beer Buzz: Paul calls it a "hobby gone out of control." He was brewing in his dorm room when he was 18. Perfectly legal to buy the ingredients, but he wasn't allowed to drink his results. And I'm sure he didn't. Actually, at first, he really didn't—it was so bad, he said, he couldn't. He was just playing around but soon got the hang of it (as one can tell from the great beer here). Mike McElwain and Jerome Ebel opened the brewery first in a 1920s former Ford Dealership in Junction City in a small brick building with a flapping screen door that opened right out onto the highway through town. Paul called it a "glorified homebrew system," and he did the boils in a 300-gallon cheese starter tank with a commercial hot water heater element attached to the bottom. Converted dairy tanks functioned as fermenters and the whole operation was built by hand. After 3 years Paul and Clint Schultz bought the brewery and soon after Anello Mollica

took Clint's place. Success led to expansion and Central Waters started a brewpub in Marshfield (now the independent Blue Heron) and moved the brewery into new digs in Amherst in 2006. The current brewing facility is the first green-powered brewery in the state (though no longer the only). Besides energy efficient lights and equipment and radiant-heat flooring, they have a bank of twenty-four solar collectors. In October 2011, they added 20,000-watt solar photovoltaic panels which provide 20% of their annual power needs. Hop Harvest uses totally local ingredients (even the hand-picked hops). As they like to say at the brewery: "Making the world a better place, one beer at a time." Their Barleywine has gotten a couple of awards, and Bourbon-Barrel Barleywine and Bourbon Barrel Cherry Stout have both taken gold at Great American Beer Festival.

Stumbling Distance: *Tomorrow River Supper Club* (9971 Cty Rd KK, 715-824-3113), a block off the end of Main St, is a notable local restaurant with a Friday fish fry (haddock and pike) and also bluegill, pan-fried walleye, prime rib (Sat) and deep-fried cheese curds. They open Wed–Sun at 4 PM and serve bottled Point and Central Waters beers. Pack a cooler full of the local brew and go canoeing on the Crystal River with the folks at *Ding's Dock*, 12 miles away near Waupaca. Take Hwy 10 east to 54, take a right and go until a left on Cty QQ through the village of King. Then take a right on Q and it's a mile down the road on the left. They drop you and your canoe off at the mouth of the river and you take 2.5–3 hours to float down 11 miles of river for about $16 per person (two people per canoe).

TRIBUTE BREWING CO.

Founded: February 2012
Brewmaster: Marc O'Brien
Address: 1106 Bluebird Road • Eagle River, Wisconsin 54521
Phone: 715-480-2337
Website: www.tributebrewing.com
Annual Production: Too soon to tell, but they have a 7-barrel system
Number of Beers: 4–8 of their own on tap, plus 10–12 guest Wisconsin beers

Staple Beers: (subject to change)
» BLUEBERRY WHEAT
» DORTMUNDER
» HELLES
» IPA

Rotating Beers:
» OKTOBERFEST
» VANILLA STOUT
» … and more planned!

Most Popular Brew: Can't say yet!

Brewmaster's Fave: His IPA.

Tours? By appointment.

Samples: Yes, a sample platter of their beers.

Best Time to Go: The taphouse is open Mon–Fri 4–9 PM and Sat 3–9 PM

Where can you buy it? Only here, for now. They fill growlers.

Got food? Free peanuts—throw the shells on the floor.

Special Offer: $1 off your first pint.

Directions: From downtown Eagle River head north on Highway 45 to Airport Road. Go left here and the next street is Bluebird Road. Go left again (south) and the brewery is on the left side.

The Beer Buzz: This isn't founder Bill Summers' first involvement with the craft beer scene. He and a few others originally started Eagle River's Great Northern Beer Festival (greatnorthernbeerfestival.com). Now he and his wife VaLynda run the fest with the help of volunteers. After the

short-lived Loaf & Stein brewpub came and went in the late 90s, there
was really no craft beers for locals to enjoy. Bill did some research and
visited a lot of places to see what sort of place might work for a brewpub.
In the 1990s the trend was to buy an old brick building downtown somewhere (as South Shore in Ashland or Angry Minnow in Hayward) and
refashion it into a pub. But then he saw brewers moving into industrial
parks and airport hangars. In the end, Bill felt this model made a more
casual atmosphere, made clients comfortable, and gave everyone more
space. They were more talkative and laid back.

Bill found this building out near the highway and the airport and decided
it was perfect. The former home to a log home design company and their
woodcrafting shop, it had a good vibe. "Like going into a garage party, a
keg in the corner." In fact, the brewery opens a garage door in nice weather
for some good air. The style is all industrial: Barrels under the bar, cement
floor, warehouse lighting, and galvanized metal utility panels along the
walls. A couple of antennae towers frame the bar. You can also see Bill's
collection of over 90 growlers.

Brewer Marc is president of the L.U.S.H. homebrew club in Eagle River
and has won some awards for his homebrews. He and Bill were at a club
meeting at Minocqua Brewing Co. a few years ago and tossed around
the idea of going pro. And in 2012 that happened. Don't expect a huge
operation. They'll do a few kegs locally, maybe some bottles in the future.
No pool tables, games or jukebox. What you'll get here is just a great place
to hang out, talk craft beer, and try a few of them.

Bill jokes that the brewery name comes from his ride: a Mazda Tribute.
But actually they wanted a simple name, and tribute comes into play with
the beer names: All will be "tributes" to people, places or things in the
Northwoods.

Stumbling Distance: Eagle River is on the Chain of Lakes, the largest
inland fresh water chain of lakes in the world with 28 connected bodies
of water. So boaters, fishermen, and paddlers will find Nirvana here. Right
across the street from the brewery is the *World Championship Snowmobile
Derby Track* (derbytrack.com). *Leif's Café* (800 N Railroad St, 715-
479-2766) is walking distance, and is famous for breakfast and brunch.
Riverstone Restaurant & Tavern (riverstonerestaurant.com, 219 Railroad
St, 715-479-8467) has an eclectic dinner menu, a Friday fish fry, and very
good wine and beer list.

PIGEON RIVER BREWING CO.

Founded: July 18, 2012
Head Brewers: Nathan Knaack and Matthew Wichman
Address: W12710 U.S. Highway 45 • Marion, WI 54950
Phone: 715-256-7721
Website: www.pigeonriverbrewing.com
Annual Production: 600–700 barrels
Number of Beers: 2–7

Staple Beers:
 » PIGEON BLONDE ALE
 » SLIPPERY RICHARD OATMEAL STOUT

Rotating Beers:
 » Some Seasonals

Most Popular Brew: Too soon to tell!

Brewmaster's Fave: Slippery Richard Oatmeal Stout.

Tours? Yes, if the brewers are there, you can ask.

Samples: Yes, sample platters.

Best Time to Go: Hours are Wed–Fri 4 PM–close, Sat–Sun 11 AM–close. Closed Mon–Tues. These may change, so watch the website.

Where can you buy it? Growlers on site.

Got food? Yes, locally handcrafted pizza.

Special Offer: A free pint.

Directions: The brewery is at the west edge of town on the south side of Highway 45 set back a bit from the road.

The Beer Buzz: Nate and Matt grew up in the same town of 1200 or so, yet didn't meet until they both ended up at the University of Wisconsin-Platteville. For a short while the university even had its own microbrewery in the student union. Nate had already started brewing in high school, and both he and Matt joined the UWP Homebrewing Club. (Nate was president.) They decided early on that brewing was something they wanted to do professionally and set up a five-year plan to make it happen back in Marion.

Nate then married his high school sweetheart Kayla, a UW business graduate who has been instrumental in getting the administrative details of the whole project in order. "Without her we wouldn't be where we're at," says Nate. When the right place opened up for a brewpub in the fall of 2011, Nate and Kayla picked it up, planning to wait until they were ready for the next step. But two weeks later, O'so Brewing called; they were in the midst of a big move and upgrade and were looking to sell their old brew system. Things just kept falling into place. Kinda like an avalanche, all at once, until Pigeon River Brewing opened for business on July 18, 2012 in honor of the feast day of St. Arnold of Metz, patron saint of brewers.

The 5000 square foot facility was previously a restaurant and bar with a banquet hall. So one side was ready to handle a brewpub, while the banquet hall required more remodeling to become a brewhouse. You can see right into it through windows from the bar side. The brewpub has a warm atmosphere about it, with old breweriana on the walls for decoration. Nate even bought the actual cast-iron lions from the old Kingsbury Brewery (weighing 40 lbs a piece).

According to Nate, their mission is to "keep people excited about local beers they may not have heard of." So along with their own brews you can get more than fifty other brands of mostly Wisconsin beer.

Stumbling Distance: As Nate puts it, Marion is "sitting at the gateway to the Northwoods" on Highway 45. A snowmobile trail crosses the property. An area special event that draws a big crowd is Caroline Lions Colorama (carolinelionscolorama.com), the first weekend of October. Of other local interest is *Dupont Cheese Inc.* (dupontcheeseinc.com, N10140 Hwy 110, 800-895-2873) five miles south on 110 which makes some stellar cheeses.

BLUE HERON BREWPUB (WEST 14TH RESTAURANT)

Founded: 2005
Brewmaster: Corey Nebbeling
Address: 108 W 9th Street • Marshfield, WI 54449
Phone: 715-389-1868
Website: www.blueheronbrewpub.com
         www.west14threstaurant.com
Annual Production: 300 bbls
Number of Beers: 10–12 on tap

Staple Beers:
» HONEY BLONDE (made with local Hauke Honey)
» LOCH NESS SCOTCH ALE
» TIGER'S EYE (English mild with pale ale malt and English Fuggles hops)

Rotating Beers:
» DUBILEE DUBBEL
» GRAPEFRUIT IPA
» HOW NOW BROWN ALE
» IRISH RED
» OKTOBERFEST
» OL' BLUE'S LIGHT CREAM ALE
» PANTHER PORTER
» PARKIN'S PILZ (German-style pilsner)
» POSSIBLY WOBBLY BARLEY WINE
» pREDator
» RED, WHITE & WHEAT AMERICAN HEFEWEIZEN
» RYEzome RED (American Amber with 25% rye)
» STRANGERS IN THE DARK AMERICAN STOUT
» TAPPER'S TRIPEL

Most Popular Brew: Honey Blonde (or Grapefruit IPA when it's on)

Brewmaster's Fave: All the IPAs and then maybe stouts

Tours? Yes, by appointment, usually Saturdays.

Samples? Yes, six 3-oz. samples for $4.50 or ten for $8.

Best Time to Go: Happy Hour is 3–6 PM Mon–Fri; 11 AM–5 PM Sat. Closed Sundays.

Where can you buy it? Growlers here in the pub. On tap at O'so Brewery in Plover and Down Under in Stratford.

Got food? Outstanding food, in fact! Full menu with pizza. Pasta alla Phil is a big hit (bowtie pasta with 3 cheeses, chicken, bacon in a creamy sauce). Fried pickle slices—crazy, but true—and excellent. Upstairs is fine dining (but no tie required). From grilled ribeye to alligator stir-fry, this is great stuff. Beer cheese soup with andouille sausage. Friday night Fish Fry! (Closed Sunday evenings.)

Special Offer: A pint of beer.

Directions: Coming into town on Business Hwy 13 (Central Ave), look for 9th St on the south side and the brewpub is on the corner on the west side across 9th from Holiday Inn.

The Beer Buzz: I was thrilled to death to know that my birth home was to have a brewpub. In 2005, Central Waters Brewery got together with Marshfield's finest restaurant and set up a brewpub/restaurant in this renovated brick creamery. The Parkin family built this dairy processing plant in 1941 and operated it until 1966. The ice cream here was tops and the family figured prominently in the so-called milk wars when grocers and dairy farmers formed the first cooperatives. The "Got milk?" people are part of that organization that John Parkin helped put together. Now you can still see some ice cream molds and some painted bricks on the wall which were used to match label colors on the ice creams. Check out the We Want Beer photo near the restrooms—anti-Prohibition marchers all decked out in suits and fedoras. Who said beer drinkers didn't have class?

Marshfield hadn't had its own beer since local mail-order cheese pioneer John Figi made an attempt to keep the Marshfield Brewery alive after its long run from 1889 to 1965. Figi Brewing Co. lasted less than two years. In 2008, the brewpub became independent of Central Waters Brewery and

was renamed Blue Heron and Craig Ziolkowski was hired as brewmaster. Craig handed the mash paddle off to local award-winning homebrewer Travis Skroch in May of 2009 who in turn passed it to Corey in April 2011. Corey was a geography major who bounced around out west and in Alaska a bit before landing an unpaid apprenticeship at Lander Brewing in Wyoming for a year. Then he and his wife moved to Michigan where he worked for Short's Brewing as an assistant fill operator for a few months and before finding the Blue Heron gig online. He took silver (86) at the BTI World Beer Championship for Dubilee Dubbel and Red, White & Wheat in 2011 and 2012, respectively.

A small gift shop by the door sells the pub's paraphernalia. The pub has free WiFi and a couple TVs for sports.

Stumbling Distance: At the Central Wisconsin Fairgrounds east on 14th Street you will find the *World's Largest Round Barn.* Come on, it's at least a photo opp! Just north of town off Cty Hwy E, *JuRustic Park* (www.jurustic. com, M222 Sugar Bush Ln, 715-387-1653) is a collection of large critters fashioned out of scrap metal. For fresh cheese curds and a great variety of other cheeses (including aged varieties), don't miss *Nasonville Dairy* (nasonvilledairy.com, 10898 Hwy 10 West, 715-676-2177) The world's largest block of cheese? Well, at least the container for it. Head west on Hwy 10 to Neillsville and you can't miss this roadside attraction with a talking cow and the Wisconsin Pavilion from the 1964 World's Fair.

WHY CREAMERIES?

And gas stations?!? You may notice that some of the breweries occupy buildings with similar stories. More than a couple are renovated creameries from the early part of the twentieth century. Why such a common brewing site? Sloped tiled floors with drains in the middle—lots of filling and draining and mopping goes into the brewing process. Plus some of the old stainless steel dairy tanks are perfectly suited for brewing beer. Who knew?

Minocqua Brewing Company

Founded: 1997 / January 2006
Brewmaster: Ryan White
Address: 238 Lake Shore Drive • Minocqua, WI 54548
Phone: 715-356-2600
Website: www.minocquabrewingcompany.com
Annual Production: 400 bbls and growing each year
Number of Beers: 7–8 at all times

Staple Beers:
> » Bare Naked Brown Ale
> » Minocqua Pale Ale
> » Pudgy Possum Porter
> » Roadkill Red Ale (8.5% abv)
> » Whitey's Wheat Ale
> » Wild Bill's Wild Rice Lager (made with native Wisconsin rice)

Rotating Beers:
> » Dark Dwarf (Black IPA)
> » Hefeweizen
> » Honey Cranberry Ale (for Beef-A-Rama using local cranberries)
> » Oatmeal Stout
> » Scottish Ale
> » Vanilla Cream Ale

Most Popular Brew: Red Ale or Wheat Ale

Brewmaster's Fave: Either the Pale Ale or the Wild Rice Lager.

Tours? No.

Samples? Yes, $11 for seven 5-oz. beers.

Best Time to Go: Summer when the town goes from Unincorporated to almost 200,000 people. Winter brings in snowmobilers. Beef-A-Rama shouldn't be missed! Closed on Mondays, otherwise open 11 am–close. Watch for live entertainment on the weekends in the upstairs Divano Lounge.

Where can you buy it? Growlers and taps only .

Got food? Yes! Expect a pub menu but with a gourmet twist. Beef and brie or pulled pork open-face sandwiches are popular. Try the wheat ale and smoked gouda soup or the open face brat with onions and beer kraut. All cheeses are made in Rudolph, Wisconsin. Also there's a Friday night fish fry serving perch and cod.

Special Offer: A free pint!

Directions: Hwy 51 splits into two one-way streets, northbound and southbound, in the middle of town at Torpy Park. Take the southbound branch and the brewery is next to Torpy Park to the west.

The Beer Buzz: Like the mythological Phoenix rising

literally from its own ashes, the MBC, under new ownership, came back in 2006 and started brewing again after fire destroyed much of the guts of the building. The brewpub/restaurant is located in a 1927 brick Masonic Temple—I asked if there were any secret rooms; they *claim* they didn't find any. Brothers Ryan and Dustin White, along with their parents, salvaged the place and re-opened it even as they were restoring the second floor. In 2009 they added the upstairs Divano Lounge which has become a nice source of good live music in the community bringing in big names from around the Midwest. Music tends toward folk, bluegrass, and originals. The lounge also functions as an event space or just a nice option for drinks while you're waiting for a table in the restaurant downstairs. There's always something going on in the summer around Minocqua and the MBC has a nice downtown location right on the water and next to a small shady park.

Stumbling Distance: *The Cheese Board* (www.thecheeseboard.com, 8524 Hwy 51, 877-230-1338) has a variety of Wisconsin cheeses and does gift boxes. *Otto's Beer & Brat Garden* (509 Oneida St, 715-356-6134) serves Sheboygan brats and over 80 different beers. The outdoor beer garden makes this a great summer hangout. Perhaps the quirkiest time to come here is for *Beef-A-Rama* (www.minocqua.org, 800-446-6784). First celebrated in 1964, the annual festival is the last Saturday in September. Friday night is a kickoff with polka music, then the next day 1500 lbs. of beef is roasted for the 10,000 or so that come out for the event. An arts and crafts fair is part of it, but the central moment is the Parade of Beef and sandwiches from the roasters along the sidewalks downtown.

O'so Brewing Company

Founded: 2007
Head Brewer: Mike Krause
Address: 1812 Post Road, Plover 54467
Phone: 715-254-2163
Website: www.osobrewing.com
Annual Production: 4500 bbls
Number of Beers: 10 packaged, a 1-off each month. Who can count?

Staple Beers:
  » The Big O (sort of a farmhouse ale)
  » Hopdinger (APA)
  » Hopwhoopin'
  » Memory Lane (German-style pilsner)
  » Night Train (Oatmeal Porter)
  » Rusty Red

Rotating Beers:
  » Black Scotch Ale
  » Dank (Imperial Red)
  » Doe in Heat
  » The Dominator Dopplebock
  » Lupulin Maximus (with a hop cone in the bottle!)
  » O-toberfest
  » Picnic Ants Imperial Saison
  » 3rd Wheel Belgian-Style Blonde
  » so many more to come and go.

Most Popular Brew: Hopdinger

Brewmaster's Fave: He likes the stuff he's been putting in barrels.

Tours? Yes, Saturdays at 2, 3 and 4 PM, with a $2 donation to a different local charity each month.

Samples? A flight of as many samples as you want from the 40 taps at $2 each.

Best Time to Go: The Tap House is open 3–9 PM Mon–Fri, Noon–9 PM Sat.

Where can you buy it? All over Wisconsin only (check the website). Bottles, growlers, and kegs for sale, as well. Bottles, growlers, and kegs for sale, as well.

Got food? Bring your own or order in; it's all cool. Restaurants all around them.

Special Offer: 10% off of O'so merchandise with this book.

Directions: From I-39/US-51, take Exit 153 at Cty Rd B/Plover Road heading west. Take the first left on Village Park Drive and you will go 1.5 blocks and see O'so across the big parking lot on your right.

The Beer Buzz: Marc Buttera started homebrewing in 1994. His first brew? Barleywine. Not a bad start, but he soon found there was no place to get supplies. So he and his wife Katina opened one: Point Brew Supply. "It was so tiny," says Katina, "customers had to wait in the hall for the previous customer to check out." After the second location, the couple moved into a new location, opening a brewery adjoining the supply shop.

Brewer Mike started on repurposed dairy equipment and used equipment from Central Waters and the now defunct Falls Brewery and Denmark Brewing. But the growth was stupendous and this wasn't going to be enough to keep up. In November 2011, O'so opened some much bigger digs. The brew supply is still next door, but now there is room to move (and grow) in a big brewing area which lies behind the windows from an also sizeable Tap House. There are 40 beers on tap here, not just the O'so line up and rotating special O'so brews, but also an assortment of other Wisconsin craft beers. Check out the yellow rubber duckies in the brewhouse. These are reminders—to take a gravity reading, for example—which Mike leaves perched around the room, an alternative to tying a string around his finger. He doesn't leave for the day until all his ducks are in a row.

The brewing philosophy is "freestyle," thinking outside the box. A bit of whimsy goes a long way in helping a good brewer stand out in the crowd. They mostly brew ales, with a few lagers from time to time—Dopplebock, Oktoberfest, and the like. The name of the brewery comes from an old picture in a local restaurant with a delivery truck from O'so Beverage Co. and it's claim: "O'so Good!" An appropriate name for a super good beer. An "O" is worked into all the labels.

O'so is very into their local community, thus the donation of their tour fees to different charities each month. Part of the proceeds from one of their beers, Memory Lane, goes to the Alzheimer's Association of Wisconsin. It's nice to be able to drink for a good cause!

Stumbling Distance: Next door is *Mikey's* (mikeysbarandgrill.com, 3018 Village Park Dr, 715-544-0157) serving good food and 40 beers on tap (anyone kicked out of O'so at 9 generally goes here). *Bamboo House* (ploverbamboohouse.com, 715-342-0988), also next door, is an Asian bistro, serving Chinese, Japanese and Southeast Asian fare. The brewery's location is right behind a big home center, so ladies, if your husband says, "I gotta run to Menard's and pick something up," he might not be back as quickly as you expected.

Rhinelander Brewing Co.

Founded: 1882
Brewmaster: Kris Kalav
Address: 59 South Brown St., Rhinelander, WI 54501
Phone: 715-550-2337
Website: www.rhinelanderbrewery.com
Number of Beers: 7

Beers:
  » Rhinelander Original
  » Rhinelander Export Lager
  » Rhinelander Light
  » Chocolate Bunny Stout
  » Mystical Jack Traditional Ale
  » Imperial Jack Double IPA
  » Thumper American Pale Ale

Most Popular Brew: Rhinelander Original

Best Time to Go: Soon. We hope.

Where can you buy it? Statewide in bottles. On tap here in Rhinelander.

Tours? Nothing to tour yet, however, some people stop in to say hello.

Special Offer: Not participating.

The Beer Buzz: I think we need to call this a resurrection in progress. That founding date is the real deal. Rhinelander has been around a long, long time. Founded by Otto Hilgermann and Henry Danner, it was once one of Wisconsin's dominant breweries. Prohibition stopped the beer flow but it picked right up again until 1967 when the brewery closed. But there were too many fans about, and Joseph Huber Brewery in Monroe (now Minhas Craft Brewery) soon bought up the label and recipe and brought it back to the market. Have you ever heard of a "Shorty"? Rhinelander was the first to put out the squat little 7-ounce bottles of beer. Sort of a little pick-me-up I guess.

But the story doesn't end in Monroe. In 2009, Jyoti Auluck bought up the brands and assets and has intentions of building a brewery again back in Rhinelander. Minhas, in the meantime, does all the brewing, and they added a few craft brews to the lineup in late 2011. For now, Rhinelander is a two-room office downtown. Brenda, the marketing coordinator, holds down the fort and says she gets walk-in traffic all summer. There's no tour; just some posters on the wall, some old cases. I think most people just want to chat about old Rhinelander beer memories. And what's wrong with that?

Stumbling Distance: *Bugsy's Sports Bar/Brown Street Brewery* (16 N Brown St, 715-369-2100, bugsyssportsbar.com) hasn't gone out of business, but—at least in the short-term—they have stopped brewing. You never know—give 'em a call. *Rhinelander Logging Museum Complex* (www.rhinelanderchamber.com, Business Hwy 8, 715-369-5004) is free but only open Memorial Day to Labor Day. A logging camp replica and an old Soo Line depot are part of a fascinating look into the hodag-fearing, beer-drinking life of the loggers. *Hodag Country Festival* (www.hodag.com, 715-369-1300) is a long weekend event in mid-July that draws over 40,000 and features some big names in country music and plenty of space to camp. Tickets go on sale the November before! Fishing is big here including the *Saldo Hodag Muskie Challenge* with a $20K prize and the *Ice Fishing Jamboree* the second weekend in February. Contact the Chamber of Commerce for lots more information (www.rhinelanderchamber.com, 800-236-4346).

Stevens Point Brewery

Founded: 1857
Brewmaster: John Zappa
Address: 2617 Water St, Stevens Point 54481
Phone: 715-344-9310 / 800-369-4911
Website: www.pointbeer.com
Annual Production: 100,000 bbls
Number of Beers: 16 (also 5 gourmet soft drinks)

Photograph courtesy of Point Brewing Co.

Staple Beers:
- » Cascade Pale Ale
- » Point 2012 Black Ale
- » Point Amber
- » Point Belgian White
- » Point Burly Brown
- » Point Drop Dead Blonde
- » Point Special Lager

Rotating Beers:
- » Point Nude Beach Summer Wheat
- » Point Oktoberfest
- » Point St. Benedict's Winter Ale
- » Point Three Kings Ale
- » Whole Hog Limited Edition Brewmaster's Series: Barley Wine, Raspberry Saison, Six-Hop IPA, Russian Imperial Stout, Pumpkin Ale

Most Popular Brew: Point Special Lager

Brewmaster's Fave: Cascade Pale Ale

Tours? Yes, $3 for a 45-minute tour. Jun–Aug Mon–Sat 11 AM–2 PM on the hour; Sept–May Mon–Fri 1 PM, and Sat 11, 12, 1 and 2. Free gift at the end of the tour! Reservations recommended (800-369-4911)!

Samples? Yes, two 10-oz. samples with the tour.

Best Time to Go: Any season! *Pointoberfest* in late September is an annual fundraiser promising plenty of Point beer, live music and local food vendors. Admission is limited to 1000 tickets, $20 in advance/$25 at the door.

Where can you buy it? Besides Wisconsin, look throughout the Midwest and beyond. Over 20 states!

Got food? Nope.

Special Offer: Buy one get one free brewery tour.

Directions: Look for Francis St off Business Hwy 51 just north of Forest Cemetery. Go west on Francis to Water St.

The Beer Buzz: This is the fifth oldest continuously running brewery in the US, and it was the site of my first *pils*-grimage back in 1988 when a retired brewery employee Bill ("Bilko") still did the tours. I clearly recall him jabbing me in the shoulder and saying, "And you know what *kreusening* is, dontcha?" I didn't. Partners Frank Wahle and George Ruder started making Point Special Lager back in the mid-1800s. They supplied the troops during the Civil War. Prohibition, of course, meant near-beer and soft drinks, but the brewery survived those dry years and the Great Depression (notice the one started before the other) and came back with Point Bock. Mike Royko, a syndicated columnist from Chicago, declared Point Special the best beer in America in 1973, but for the longest time it remained a very local brew, and even in the 80s I still remember saying, "When you're out of Point, you're out of town." Finally, in the 90s Point crossed state lines and became available in Minnesota and Chicagoland. They do some contract brewing now too, and they brought back Augsburger. And like Leinie's, though a large regional brewery, they have moved beyond the standard American pilsners and offer various alternatives. Back in 2003 Point Special took the Gold at Great American Beer Festival beating Bud and Miller. In 2009 the brewery introduced a line of extreme beers with bold flavors and higher alcohol content called Whole Hog Limited Edition Brewmaster's Series. The brewery also purchased James Page brand beer in 2005 and began producing it for sale in the Minnesota market. In 2012 the brewery added yet another expansion, increasing their capacity to 120,000 barrels!

Stumbling Distance: Hanging around town you should head to The Square—the historic downtown hosts a number of taverns (more than 10!) all serving the hometown brew. *Rusty's Backwater Saloon* (www.rustys.net, 1715 West River Dr, 715-341-2490), five miles southwest of Point off Cty P, is known for amazing Bloody Marys and also serves Cajun smelt, cheese curds, a variety of sandwiches and a fish fry. *SentryWorld* (www. sentryworld.com, 601 Michigan Ave North, 866-479-6753) is a Robert Trent Jones Jr.-designed par 72 golf course, a must for golfers. Colors are phenomenal here in fall. A twenty-minute drive away in Rudolph is *Wisconsin Dairy State Dairy Co.* (6860 State Rd 34, 715-435-3144) which offers free tours and fresh cheese curds and ice cream. The *Bottle Stop* (35 Park Ridge Dr, 715-341-7400) is an awesome liquor store with deep knowledge of Wisconsin craft beer! Generally, the third weekend in July, Wittenberg (45 minutes northeast) hosts *Crawdadathon* (a crawdad boil and street dance) and Point provides the beer (and some prizes). Call *Klinkers Bar and Grill* (207 W Vinal St, Wittenberg, 715-253-2207) for info.

Bull Falls Brewery

Founded: September 2007
Brewmaster: Mike Zamzow
Address: 901 E Thomas Street
Wausau, WI 54403
Phone: 715-842-2337
Website: www.bullfallsbrewery.com
Annual Production: 900 bbls
Number of Beers: 7 plus seasonals

Staple Beers:
- » Bavarian-Style Hefeweizen
- » Bull Falls Marathon (a revived regional Marathon City Brewery recipe)
- » Five Star Ale (English Amber Ale)
- » Holzhacker Lager (Munich-Style Lager)
- » Nut Brown Ale
- » Oatmeal Stout
- » Zwickel Pils

Rotating Beers:
- » Bourbon-Barrel Oatmeal Stout
- » Edel Bock (Maibock)
- » Midnight Star (Schwarzbier)
- » Oktoberfest
- » Opti-Lager (Munich-style Lager, brewed for Wisconsin Valley Fair)
- » Rauchbier (Bamberg-style Smoked Lager)
- » Traditional Bock
- » Weizenbock
- » White Water Ale

Most Popular Brew: Five Star Ale

Brewmaster's Fave: Midnight Star Lager

Tours? Yes, groups of 10 or more and by appointment.

Samples? Five for $5.

Best Time to Go: Mon–Fri 4 pm–close, Sat 1 pm–close. Closed on Sundays!

Where can you buy it? Growlers , a few grocery stores and many restaurants and taverns in the greater Wausau area.

Got food? Free shell-on peanuts and menus from some local places that deliver pizza and sandwiches.

Special Offer: Buy 1 beer, get 1 free.

Directions: From Hwy 51 take N Mountain Road (Cty Rd NN) east to River Dr at Lake Wausau. Then go north until Thomas St and go right to the end.

The Beer Buzz: Big Bull Falls, was the original name of Wausau during the lumber era when giant White Pine we're prevalent in northern Wisconsin. The Bull Falls waterfalls are located right in the city on the Wisconsin River which runs through town. That stretch of the river provides an Olympic-caliber course for whitewater kayaking and canoeing during the summer in Wausau. Bull Falls Brewery was named after the original city name: Big Bull Falls.

Let this be a warning to wives everywhere: "My wife got me a beer kit ten years ago," says Mike. Prior to this he was and still is a co-owner of a software company that develops and markets software to county Social and Human Service Departments in Wisconsin. Someone informed him of some brewing equipment up in Eagle River that had been sitting on the market for a while. He got a good deal on it and then stored it locally for five years. Mike and Don Zamzow bought the current brewery building in 2007 as well as a used 10-barrel system that was located in Stevens

Point, Wisconsin. They then sold the smaller 3-barrel Eagle River system to a place out in Peekskill, New York without ever having brewed a batch in it. When Mike and partners submitted a Bull Falls Brewery trademark they received a challenge. "Yours is too close to ours and it will cause confusion in the market place." The offended company? Red Bull. An attorney from California argued that someone might confuse Red Bull with the local microbrewery. One option was to go to Federal court to tell them they were ridiculous. Unfortunately, ridiculous people with money versus reasonable people

without it… well, you know how THAT ends. After four years a three-page agreement was developed. Bull Falls can't use any bovine animals in their advertising. The words Bull and Falls cannot be separated. The colors blue and silver are not to be used in the fashion they do. And they are not allowed to brew root beer and call it Bull Falls Root Beer.

An interesting beer note: Mike's great uncle Walter A. Zamzow was treasurer of the now defunct Marathon City Brewing Company which closed in 1966. The brewery had been brewing beer for over 100 years. Mike had been searching for the recipe for Marathon Superfine Lager. The son of a worker who was involved with tearing down the old Marathon City Brewing Co. building had the log book from 1954 which his father had found during the demolition. Inside was a July 30, 1954 recipe for Marathon's beer. In 2009, Mike brought it back and reintroduced the beer to the community as Bull Falls Marathon. The resurrected brew is available every year in Marathon, Wisconsin, on Labor Weekend at the Marathon Fund Days celebration, as well as at the Bull Falls brewery taproom. Like traveling back in time.

Stumbling Distance: *Angelo's Pizza* (www.angelospizzawausau.com, 1206 N 6th St, 715-845-6225) is good for ordering in at the brewery tasting room. *City Grill* in the *Jefferson Street Inn* (www.jeffersonstreetinn. com, 203 Jefferson St, 715-848-2900) is also a good spot for eats. *Red Eye Brewing* isn't far away and also serves great food.

THE GREAT DANE PUB AND RESTAURANT

Founded: 2009
Brewmaster: Pete McCabe
Address: 2305 Sherman Street • Wausau, WI 54401
Phone: 715-845-3000
Website: www.greatdanepub.com
Annual Production: 1200 bbls
Number of Beers: 12

Staple Beers:
   » CROP CIRCLE WHEAT ALE
   » EMERALD ISLE STOUT
   » GEORGE RUDER'S GERMAN PILS
   » LANDMARK LITE ALE (pilsner)
   » OLD GLORY APA
   » SPEEDWAY IPA
   » STONE OF SCONE SCOTCH ALE

Rotating Beers:
   » DUNKBRAU
   » IMPERIAL RED ALE
   » SAISON
   » SPRUCE TIP PORTER
   » ÜBER BOCK
   » ...and a rotating beer engine choice

Most Popular Brew: Stone of Scone Scotch Ale

Brewmaster's Fave: Whatever specialty we have on tap but Crop Circle or Emerald Isle.

Tours? By chance or appointment but always welcomed.

Samples? Yes, a couple 2-ounce tasters, side by each, dontcha know, or sampler platters of as many 4-ounce tasters as you want for $1.50 each.

Best Time to Go: Happy hour 4–6 PM with free popcorn. Each day there's a Brewer's Choice, $2.50 for a pint.

Where can you buy it? 100+ tap accounts around the state. On-site growlers, pub kegs, half barrels (with 24-hour notice). In 2012 the Dane did its first bottles with Imperial Red Ale, available in house. See their Madison/Fitchburg locations in Zone 1.

Got food? Yes, a full menu of soups, salads, burgers, and entrees. The bratburger (created on a dare) is an original with bacon on a pretzel bun. Beer, brat and cheese soup is Wisconsin in a bowl. Beer bread is standard, fish and chips available, and a load of other great dishes. Friday night pilsner-battered fish fry!

Special Offer: A free 10 oz. beer

Directions: From Interstate 39/Highway 51 take Exit 191 heading east on Sherman Street. The Dane is right there on the right (south) side of the road just a stone's throw from the exit.

The Beer Buzz: Located just off the highway, and thus convenient to anyone heading past Wausau for the Northwoods, this place originally opened in 2000 as Hereford and Hops, a grill-your-own steakhouse with a rather nice brewpub. A few good brewers passed through and on to other gigs and when the steakhouse didn't make it, the venerable Great Dane from Madison stepped in. The pub has plenty of parking, and inside you'll find the brewhouse behind glass and open to daylight from the other side. Circular booths in the main bar make a stylish lounge atmosphere while billiards, darts and the usual Dane shuffleboard give you something to do

with your hands when you're not holding a beer. A beer garden with an outdoor bar was added in 2011 with room for 100. A fireplace takes the bite out of winter. Six TVs pipe in important games. If you have a wedding or work party, the Dane has private space for up to 300!

Brewmaster Rob's experience goes way back. He went to college with Great Dane founder Eliot Butler and has been corporate brewmaster since the Dane's inception in its first location in Madison. He came to Wausau to get this Dane up and running until Pete took over. Pete was a lost poli-sci student who didn't want to be a lawyer anymore who got a job as a bouncer in the downtown Dane in Madison. He moved up to bus boy, then into the brewhouse making his way to assistant and finally head brewer when he came to Wausau.

Stumbling Distance: *Rib Mountain* is more of a hill, but we take what we can get here in the Midwest. At one billion years old, it is one of the oldest geological formations on the planet. And what do we do with it? Ski on it. *Granite Peak Ski Area* (www.skigranitepeak.com, 3605 N Mountain Rd, 715-845-2846) offers 72 runs as well as lodging and lessons. From Hwy 51 take Cty Hwy NN and the entrance is just over half a mile down. The state park here at the top charges a fee and offers camping, trails, and picnic areas. Exit 51 Cty Hwy N West. Turn right (west) at the first intersection (Park Dr) and go about 2.5 miles to the top. Get a close-up look at some whitewater with *Wausau Kayak Canoe Corporation* (www.wausauwhitewater.org, 1202 Elm St, 715-845-5664). They offer training courses for all levels and if you prefer to stay dry come see one of three national and international competitions.

RED EYE BREWING COMPANY

Founded: 2008
Brewmaster: Kevin Eichelberger
Address: 612 Washington Street • Wausau, WI 54403
Phone: 715-843-7334
Website: www.redeyebrewing.com
Annual Production: 500 bbls
Number of Beers: 5 on tap, more to come

Staple Beers:
- » BLOOM (Belgian White),
- » THRUST! (American-style IPA),
- » SCARLET 7 (Belgian-style dubbel with caramelized black mission figs)

Rotating Beers:
- » GERMAN PILS
- » IMPERIAL STOUT
- » LEMONGRASS RYE
- » NITRO ENGLISH NUT BROWN
- » OKTOBERFEST (Fastest Seller!)
- » PUMPKIN ALE
- » RYE PORTER
- » SERENDIPITY DOUBLE IPA
- » VIENNA LAGER
- » TARTAN TODDY SCOTCH ALE
- » VERUCA STOUT

Most Popular Brew: Bloom

Brewmaster's Fave: Ask him, why don'tcha?

Tours? Yes, by appointment.

Samples? Yes, 4 samples for $5.

Best Time to Go: Happy hour is 4–6 PM, 6 days a week. Closed on Sundays.

Where can you buy it? Growlers on site, some draft accounts.

Got food? Definitely. Try the wood-fired oven pizzas. The menu offers paninis, wraps, soups, and salads as well. For a gourmet take on Wisconsin's beer cheese soup, check out Scarlet 7 Bisque made with the beer of the same name, brie and mushrooms.

Special Offer: A pint of beer.

Directions: From Hwy 51 take the Hwy 52 exit east which becomes Stewart Ave. Follow it across the Wisconsin River. It splits and as you go right it becomes one-way. Follow it and it becomes First St, then Forest St. before it joins Grand Ave. Do not follow this to the right; rather stay left and turn onto 6th St and continue two blocks to Washington St and turn right.

The Beer Buzz: Kevin used to brew over at the now defunct Hereford and Hops (which reopened as The Great Dane.) He is a creative brewer making some remarkable stuff and really likes Belgians (you may notice that two of the house beers are Belgian). He bought a brew system that had been sitting for four or five years for a good price and opened Red Eye. His promise: "Red Eye Brewing Company will never serve a beer that is not worthy of the most articulate beer drinker's palette."

He's also serious about his pizza. The oven came all the way from Italy. They ferment the dough overnight and hand toss it as it should be for an Italian pie. Most of the food is locally sourced and there is no deep fryer here. Plus, every item on the menu is paired with one of the beers. Watch for the Black Eye Series which features super premium beers in limited batches. This is Kevin showing off. Good stuff and worth marking the calendar for. A lot of people stop in frequently to fill their growlers and Red Eye has become a social center for cyclists, especially after a day's ride.

Stumbling Distance: You are just minutes from *Bull Falls Brewery*.

ZONE 5

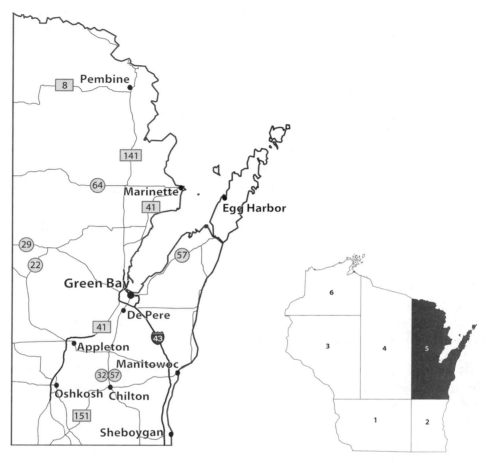

Appleton: Appleton Beer Factory
Appleton: Fox River Brewing Co.
Appleton: Stone Cellar Brewpub / Stone Arch Brewhouse
Chilton: Rowland's Calumet Brewing Co.
Egg Harbor: Shipwrecked Brew Pub
Green Bay: Cheeseheads
Green Bay: Hinterland Brewery
Green Bay: Legends Brewhouse and Eatery
Green Bay (De Pere): Legends Brewhouse and Eatery
Green Bay: Stillmank Brewing Co.
Green Bay: Titletown Brewing Co.
Manitowoc: Courthouse Pub
Marinette: Rail House
Oshkosh: Fox River Brewing Co.
Pembine: Black Husky Brewing Co.
Sheboygan: 3 Sheeps Brewing Co.

Appleton Beer Factory

Founded: December 2012
Brewers: Ben Fogle and Carl Pierce
Address: 603 West College Avenue • Appleton, WI 54911
Website: www.appletonbeerfactory.com
Annual Production: 600 bbls
Number of Beers: 6 on tap, room for 20

Staple Beers:
- » Amber
- » APA
- » Belgian Wit
- » Black
- » Blonde
- » Brown
- » Oatmeal Stout
- » Wefeweizen

Rotating Beers:
- » Several seasonals!

Most Popular Brew: Too soon to tell!

Brewmaster's Fave: "Mostly ales. Amber, Brown, Black, IPA, Hefe…"

Tours? Yes.

Samples: Yes

Best Time to Go: Whenever they're open!

Where can you buy it? Only here at first, but then in draft accounts around town. Bottling is in the future.

Got food? Yes. Jeff's wife Leah is the executive chef and is developing a beer-centric menu.

Special Offer: A free pint of their beer!

Directions: Easy peasy: From Hwy 41 just take College Avenue east into town. The "factory" will be on your right just after you cross the railroad tracks.

The Beer Buzz: I've had a few brewers say they are putting their own system together, meaning recycling some dairy equipment or other clever re-engineering, but when Jeff Fogle showed me his operation I was dumbfounded. He is literally building it. He was a pipe welder for Anheuser Busch and ended up in design management for them, working on multi-million dollar projects. So welding together some tanks from sheets of metal was just a tiny version of what he used to do.

The "factory" looks the part set in a 1940s brick auto-parts building. The front bar/tasting room, meant to feel like coming into the factory office space, looks past the bar through glass on the brewhouse and the kitchen in back. Recycled wood was used for the tables. The brewing equipment is in back in a high-ceiling production room and will incorporate a gravity-feed system. This will be off to the side and share the space with Phase 2 of the construction, a sort of communal beer hall. Phase 3 will add an upstairs pub room with another bar. And who knows? Maybe a terrace as well. There are no mugs hanging on the wall, but there is still a "pint club" with free membership: Drink beer, earn points, get stuff.

Jeff's son Ben, a mechanical engineer is in charge of the brewing. Jeff learned from his own father in 1983 and then passed the pleasure on to his son Ben in 2005. Rounding off Team Fogle is Ben's wife Mairi who also works here.

Stumbling Distance: If you need your Wisconsin cheese fix, head over to *Arthur Bay Cheese Company* (237 E Calumet St, 920-733-1556) for the best selection in town.

FRATELLOS RESTAURANT AND BREWERY (FOX RIVER BREWING CO.)

Founded: 1998
Brewmaster: Kevin Bowen
Address: 4301 W. Wisconsin Avenue • Appleton, WI 5491
       (inside Fox River Mall)
Phone: 920-991-0000
Website: www.foxriverbrewing.com
Annual Production: 600 bbls
Number of Beers: 8

Staple Beers:
  » BUZZIN' HONEY ALE
  » CABER TOSSING SCOTTISH ALE
  » FOX LIGHT (Kölsch)
  » WINNEBAGO WHEAT (Hefeweizen)

Rotating Beers: Four lines including a fruit, dark, hoppy, and seasonal beer which may feature:
  » ABBEY NORMAL (Belgian dubbel)
  » BLÜ (blueberry ale)
  » CHERRY BRAU
  » FOX TAIL PALE ALE
  » FOXTOBERFEST
  » HOPPY FACE IPA
  » PAINE'S PILSNER
  » PEACHES ALE
  » SLAM DUNKEL (dark lager)
  » TITAN PORTER
  » TROLLEYCAR STOUT
  » VADER'S IMPERIAL STOUT

Most Popular Brew: Caber Tossing Scottish Ale

Brewmaster's Fave: Maibock, Hoppy Face, Fox Tail Pale. He likes seasonal beers and prefers dry, bitter and hoppier stuff.

Tours? On request, call ahead.

Samples? Eight 5.5-oz. beers for $10

Best Time to Go: When you're going mad from being in the mall too long!

Where can you buy it? Bottles, growlers, quarter- and half-barrels and some local taverns serve it. On site as well as the other Fratellos locations in Oshkosh and Fratellos of Appleton.

Got food? Of course. Fratellos features a variety of steaks, seafood, pastas, sandwiches, and pizzas and much more on their full menu.

Special Offer: $2 pint on your first Fox River beer, additional pints regular price.

Directions: From Hwy 41 take the College Ave exit and go east to S Appleton St. Go right (south) and take a right on Water St before crossing the Fox River. It's inside the mall.

The Beer Buzz: Fratellos and Fox River Brewing Co. could be the highlight to a giant shopping mall trip for any true-brew connoisseur. This food court couldn't get any better – it boasts a brewery with a restaurant inside it! Kevin is working double duty, with this location and Oshkosh's Fox River Brew Co. (but each is brewed on site). Fratellos Fox River Mall incorporates the waterfront theme of its sister locations with an interior highlighting deep-water blues and a freshwater feel. There is an open kitchen, pizza oven, and an outdoor patio for the summer season. Serving lunch and dinner daily, their full menu offers steaks, pasta, seafood, pizzas, and sandwiches to accompany the handcraft beers. Kevin Bowen started at the restaurant in Oshkosh years ago and he began helping out in the brewery: cleaning kegs, filling bottles and such. After studying at Siebel Institute he worked for a few other brewhouses before returning to Fox River Brewing Co.

Stumbling Distance: The former *White Clover Dairy,* now part of Arla Foods, is a cheese store in nearby Kaukauna. You can see havarti being made at the factory and then buy some great cheddars, gouda, edam and more in the little white house next door. (489 Holland Ct, Kaukauna, 920-766-5765 ext.2; Mon–Fri 9–5, Sat 8–1) Take Hwy 441 around the east side of Appleton and take Cty CE (Holland Rd) east to Holland Ct.

Look for Fratellos and the Fox River Brews in Oshkosh and a second Appleton location:
- » 1501 Arboretum Drive, Oshkosh, WI 54901 (920) 232-2337
- » 501 West Water Street, Appleton, WI 54911 (920) 993-9087

Stone Cellar Brewpub

Founded: 2004
Brewmaster: Steve Lonsway
Address: 1004 S Olde Oneida Street • Appleton, WI 54915
Phone: 920-731-3322
Website: www.stonecellarbrewpub.com
Annual Production: 2500 bbls
Number of Beers: 10–13

Staple Beers:
- » English Six-Grain Ale (corn, barley, oats, rice, wheat, rye)
- » Houdini Honey Wheat
- » Marquette Pilsner
- » Pie-Eyed IPA
- » Stone Cellar Stout
- » Tilted Kilt Scottish-style Ale
- » Vanishing Vanilla Stout

Rotating Beers:
- » Adler Brau
- » Blind-Sided Barleywine
- » Caffeinator
- » Dark Lager
- » Masterpiece Porter
- » Pumpkin Spice
- » ...and fruit beers in summer

Most Popular Brew: Scottish-style Ale

Brewmaster's Fave: IPA

Tours? Yes, by appointment.

Samples? Yes, ten–thirteen 4-oz. samples for $7.50.

Best Time to Go: 11AM–close daily, except for a few holidays. The beer garden is awesome in the summer and often features live music on Tuesdays.

Where can you buy it? Growlers, six-packs, and on tap at numerous Fox River Valley pubs.

Got food? Yes, lunch and dinner. Bangers and mash, shepherd's pie, goulash, fish and chips, Scotch egg, deep-fried Wisconsin cheese curds, ale-steamed shrimp, cheese, sausage and beer for two, burgers, pizzas, and a Friday fish fry.

Special Offer: Not participating.

Directions: Yes, lunch and dinner. Bangers and mash, shepherd's pie, goulash, fish and chips, Scotch egg, deep-fried Wisconsin cheese curds, ale-steamed shrimp, cheese, sausage and beer for two, burgers, pizzas, and a Friday fish fry.

The Beer Buzz: Situated between the locks in a building called Between the Locks, this brewery carries on a long tradition on this site. In 1858 Anton Fischer, a German immigrant, founded the first brewery in Outagamie County and helped build the Fox River canal system. His Fischer Brewery was sold just a couple years later to Carl Meunch, a foreman from the Schlitz Brewery in Milwaukee. In 1884 the building lost a battle with fire and needed to be rebuilt. George Walter Brewing Co., the

producer of Adler Brau, lasted until 1972. When the old building was converted into a little collection of stores and offices, Adler Brau Brewery and Restaurant tried to make a go if it as a microbrewery. In 2004, father and son partners Tom and Steve Lonsway took over the tradition. And one more thing: the building is haunted by "Charlie."

While studying science in college, Steve went to England for a semester and fell in love with beer history and beer itself and decided it had to be his career. "Beer is such a part of the culture there." And so it is here as well. He started Homebrew Market (1326 N

Meade St, 800-261-2337, homebrewmar-
ket.com) in 1993 which sells ingredients
and equipment for making beer, wine,
and soda. He attended Siebel Institute
in Chicago and then for six years did the
brewing for both Fox River Brewing Co.
locations until breaking out on his own. His
brews have gotten some awards: Marquette
Pilsner (Gold), Between the Locks (Silver)
2005, and others for Barleywine, Six-Grain,
Stout, and Scottish-style Ale.

You may notice the beers are under the
trade name Stone Arch Brewhouse. This
is all still Stone Cellar, but in order to get
approval to sell his beer offsite, Steve had to
change the name. Still the same beer, still
the same location. The only thing different
is a new tap room alongside the brewhouse.

Stumbling Distance: *Skyline Comedy Café* is in the same building. Stop
in at the *Outagamie Museum* (330 E College Ave, 920-733-8445, $5, open
Tues–Sat 10–4, Sun 12–4, add Mon during summer) and see A.K.A.
Houdini, an exhibit dedicated to the famous escape artist, an Appleton
native (or so he claimed). *Simon's Specialty Cheese* (www.simonscheese.
com, 2735 Freedom Rd, Little Chute, 920-788-6311, north on Hwy 41
exit Freedom Rd) has the fresh cheese curds as well as over 100 types of
cheese (free samples), various fudge flavors (more samples), and a cheese
mini-museum with a video about the cheese making process. *Octoberfest*
(www.octoberfestonline.org) as well as *License to Cruise* (a classic car show)
and *Applefest* are held downtown on College Ave in late September. "A
mile of fun," as they call it.

ROWLAND'S CALUMET BREWING (ROLL INN BREW PUB)

Founded: Sept. 1990, first beer on tap
Brewmaster: Patrick Rowland
Address: 25 N. Madison Street
Chilton, WI 53014
Phone: 920-849-2534
Website: www.rowlandsbrewery.com
Annual Production: 400 bbls
Number of Beers: 20 per year, 11 on tap

Staple Beers:
- » CALUMET AMBER
- » CALUMET DARK
- » CALUMET OKTOBERFEST
- » CALUMET RYE
- » FAT MAN'S NUT BROWN ALE

Rotating Beers:
- » BITTER BITCH BELGIUM ALE
- » BUCHOLZ ALT (formulated with Luther from Lakefront Brewery)
- » CALUMET BOCK
- » CALUMET ICE
- » CALUMET KOLSCH
- » CALUMET PILSNER (the brewer's grandfather's recipe, a 1950 Coal miner from West Virginia)
- » CALUMET WHEAT
- » CONNOR JOHN'S SCOTCH ALE
- » DETENTION ALE
- » GUIDO'S GRAND IMPERIAL STOUT
- » HONEY LAGER
- » HUNTER'S CHOICE
- » KELLY'S IRISH RED LAGER
- » MADISON STREET LAGER (a pre-Prohibition pilsner)
- » MITTNACHT PILSNER (Schwarz Bier)
- » MORTIMER'S ALE (English-style ale formulated with Kirby Nelson of Wisconsin Brewing Co.)
- » TOTAL ECLIPSE

Most Popular Brew: A dead heat: Amber, Nut Brown, or Oktoberfest

Brewmaster's Fave: "Whatever we have the most of—we make it exactly the way we like it"

Tours? Yes, by appointment.

Samples? Yes, $9 for eleven 3-oz. beers and a root beer.

Best Time to Go: The local street party in August, Crafty Applefest, or the brewery's famous Wisconsin Micro Brewers Beer Fest in May (Closed Mondays, except holidays).

Where can you buy it? Growlers on site or 45+ area bars with draft accounts.

Got food? Pickled eggs and turkey gizzards? You make the call. "Eight or nine beers and it'll be the best food you ever had in your life." Also popcorn and pizzas made in Fondulac.

Special Offer: A free 7 oz. glass of the reason they're in business so long.

The Beer Buzz: Built around 1870, the building was Chilton's first firehouse and later city hall. At one time church services were held upstairs. John Diedrich made a tavern out of it in 1937, officially (though the back bar's mirror indicates 1926, so it may have been a speakeasy during Prohibition). Bob and Bonita Rowland opened the bar in '83. As the drinking age went from 18 to 19 and then to 21, Bob dealt with a lagging customer base and decided to take his home-brewing public. The Old Calumet Brewing Co. closed in 1942 when the Feds made an example of them for not paying beer taxes, and Bob saw it fit to adopt the name for what in 1990 was the 3rd smallest brewery in the US in the smallest city to have one. Madison Street Lager, a pre-Prohibition American-style lager, was formulated by Bob and Carl Strauss, the former head at Pabst for 40 years. Calumet Ice was the result

of an equipment malfunction and the engineer sent out by the company to find the problem was Dan Carey, now the brewmaster at New Glarus Brewery. There's a handwritten note behind the bar from Kirby at Capital Brewery. As Bob once put it, "Brewers in Wisconsin are like cohorts in the same crime." Bob's son Patrick carries on this awesome family tradition. This is a true tavern, not to be missed, and laden with breweriana and some great stories. Small town prices are a bonus!

Stumbling Distance: *Vern's Cheese* (www.vernscheese.com, 312 W. Main St, 920-849-7717) has fresh curds on Tues and Thurs evenings (or the following mornings) and various string cheeses besides a huge selection of other cheeses. *Ledge View Nature Center* (W2348 Short Rd, 920-849-7094) is a 105-acre wooded park with a 60-ft observation tower and a couple miles of hiking trails. $6 scheduled tours are available for three natural caves here. Expect to get dirty and you might want to do this *before* you hit the brewpub. The park is free and open from dawn till dusk, but only till 4:30 at the office. Pick strawberries, buy honey or maple syrup, go on hay rides and explore a corn maze in fall at *Meuer Farm* (meuerfarm.com, N2564 Hwy 151, Chilton, 920-418-2676).

LOCAL INGREDIENTS—BRIESS MALT

Beer can only be as good as its ingredients. Garbage in, skunk beer out. So we are fortunate to have the Briess Malt and Ingredients Co. (www.briess.com), North America's leading producer of specialty malts, right here in Chilton, Wisconsin. Briess produces over 50 styles of malt—more than any other malting company in the world! Ignatius Briess started malting barley back in the 19th century in Moravia in what is now the Czech Republic. World Wars do little for business and so grandson Eric brought the operation to the US in the 1930s. Great-grandson Roger saw that craft brewers could not buy in quantities as big as a box car and, sensing the coming trend toward hand-crafted microbrews, had the brilliant notion to start producing and bagging specialty malts in the 1970s. Specialized roasters were necessary to get the darker malts. You'll find bags of Briess Malt in the back rooms of nearly all of the microbreweries in Wisconsin. Now *that's* some local beer.

SHIPWRECKED BREW PUB

Founded: 1997
Brewmaster: Rich Zielke
Address: 7791 Egg Harbor Rd, Egg Harbor 54209
Phone: 920-868-2767, 888-868-2767
Website: www.shipwreckedmicrobrew.com
Annual Production: 800 bbls
Number of Beers: 9 on tap

Staple Beers:
» BAYSIDE BLONDE ALE
» CAPTAIN'S COPPER ALE
» DOOR COUNTY CHERRY WHEAT
» LIGHTHOUSE LIGHT
» PENINSULA PORTER

Rotating Beers:
» INDIA PALE ALE
» PUMPKIN PATCH PUMPKIN ALE
» SPRUCE TIP ALE
» SUMMER WHEAT

Most Popular Brew: Door County Cherry Wheat

Brewmaster's Fave: IPA

Tours? No.

Samples? Yes, seven 3-oz. samplers for $5.

Best Time to Go: In summer Door County is swarming with tourists and you may have to wait to be seated. Late spring or early fall might be better times to go if you want to avoid the crowds. From about Nov–Apr they are only open Fri–Sun with special hours around the holidays.

Where can you buy it? Growlers on site and kegs on order and throughout Wisconsin. Six-pack bottles all over Wisconsin and in the Chicago and Twin Cities areas.

Got food? Yes, a fine menu including beer-boiled brats, pulled pork sandwiches, fried cheese curds, and a chicken dish made with Door County cherry wine sauce.

Special Offer: $1 taps during signature visit (for bookholder only).

Directions: Highway 42 passes right through town and the pub is right on it at the bend in the road where Horseshoe Bay Dr connects from the west.

The Beer Buzz: Owned by the Pollmans of the Door Peninsula Winery (and Door County Distillery), this is currently the only brewpub in the ever popular Door County. The brewpub was merely an idea for a good place to hang out and get a beer, and the food developed after that. The place dates back to the late 1800s when it attracted lumberjacks and sailors looking for a drink. Al Capone frequented the bar, and tunnels beneath it functioned as potential escape routes to other parts of the town. Shipwrecked also is known for its spirits—not whiskey and the like, but the ghostly kind. One of several frequently spotted apparitions is Jason, Capone's illegitimate son who hanged himself (perhaps with help) in the attic. Ask about the other haunts.

Brewer Rich brewed in Colorado for 12 years at Estes Park Brewery. He had been tending bar and moved over to the brewery side and just "kinda lucked into it." He moved to Door County in 2008 inheriting the recipes at Shipwrecked and adding some of his own such as the IPA. While he misses the mountains sometimes, he was landlocked in Colorado and loves the water and endless shoreline of Door County.

Stumbling Distance: *Door Peninsula Winery* (www.dcwine.com, 800-551-5049, 5806 Hwy 42) is ten minutes south in Carlsville. Tours are $3 and 45 wines are on hand for free tasting. Also, attached to the winery is *Door County Distillery* (doorcountydistillery.com, 920-746-8463) which produces vodka, fruit-infused vodka, gin, and (soon) whiskey. The distillery is open Fri-Sat with free tastings, but you can taste the tipple on other days at the winery as well. Door County is famous for its cherries and the season starts around mid-July. There are places to pick them or just stop at one of many roadside stands. Fish fries are less common than the fish boil, a tradition unique to Door County. *Pelletier's* (920-868-3313, Fish Creek, open May–Oct) is recommended for theirs. Whenever traveling up here during early spring, late fall and winter, it is advisable to call ahead to see what is open. Many places in Door County shut down during the off season. Too tired to stumble? There are eight guest rooms above the bar *(Upper Deck Inn at Shipwrecked)!*

CHEESEHEADS

Founded: 2003
Brewmaster: Ken Novak
Address: 940 Waube Lane • Green Bay 54304
Phone: 920-339-8970
Website: www.cheeseheadsrestaurant.com
Annual Production: 84 bbls
Number of Beers: 4 on tap

Staple Beers:
  » C-WOOD HONEY WHEAT
  » CLAYMAKER LIGHT
  » A-ROD AMBER
  » DOUBLE D DUNKEL

Most Popular Brew: A-Rod Amber

Tours? If Ken's out there, otherwise try to make an appointment.

Samples? Yes, $3.25 for four 3-oz. samples

Best Time to Go: Friday and Saturday nights, Packer game days. Fridays the beers are on special. Happy Hour is 2–6 PM Mon–Fri—shake dice against the bartender and get a free beer.

Where can you buy it? On-site growlers with very cheap refills

Got food? Yes, pizza buffet, broasted chicken, Friday fish fry (perch), beer cheese soup, wings, and ribs are notable.

Special Offer: Buy one housebrew, get one free

Directions: This is just off US Hwy 41 at the Oneida St exit. Go west and it is on your right.

The Beer Buzz: As the name and website indicate, the term Cheesehead is not considered derogatory; it's a badge of honor. This restaurant and brewery, dedicated to all things Wisconsin and fiercely loyal to the Green Bay Packers, used to be one of the Legend's Brewhouses. The ownership and brewer remain the same, but the place has changed things up a bit on the menu and atmosphere. A pizza buffet and broasted chicken are now served. Ingredients are locally sourced as much as possible and the pizza is as handcrafted as the beer. Along with the collection of televisions there is a pool table and free WiFi is available. If you are in town for a Packers game just follow Oneida St. to Lombardi Ave. They offer free shots when the Packers score and free pizza during half time. Brewer Ken is doing triple duty as he comes here for the brewing and handles the two Legends locations as well.

Stumbling Distance: This is close to *Lambeau Field*, the *Packer Hall of Fame*, and the Packers' practice field.

Hinterland Brewery
(Green Bay Brewing Co.)

Founded: 1995
Brewmaster: Joe Karls
Address: 313 Dousman Street • Green Bay, WI 54303
Phone: 920-438-8050
Website: www.hinterlandbeer.com
Annual Production: 5000 bbls
Number of Beers: 14+

Staple Beers:
- » Amber Ale
- » India Pale Ale
- » Luna Stout
- » Pale Ale
- » Pub Draught (pale ale-style, under nitro)

Rotating Beers:
- » Bourbon-Barrel Doppelbock
- » Bourbon-barrel Stout
- » Door County Cherry Wheat
- » Grand Cru
- » Maple Bock
- » Oktoberfest
- » Saison
- » White Out Bourbon-Barrel Imperial IPA
- » Whiteout Imperial India Pale Ale
- » Winterland

Most Popular Brew: Luna Stout

Brewmaster's Fave: "Depends on my mood and time of the year."

Tours? Yes, Saturdays by appointment. Cost is $5 and includes two beers.

Samples? Yes, eight beers for $14.

Best Time to Go: In late summer and early fall there are lots of area events. Packer game days. Summer is the slowest time of year, but the courtyard patio is a great place to hang outside. Happy hour is 4–7 PM Mon–Sat.

Where can you buy it? Bottles and drafts of most brews are available in Green Bay, Milwaukee, Madison, Door County, and throughout the state of Wisconsin. Illinois, Iowa, Indiana, Minnesota and Ohio now also have it!

Got food? Yes, but don't expect greasy pub fare—this is a high-class menu. Seafood is flown in daily from Maine and Hawaii.

Special Offer: A glass of their beer.

The Beer Buzz: Broadway Street, once famous for seedy bars, now has a collection of fine restaurants and shops. Beer meets class in this upscale and classy restaurant/pub on the corner of Dousman and Broadway, just west of the Fox River. This is Packerland, after all—the building was formerly a meat-packing plant and the hook receptacles can still be seen in the ceiling. Sound like a dismal place? Not on your life! The atmosphere is relaxed, the décor elegant. The upstairs lounge has an eclectic music library and is a popular post-work-day gathering place. The menu includes a lot of local game and a wood-fired oven is on hand for some fine pizzas. Founder Bill Tressler studied journalism in college and started editing brewing magazines in the 90s. So the logical step, of course, was to open a brewery. Rahr Green Bay Brewing Co. was the longest running brewery in the city, operating from 1858 to 1966, and the corporation name here is a nod to them. Hinterland was the first brewpub to bring hometown brew back to Green Bay. The beers have won seven medals including two Silver medals for the Pale Ale and a World Champion medal for Maple Bock. Hinterland ships its beers to its second fine-dining location down in Milwaukee (222 East Erie Street, 414-727-9300).

Stumbling Distance: *Titletown Brewing Co.* is just across the street. Look both ways—you've been drinkin'. You cannot come to Green Bay and not at least see *Lambeau Field*, the legendary home of the Green Bay Packers. *The Packer Hall of Fame* (www.packers.com, 920-569-7512) is another pilgrimage site for football fans, right across the street from the stadium. Go west 3 blocks on Dousman to take a left (south) on Ashland. This will take you to Lombardi Avenue and you will turn right (west) and you're almost there. They live and die by football in this town. Bars will be hopping on game day; streets may be empty... until the game lets out anyway.

Legends Brewhouse & Eatery

Founded: 1998
Brewmaster: Ken Novak
Address: 2840 Shawano Drive • Green Bay, WI 54313
Phone: 920-662-1111
Website: www.legendseatery.com
Annual Production: 88 bbls
Number of Beers: 6 on tap

Staple Beers:
- » Acme Amber
- » Duck Creek Dunkel
- » Founders Wheat
- » Longtail Light

Rotating Beers:
- » Claude Allouez IPA
- » Crocodile Lager
- » Half Moon Brick Belgian Tripel
- » Harvest Moon Oktoberfest
- » Ixtapa Blonde Ale
- » Jack Rabbit Red Ale
- » Rudolph's Red-Nose Ale (Christmas)

Most Popular Brew: Founders Wheat

Brewmaster's Fave: Belgian Tripel "The best beer I've ever made!"

Tours? If Ken's out there, otherwise try to make an appointment.

Samples? Yes, $5 for six 2-oz. beers.

Best Time to Go: Friday and Saturday nights, Packer game days. Fridays the beers are on special. Sunday brunch is popular. Happy Hour is 2–6 pm Mon–Fri.

Where can you buy it? Growlers on site (and cheap refills!).

Got food? Yes, Friday fish fry (perch), beer cheese soup, wings, and ribs are notable.

Special Offer: Buy one housebrew, get one free.

Directions: Head west on Shawano Ave (Hwy 29 West) off of 41 North, take Hwy 2 west to Riverdale Drive and turn right (north) and Legends is on the right, just past the *Village Green Golf Course*.

The Beer Buzz: Prior to this, Legends there was an old bar of the same name with an adjoining baseball field on this site. Thus, the name. The new building was completed in 1998, and the owners wanted a brewpub. Ken heard through a friend and got the job (nice friend!). Ken got his start homebrewing in 1993 with a kit he received as a gift, and he did his first beer on Christmas Day. He likes the hours and that no one tells him when he has to work or how to do it. The drawback, he says, "I work alone a lot. Not a lot of people to talk to."

Two large projection screen TVs are the flagships for a whole fleet of TVs piping in the day's sporting events. Sunday brunch is popular with folks staying around for noon kick-offs. Free WiFi is available and parking is off-street. They do their own root beer as well.

Stumbling Distance: Here it is, the local color you may have been scouring the pages for: *BOOYAH!* This is the regional hearty chicken-vegetable soup often made in mass quantities. *Rite View Family Dining* (2130 Velp Ave, 920-434-8981) makes 42-gallon batches. They also serve broasted chicken, Friday fish fry, cheese curds, and offer views of an old stone quarry and a yard full of peacocks.

Legends Brewhouse & Eatery of De Pere (Swan Club Banquet Facilities)

Founded: 2001
Brewmaster: Ken Novak
Address: 875 Heritage Road • De Pere, WI 54115
Phone: 920-336-8036
Website: www.legendseatery.com.
Annual Production: 88 bbls
Number of Beers: 6 on tap

Staple Beers:
» Acme Amber
» Duck Creek Dunkel
» Founders Honey Weiss
» Longtail Light

Rotating Beers:
» Claude Allouez IPA
» Crocodile Lager
» Half Moon Brick Belgian Tripel
» Harvest Moon Oktoberfest
» Ixtapa Blonde Ale
» Jack Rabbit Red Ale
» Rudolph's Red-Nose Ale (Christmas)

Most Popular Brew: Acme Amber

Brewmaster's Fave: IPA

Tours? If Ken's out there, otherwise try to make an appointment.

Samples? Yes, $5 for six 2-oz. beers.

Best Time to Go: Friday and Saturday nights, Packer game days, or after an event at St. Norbert College. Fridays the beers are on special. Sunday brunch is popular. Happy Hour is 2–6 PM Mon–Fri.

Where can you buy it? On-site growlers with super cheap refills.

Got food? Yes, Friday fish fry (perch), beer cheese soup, wings, and ribs are notable.

Special Offer: Buy one housebrew, get one free.

Directions: Cross the Fox River heading east in De Pere and then go right (south) on S. Broadway. Where the road curves and Hwy 32 continues, go straight on Cty PP until you reach Heritage Road. Then go right (west).

The Beer Buzz: This used to be Splinters Sport Bar. The new owners remodeled a bit, and moved the bar to the side. Like the other locations, this has a sports bar theme. Read a bit about Ken at the Green Bay location listing.

Sit outside on the deck during the summer. During football season, come see the Monday Night Kickoff Show. Green Bay Packer players host a live TV show talking to guests, fans and friends. You will need a reservation for the TV show. Free WiFi on site.

Stumbling Distance: *St. Norbert College* (www.snc.edu) is about all you're going to find in De Pere. The Packers stay there for training camp so autograph seekers often hunt there in summer. The campus also has the usual sporting, arts, and cultural events associated with a fine liberal arts college. Go Green Knights!

CASK-CONDITIONED ALES

Cask comes from the Spanish word for "bark" like tree bark (cáscara). The little wooden barrel holds the beer in the same way bark surrounds a tree trunk I suppose. This is Old School beer storage (think of the original IPAs on their way to India to be drunk right out of the container) and the beer is unfiltered and unpasteurized.

Cask-conditioned ale goes through its secondary fermentation right in the cask or firkin from which it is poured. The yeast is still active and so still conditioning the brew. In many cases, the cask is right behind the bar, tilted on a shelf so the beer is delivered by gravity, without added carbon dioxide. Cask ale will only last a few days if air is going in to replace that draining beer. Some casks have CO_2 breathers that allow a bit of gas in but not enough to cause more carbonation. By definition the cask-conditioning can be going on in any tank downstairs as long as it is a secondary fermentation, but the little wooden firkins behind the bar are a rare treat of authenticity.

Stillmank Beer Co.

Founded: May 2012
Brewmaster: Brad Stillmank
Address:
Website: www.stillmankbrewing.com
Annual Production: 150 barrels
Number of Beers: 1

Staple Beers:
> » Wisco Disco (unfiltered amber ale)

Most Popular Brew: Wisco Disco

Brewmaster's Fave: An Imperial IPA and a Coffee Porter in the works.

Tours? No place to tour yet!

Samples: No place to do so yet.

Where can you buy it? 4-pack 16 oz. cans, only in Northeastern Wisconsin, and just under 12 bars have them on tap.

Got food? Nope.

Special Offer: Not participating

The Beer Buzz: And here we have another work in progress. Brad Stillmank currently heads to Milwaukee on weekends to brew his beer at Milwaukee Brewing Co.'s 2nd Street Brewery. He doesn't have a place yet in Green Bay but that may change soon after this book gets printed. Therefore, we leave the address blank so you can fill it in!

Brad got his start as a homebrewer in the late 90s, throwing parties with his creations in college. The first batch was "good enough to keep me going. We were really surprised, actually, and emptied all the bottles over the weekend." In 2002 he started brewing at Ska Brewery in Colorado but left in 2007 and moved to Green Bay with his wife to start a family. He brewed for a while for the now defunct Black Forest Dining and Spirits, but has decided there is no greater joy than brewing it for yourself. Brad has certifications from the Institute of Brewing and Distilling and has judged beer competitions. He is also a Certified Cicerone™ (sis-uh-rohn), what you might call a beer sommelier. He's still waiting to quit his day job as his beer sales grow and provide that last push to his own facility. By the way, his day job? Beer distributor. Coincidence? I think not. Watch the website for his next steps.

TITLETOWN BREWING CO.

Founded: 1996
Brewmaster: David Oldenburg
Address: 200 Dousman Street • Green Bay, WI 54303
Phone: 920-437-2337
Website: www.titletownbrewing.com
Annual Production: 1700 bbls
Number of Beers: 6 year-round, about 25 new recipes/year, 12–14 beers and 2 cask ales on at a time

Staple Beers:
- » "400" HONEY ALE (blonde ale with local wildflower honey)
- » CANADEO GOLD (Kölsch)
- » DARK HELMET SCHWARZBIER
- » GREEN 19 IPA
- » JOHNNY "BLOOD" RED (Irish-style red ale)
- » RAILYARD ALE (altbier)

Rotating Beers: (the list is endless, but here are a couple)
- » BRIDGE OUT STOUT
- » DOUSMAN STREET WHEAT
- » OKTOBERFEST
- » BELGIANS
- » AMBERS
- » PORTERS
- » BROWNS
- » DOUBLE IPAs

Most Popular Brew: Green 19 IPA

Brewmaster's Fave: The beer in his glass.

Tours? Yes, by appointment or just randomly when they are free.

Samples? Yes, by appointment or just randomly when they are free.

Best Time to Go: Hoppy hour 2-6 PM, open every day. Join the Hoppy Campers Club.

Where can you buy it? On site and in growlers, and some draft accounts around the Green Bay, Madison and Milwaukee areas.

Got food? Yes, a good pub menu. Fish and chips, pizzas, artichoke dip, fresh perch on Friday,

deep-fried cheese curds, spicy beer cheese soup, the on-site baker makes beer breads. In fact, 20% of the entrees use beer in some way. The dinner entrees are excellent as well.

Special Offer: A pint o' beer!

Directions: From US Highway 41 take Shawano Ave exit and go east to Ashland Ave. Go left (north) two blocks and take a right on Dousman St. The brewpub is on the left just before the bridge over the Fox River.

The Beer Buzz: Overlooking the Fox River, Titletown occupies a former train station that is listed in the National Register of Historic Places. Built in 1898, it was a stop for the Chicago & Northwestern railway. Prior to that, it was the Fort Howard Military Reservation. This was a center of the community when the "Peninsula 400" passenger service still ran. Three presidents rolled through on whistle-stops: Taft, Franklin Roosevelt and Eisenhower. The "400" ended service in 1971 and in '87 C&NW sold the tracks to Milwaukee to Fox River Valley Railroad. By 1994, after a couple more sales, it was just an empty building. That's when founder Brent Weycker, a fellow student union employee in college with yours truly, decided he would open a brewpub so that I would have something to write about 10 years later, and so we could all drink beer again just like we never, never did on the job. No, never. Well, hardly ever.

Brewmaster David started homebrewing in 2002 and then apprenticed here for many years. When the lead position opened up, he was a brew-in. Nearly everything produced here is sold over the counter (except for just a few tap accounts). It's an impressive amount of beer, but then this is Green Bay. Railyard Alt got silver at 2008's Great American Beer Festival, Dark Helmet took bronze a year later, followed by a gold for Boathouse Pilsner in 2010. The bar's got WiFi so you can email your friends and make them jealous. (For those of you visiting from another planet, Titletown is the nickname of Green Bay, in recognition of the many championships won by the beloved Packers.) In 2011, I personally shared a growler of David's Expect the Wurst (bratwurst ale) with Al Roker when they did the Today Show right on the turf at Lambeau Field. My 1:40 of fame.

Stumbling Distance: *Hinterland Brewpub* is right across the street! Like the railroad theme going on here? Check out the *National Railroad Museum* (www.nationalrrmuseum.org, 2285 S. Broadway St, 920-437-7623) which has over 70 locomotives and cars, including Eisenhower's command train from WWII and the world's largest steam locomotive. A train ride around the grounds is available from May through September.

Courthouse Pub

Founded: 2001
Brewmaster: Brent Boeldt
Address: 1001 S 8th Street • Manitowoc, WI 54220
Phone: 920-686-1166
Website: www.courthousepub.com
Annual Production: 48 bbls
Number of Beers: Generally 5 on tap. Sometimes includes a guest brew.

Rotating Beers: Beers change monthly, so come back often.
» American Amber Ale
» Australian Lager with Tasmanian hops,
» Canadian-style Light
» Chief Wawatam Steam Lager (with Tasmanian hops, it's the official beer of the Maritime Museum and 25¢ per glass goes there)
» Czech Pilsner
» Double Bock
» Märzen
» Mexican Light
» Munich Helles (malty, mild hops, golden)
» Pub Porter
» Red Ale (high octane!)
» Scottish Ale
» Sing-Thai
» Trippel Jon
» Unfiltered Weiss
» Willinger Wheat

Most Popular Brew: Munich Helles

Brewmaster's Fave: Munich Helles (really, anything with malt, hops, and alcohol)

Tours? Yes, by appointment.

Samples? Yes, five beer samplers and a root beer for $6.00.

Best Time to Go: Friday and Saturday nights offer good dinner specials. Closed on Sundays; lunch and dinner on Saturday. This is primarily a restaurant so don't expect to stay out late here unless you can chat up the barkeeper. Watch for live music dates on the website.

GATEWAY TO WISCONSIN II

From mid-May to mid-October, the S.S. Badger (www.ssbadger.com, 800-841-4243), a coal-powered car ferry, makes the four-hour crossing of the big lake to Manitowoc from Ludington, Michigan.

Where can you buy it? Growlers on site.

Got food? Yes, serious food for both lunch and dinner. Items range from the more casual sandwiches, burgers, and wraps to steaks, seafood and other dinner entrées such as pecan-encrusted duck with Wisconsin maple syrup glazing or fresh scallops.

Special Offer: A free pint of microbrew when you bring in this book to be signed!

Directions: Take Exit 149 east off of I-43. Then travel east on 151/10/Calumet Avenue (turns into Washington St) until 8th. Street. The pub is on the southeast corner of 8th and Washington Street in Downtown Manitowoc.

The Beer Buzz: This site was originally home to F. Willinger's Beer Hall, and an old black and white photo behind the bar shows the former beer joint. The pub was rebuilt to the hall's likeness. Once there were five breweries in Manitowoc, but by the mid-70s, there was not a one. Owner John Jagemann wanted to bring back a little of that tradition and so the pub was born. Beer is not the only libation here. Since 2002, the restaurant has maintained a Wine Spectator Award of Excellence. Follow the website's blog to find out about upcoming live music.

Stumbling Distance: Look for the big cow and you'll find *Cedar Crest Ice Cream Parlor* (www.cedarcresticecream.com, 2000 S 10th, 800-877-8341). Award winning stuff. Stop in at the *Wisconsin Maritime Museum* (www.wisconsinmaritime.org, 866-724-2356) and tour the submarine U.S.S. Cobia. Twenty-eight subs were built here in Manitowoc during WWII. *Tippy's Bar, Grill and Miniature Bowling* (1713 East St, 920-553-8479) in Two Rivers (pronounced "T'rivers" by locals) serves smelt six days a week! (A small fish which is netted and then fried—and eaten—whole. It's a Wisconsin thing.) The Manitowoc VFW or Eagle's Hall are rumored to have the best fish fries, but there are tons of them here. Get your cheese fix at *Pine River Dairy* (www.pineriverdairy.com, 10115 English Lake Rd, 920-758-2233) south of 151 on Range Line Rd (since 1877). Over 250 varieties!

Rail House Restaurant & Brewpub

Founded: 1995
Brewmaster: Kris Konyn
Address: 2029 Old Peshtigo Court
Marinette, WI 54143
Phone: 715-732-4646
Website: www.railhousebrewpub.com
Annual Production: 300 bbls
Number of Beers: 20–24, 14 on tap

Staple Beers:
- » Big Mac IPA
- » Blueberry Draft
- » Bock
- » Brewer's Best Pilsner
- » Dumb Blonde
- » Honey Weiss (Honey from Crivitz, WI)
- » Imperial Pilsner
- » Irish Red Ale
- » Oatmeal Stout
- » Oconto Premium Lager
- » Scottish Ale
- » Silver Cream Pilsner

Rotating Beers:
- » Barley Wine
- » Holiday Brew
- » Oktoberfest
- » Pumpkin Spice
- » Winter Fest
- » Zummer Fest

Most Popular Brew: Silver Cream

Brewmaster's Fave: Bock

Tours? Not really.

Samples? Yes, twelve 4-oz. samples for $9, four for $3.50. All 16 plus root beer is a possibility as well.

Best Time to Go: 2-for-1 happy hour Mon–Thurs 3–6 PM, Fri 1–5 PM, Sat 12–4 PM. Menominee Water Front Festival is the first long weekend in August.

Where can you buy it? On-site growlers.

Got food? Yes, the menu offers a big variety including Italian (the muffuletta sandwich is highly recommended) and Mexican. Pizzas, beer-battered shrimp, Wisconsin beer and cheese soup, and a big Friday night fish fry.

Special Offer: A free house beer!

Directions: The pub is on the right side of US41 as you come into Marinette from the south. Turn right (east) at Cleveland Ave and take the next 2 rights. There are large signs to direct you with the Rail House and Country Inn hotel on them.

The Beer Buzz: The pub was originally in a smaller building on the same lot and in 1997 it reopened in the new facility. The Silver Cream Pilsner is a bit of nostalgia. It is a reproduction of the turn-of-the-century beer once produced by Menominee-Marinette Brewing Co. (just over the border in the Michigan sister city). The back bar here is a fantastic wood-carved affair all the way from Bavaria. Its original Wisconsin residence was a saloon in Blackwell. Two projection screen TVs are on hand for the big games, and an outdoor covered patio is the place to be in summer.

Kris began homebrewing in college using a couple of plastic pails and a big stainless kettle borrowed from his fraternity house kitchen. At first he used malt extracts and experimented with mini mashes and colder fermenting lagers. (He went to school in the cold U.P. climate of Houghton, MI after all.) One year after graduation he was having a beer with a friend in a brewpub and found himself in a brewing conversation with the owner. The conversation was in fact a cleverly disguised job interview. The next day Kris was offered the brewer position. His first batch of Scottish-style Ale was kegged a month later confirming they had the right guy for the job. Kris loves to try new beers and keeps up on the latest news and ideas in brewing in technical and scientific publications, beer reviews, magazines and homebrewing blogs and books.

Stumbling Distance: South of town on 41 is *Seguin's Cheese* (www.seguin-scheese.com, 800-338-7919) offering a vast assortment of Wisconsin's other finest product and a variety of other local yummies (mustards, jams, sauces). They even ship it. Cheese curds and aged cheddar—can you ask for much else? For you outdoorsy types, grab a growler from the brewpub and check out one of the 14 cascades that make *Marinette County* the "Waterfalls Capital of Wisconsin" (www.marinettecounty.com, 800-236-6681). More info on Marinette is found in a chapter from my book *Backroads and Byways of Wisconsin*.

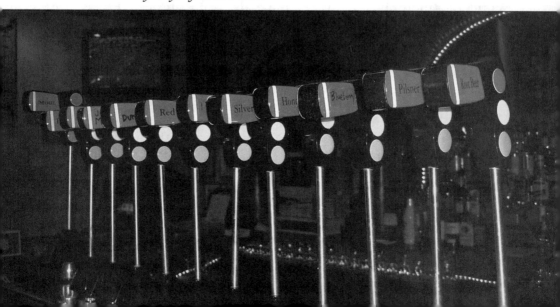

Fratellos Waterfront Brewery and Restaurant (Fox River Brewing Co.)

Founded: December 15, 1995
Brewmaster: Kevin Bowen
Address: 1501 Arboretum Drive • Oshkosh, WI 54901
Phone: 920-232-2337
Website: www.foxriverbrewing.com
Annual Production: 600 bbls
Number of Beers: 8 on tap

Staple Beers:
- » Buzzin' Honey Ale
- » Caber Tossing Scottish Ale
- » Fox Light (Kölsch)
- » Winnebago Wheat (Hefeweizen)

Rotating Beers: A fruit, dark, hoppy, and seasonal beer which may feature:
- » Abbey Normal (Belgian dubbel)
- » Blü (blueberry ale)
- » Cherry Brau
- » Fox Tail Pale Ale
- » Foxtoberfest
- » Hoppy Face IPA
- » Paine's Pilsner
- » Peaches Ale
- » Slam Dunkel (dark lager)
- » Titan Porter
- » Trolleycar Stout
- » Vader's Imperial Stout

Most Popular Brew: Caber Tossing Scottish Ale

Brewmaster's Fave: Maibock, Hoppy Face, Fox Tail Pale. He likes seasonal beers and prefers dry, bitter and hoppier stuff.

Tours? On request, call ahead.

Samples? Eight 5.5 oz beers for $10.

Best Time to Go: Summer. Live music on Friday and Saturday. Happy Hour 3–6 PM for ½ price drinks.

Where can you buy it? Bottles, growlers, quarter- and half-barrels and some local taverns serve it. On site as well as the other Fratellos locations at Fox River Mall-Appleton and Fratellos of Appleton.

Got food? Yes! Of course, Fratellos features a variety of steaks, seafood, pastas, sandwiches and pizzas and much more on their full menu.

Special Offer: $2 pint on your first Fox River beer, additional pints regular price.

Directions: In Oshkosh, cross the Fox River heading easy on Congress (Hwy 21) and it's the first street on the left. You'll see it from the bridge.

The Beer Buzz: On the banks of the Fox River, this trendy restaurant is one of the most happening spots in town. This restaurant has a view like no other and offers a family-friendly atmosphere with a separate lounge which is more oriented to the party scene. There are forty slips for boaters and the terrace outside has a large tiki bar. It's a great time in the summer (rumor has it my cousin once danced on a table here—she denies it to the last). Cross the river heading east on Congress (Hwy 21) and it's the first street on the left. You'll see it from the bridge. Kevin Bowen worked at the restaurant years ago and started at Fox River Brewing Co. in an undeclared apprenticeship working from the bottom up: cleaning kegs, filling bottles, and such. After attending Siebel Institute to study the art and science of brewing, he worked for a few other brewhouses before returning to Fox River Brewing Co. He's nabbed silver for his Kölsch in 2010 at the World Beer Cup as well as for his Abbey Normal Belgian Dubbel aged in

a brandy barrel. In fact, he has started doing more barrel-aged beers and bringing new brews into the lineup. Foxtoberfest comes on mid-Sept-Oct while Red Baron Altbier comes on tap during the EAA Fly In. Watch for a resurrected Chief Oshkosh beer!

Stumbling Distance: *EAA* (Experimental Aircraft Association) (www.eaa.org) has a museum (just off Hwy 41 adjacent to Wittman Airport, 920-426-4818, open Mon–Sat 8:30–5, Sun 10–5, $12.50) with over 250 historic planes, five theatres and a flight motion simulator. And don't miss the largest aviation event in the world. The AirVenture, when hundreds of experimental and homemade aircraft come to the week-long "Fly In" in late July, is like nothing you've ever seen. *Hughes Homemade Chocolate Shop* (1823 Doty St, 920-231-7232)—look for the open sign on the porch, walk up the driveway and to the side door, and head directly downstairs. If there is a line (which there always is) you'll have to wait on the steps. No displays or candy counters or fancy colors—just clean white boxes of chocolates that get unbelievable raves by choco-junkies. Call first—they are often closed and keep erratic hours. Best around holiday seasons. See the *Brews N Blues Festival* in the Festival section at the back of the book.

Look for Fratellos and the Fox River Brews in Fox River Mall-Appleton and a second Appleton location:
  » 4301 Wisconsin, Appleton, WI 54913 (920) 991-0000
  » 501 West Water Street, Appleton, WI 54911 (920) 993-9087

OSHKOSH BREWING HISTORY

Oshkosh's brewing history goes back a lot further than Fox River Brewing Co. Since the 1840s, the city has been home to more than a dozen breweries and a robust beer culture that continues to thrive. You history and breweriana buffs out there should check out a new book about that old profession. (I mean brewing.) Co-written by Ron Akin, a retired University professor and breweriana collector, and Lee Reiherzer, a beer columnist and blogger, this is a lively account of beer and breweries in "Sawdust City," with over 400 illustrations. Check out the Oshkosh Beer website and order yourself a copy. (oshkoshbeer@gmail.com, oshkoshbeer.blogspot.com)

Black Husky Brewing Co.

Founded: March 2010
Brewmaster: Tim Eichinger
Address: W5951 Steffen Lane • Pembine, WI 54156
Phone: 715-324-5152
Website: www.blackhuskybrewing.com
Annual Production: 200 barrels
Number of Beers: 17

Staple Beers:
  » Harold The Red
  » Pale Ale
  » Sproose Joose Double IPA (with spruce in it!)

Rotating Beers:
  » American White
  » Big Buck Brown
  » Honey Wheat
  » Milk Stout
  » …and many more

Most Popular Brew: Pale Ale or Sproose Joose.

Brewmaster's Fave: Hard to say. Depends on the time of year. Pale Ale, I suppose.

Tours? For a nominal fee. Very limited and by appointment only – don't just stop in. They have dogs, you know.

Samples: Yes, if you schedule a tour.

Best Time to Go: Visit them at various beer festivals around Wisconsin

Where can you buy it? Pembine, for sure. About 20 draft accounts in eastern Wisconsin, think I-43 corridor. Limited bottles are going to Milwaukee, Sheboygan, and few random places. They self-distribute, so check the website.

Got food? Nope.

Special Offer: A Laurel and Hardy handshake

The Beer Buzz: This is typically what a serious homebrewer ends up doing when he thinks "career change." He and his wife Toni figured they'd never retire anyway so may as well find something they could do indefinitely. "Find something you love doing, something you really believe in so that it doesn't feel like work." He thought about volunteering at another brewery, but then thought, "Why? So I can learn to clean?" There is a lot to learn and starting on your own, they felt, it was better to just dive right in, but as a nanobrewery. "Risks are smaller, and we're poor. We can't afford to borrow $500,000!" The learning curve is steep but they went from 28 barrels to 200 in a year. They bottled over 20,000 bottles by hand one year. That has gone down as they focus on kegs (80% of their business). But they are still bottling a bit.

The aim is to keep on growing slowly and organically. Half the new accounts they get contact them directly. They don't market a bunch as they are so busy. Tim is on his third generation of brewing equipment. The first kettles were made out of half barrels with the tops cut off. He then moved on to a one-barrel system. Now they have a 4.5-barrel system, all of it made from recycled dairy equipment. "I'm a hack when I do stuff, but it doesn't stop me from trying. My motto is How hard can it be?"

Stumbling Distance: *Newingham's Supper Club* (722 Main St, Wausaukee, 715-856-5966) serves local beef and buffalo, steaks and seafood, and a Friday fish fry (lake perch, cod, walleye). *Four Seasons Resort* (thefourseasonswi.com, N16800 Shoreline Dr, 715-324-5244) is a nice hotel deep in the woods along the Menomonie River, rumored to be an old hangout for Capone types from Chicago back in the day. If you're in town and you didn't get in touch with Tim or Toni, stop in at *Pembine Food Depot* (N18678 Hwy 141, 715-324-6499)—they have Black Husky beer.

3 Sheeps Brewing

Founded: February 2012
Brewmaster: Grant Pauly
Address: 1327 North 14th Street • Sheboygan, WI 53081
Phone: 920-395-3583
Website: www.3sheepsbrewing.com
Annual Production: 1500 bbls
Number of Beers: 4 plus seasonals

Staple Beers:
- » Baaad Boy Black Wheat
- » Cirque Du Wit
- » Really Cool Waterslides IPA
- » Rebel Kent The First Amber (formerly known as Enkel Biter)

Rotating Beers:
- » Ginger Coffee Stout

Most Popular Brew: Really Cool Waterslides IPA

Brewmaster's Fave: "I'm a hop head: the IPA"

Tours? Yes, but groups of 5 or more and by appointment only.

Samples: No, but get a sampler flight at Hops Haven upstairs.

Best Time to Go: Tuesday-Saturday 3 to close (3-6 is Happy Hour). On Tuesdays from 3 to close pints are 2 for $5.

Where can you buy it? At Hops Haven upstairs and in growlers there, but also in an area from Green Bay to Racine, and in Madison and Milwaukee on tap. Some bottles in eastern Wisconsin. There's a tapfinder on the website.

Got food? Well, the bar upstairs Hops Haven serves the beer and shares the space with a restaurant, so yes. Pizza, paninis, sandwiches, salads and some beer worked into a few recipes.

Special Offer: Not participating

The Beer Buzz: "So many great breweries in Sheboygan have been forgotten," says Brewer Grant. True the brewing history goes way back to 1847 with Gutsch Brewing Co., a year before Wisconsin's statehood. After

Prohibition knocked Gutsch out, the still-familiar Kingsbury took over in 1933 brewing until 1974. Heileman had already bought them in 1963 so one could still go "swinging with the King" even after that brewery closed its doors. In fact, 3 Sheeps takes over where another great brewery left off: Hops Haven. 3 Sheeps is set up in the basement of the same building but you will still find Hops Haven on the sign because the restaurant that took over the bar portion has kept the name.

In 2005, Grant started homebrewing when his wife bought him a brew kit. Once he started counting yeast cells, he figured this was getting serious. He took some coursework at the Siebel Institute and when Hops Haven's former location and equipment became available, he made the leap. Rather than trying to develop a menu and tavern, he decided to just brew the beer and let other entities operate the other two aspects of this unusual all-in-one arrangement.

Grant's amber was first named Enkel Biter. However, many drinkers kept thinking it was Enkel Bitter (seeing double, as can be expected) and so the name was changed to Rebel Kent the First to avoid the suggestion that this was a bitter beer. Funny story about his IPA's name. It comes from a t-shirt that shows a little boy at a crossroads forced to choose: Fame, Fortune, Success? or REALLY COOL WATERSLIDES! Perfectly expresses Grant's choice to leave the financial security of a job he was not passionate about to take the risk on something he really enjoyed.

Stumbling Distance: *Schulz's Restaurant* (1644 Calumet Dr, 920-452-1880) a few blocks up the street is a good place for a burger or a brat. *Legend Larry's* (www.legendlarrys.com, 1632 Michigan Ave, 920-458-9464) is the place for wings. A history of awards backs that statement up. *Charcoal Inn* (1313 S 8th St, 920-458-6988) has a charcoal grill (big surprise, given the name) for brats and burgers. The Sheboygan area is home to a Wisconsin classic: Johnsonville Brats (bratwurst, not rotten children). Check out *Brat Days* (www.sheboyganjaycees.com) in August—1000s of brat eaters, live music and a brat eating contest with serious competitors from around the world. By the way, brats are "fried" in Sheboygan. A "grill out" or "cook out" is referred to as a "fry out."

ZONE 6

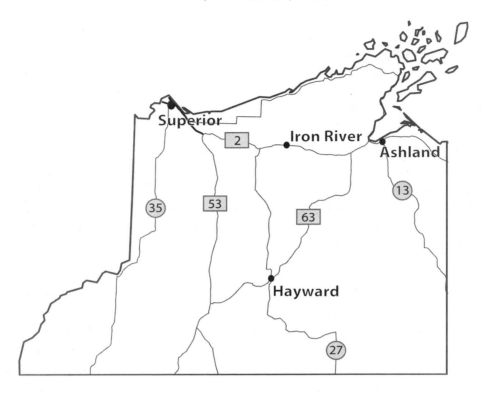

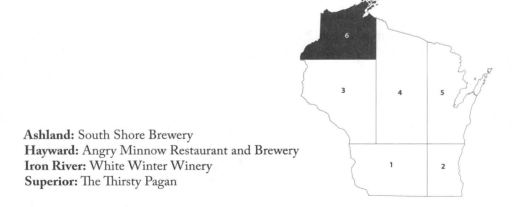

Ashland: South Shore Brewery
Hayward: Angry Minnow Restaurant and Brewery
Iron River: White Winter Winery
Superior: The Thirsty Pagan

SOUTH SHORE BREWERY (IN L.C. WILMARTH'S DEEP WATER GRILLE)

Founded: May1995
Brewmaster: Bo Bélanger
Address: 808 W Main Street • Ashland, WI 54806
Phone: 715-682-9199
Website: www.southshorebrewery.com
Annual Production: 1600 bbls
Number of Beers: 7 on tap, 23 throughout the year

Staple Beers:
- » AMERICAN PALE ALE
- » BELGIAN TRIPLE
- » INLAND SEA PILSNER
- » NORTHERN LIGHTS CREAM ALE
- » NUT BROWN ALE (it's English-style and they've got the darts and crusty bread to go with it)
- » RED LAGER
- » RHOADES' SCHOLAR STOUT

Rotating Beers:
- » APPLEFEST ALE (with local cider direct from the orchard)
- » BELGIAN-STYLES SAISON AND TRIPPEL
- » BITTER BLONDE
- » BOURBON-BARREL COFFEE-MINT STOUT
- » BRACKET
- » ESB
- » IRISH MILK STOUT
- » MAIBOCK
- » PORTER
- » PUMPKIN BEER (with maple syrup sweetener)
- » SCHWARZBIER
- » STREET CORNER 40 MALT LIQUOR
- » WHEAT DOPPELBOCK
- » ...Special beers for special events

Most Popular Brew: Nut Brown Ale

Brewmaster's Fave: Inland Sea Pilsner

Tours? Yes, best by appointment.

Samples? Yes, a rack of six for $4.50

Best Time to Go: Any time, check for local festivals: Whistlestop Marathon, Blues and Brews (second weekend in Oct.), Applefest in Bayfield (first weekend in Oct.), Bay Days in Ashland (mid-July), Red Clay Classic (WISSOTA-sanctioned stock-car race), Firehouse 40 Bike Race, Fat Tire Bike Race, Birkebeiner cross-country-ski race in Hayward, etc.

Where can you buy it? Growlers on site, bottles distributed throughout much of Wisconsin, western Upper Peninsula Michigan, North Shore of Minnesota, Duluth Metro area, and limited Twin Cities locations.

Got food? Yes, salads, sandwiches, and entrees. Walleye fish fry on Fridays and fresh Lake Superior whitefish. Beer cheese soup, ham, mushroom and wild rice soup, pale ale onion soup, and a stout BBQ sauce put the brews in the kitchen. They use malt flour or wort reduction on desserts.

Special Offer: 10% off South Shore Brewery merchandise.

The Beer Buzz: Ashland Brewery made a run from 1886 to 1892, and Ashland Brewing Co. served the city from 1901 to 1937, and it wasn't until South Shore opened up in a renovated railway station that local brew returned to Chequamegon Bay. Originally, the brewery operated with the Railyard Pub in the historic Soo Line Depot downtown. But fire and buildings don't mix and when they did anyway, the brewery relocated to join Deep Water Grille in one of three Main Street buildings built by Lewis Cass Wilmarth (1833–1907), Ashland's fourth mayor. The brownstone accents and footings are all locally mined, and the cornerstone dates the structure at 1895. The restaurant is the best in town and it doesn't hurt to have fresh beer on tap. The bar shows some antique stained glass and serves free popcorn. Brewmaster Bo likes to push the envelope a bit on some things. (See the peppermint in that coffee stout!) This is some high quality stuff and an adventuresome spirit. All of the base malt used in South Shore's beers is grown right there in the Chequamegon Bay / Bayfield Peninsula area—that's some impressively local beer. Bo collaborates with Iron River mead maker Jon Hamilton at White Winter Winery to make bracket, a sort of cross between mead and ale and precursor to modern beers. Bo's Nut Brown Ale is so popular he says he could get by on that brew alone. With all the continued success, expect to see more growth from South Shore.

Stumbling Distance: *Frankie's Pizza* (1315 Lake Shore Dr E, 715-682-9980) is the great greasy variety you can't get enough of (does carry out). *Ashland Baking Company* (ashlandbakingco.com, 212 Chapple Ave, 715-682-6010) is an artisan bakery bringing a bit of Europe to the Northwoods. South Shore hosts a Brew Fest as part of the larger *Whistlestop Marathon and Festival* (www.whistlestopmarathon.com, 800-284-9484). Great blues concerts, a Lake Superior fish boil, pasta feed, and running events the second full weekend in October. *Applefest* (www. bayfield.org) is the weekend before up in Bayfield and South Shore hauls out the specialty Applefest Ale for it. 60,000 people turn out for this massive celebration of Wisconsin apples. A rare roadside attraction might be the so-called *"Plywood Palace"* out in nearby Moquah, an odd little tavern that looks like it was nailed together by some fellas that already had a few. *Big Top Chautauqua* (www.bigtop.

org, 888-244-8368) is an outdoor music/theatre venue that runs all summer up in Bayfield. *Stage North* (www.stagenorth.com, 123 W Omaha St, 715-373-1194) in Washburn runs music and theater events year round.

Angry Minnow Restaurant and Brewery

Founded: September 2004
Brewmaster: Jason Rasmussen
Address: 10440 Florida Avenue • Hayward, WI 54843
Phone: 715-934-3055
Website: www.angryminnow.com
Annual Production: 670 bbls
Number of Beers: 6–7 on tap, 12–14 per year

Staple Beers:
- » Honey Wheat
- » Minnow Light
- » Oaky's Oatmeal Stout (under nitrogen!)
- » River Pig Pale Ale
- » Rye IPA

Rotating Beers:
- » Belgian Blonde
- » Doppelbock
- » Hefeweizen
- » Imperial IPA
- » Last Notch Wheat
- » McStukie's Scotch Ale
- » Oktoberfest
- » Pilsner
- » Smoked Porter
- » …and a couple Belgians around winter

Most Popular Brew: River Pig Pale Ale

Brewmaster's Fave: Rye IPA, River Pig Pale Ale, Stouts in winter

Tours? Yes, by appointment or by chance.

Samples? Yes, $10 for six 6 oz. samples.

Best Time to Go: Muskiefest is third week in June each year and the Birkebeiner in late February.

Where can you buy it? They self-distribute, so growlers at the bar and kegs and cans only in the Hayward area. River Pig Pale Ale and Oaky's Oatmeal Stout are the only brews available in cans either at stores or the brewpub.

Got food? Yes. The menu featuring everything from sandwiches to full meals changes regularly. The emphasis is on locally sourced ingredients. Burgers are popular. Fresh whitefish and perch come from Lake Superior, and crayfish are on the menu. Deep-fried cheese curds are still here, and Friday features the traditional fish fry (walleye, perch, and whitefish). Look for the Lake Superior whitefish sandwich.

Special Offer: A free pint *and* ½ off an appetizer!

Directions: Look for Florida Ave to intersect with Hwy 63 just four blocks south of the junction with Hwy 27.

The Beer Buzz: Lumber put Hayward on the map back in the nineteenth century, and the Angry Minnow has inherited a bit of its legacy. The restaurant and brewery occupy a restored 1889 brick building that once served as the offices for Northwest Lumber Co. Exposed brick, hardwood floors, tasteful lighting, and a good menu are notable enough. But like anything, add some great beer and it's all a little bit better. Brewmaster Jason got his start at the Great Dane in Madison as an apprentice and then returned to his hometown to show the results. The name was a twist on the local icon, the massive and elusive muskellunge (that's muskie to you and me). Hayward has the record for the largest one caught. So the pub went with the little guy on the hook who does all the work of catching the big fish. Appropriate for the brewpubs that are the little guys in the beer industry and yet really doing the most impressive work. The bar offers Wi-Fi.

Stumbling Distance: OK, no one goes to Hayward—angler pro or not—without stopping in to see the giant muskie (over 4 stories tall!) at the

National Fresh Water Fishing Hall of Fame (www.freshwater-fishing.org, 10360 Hall of Fame Dr, 715-634-4440). Go, and at *least* take a photo. The museum itself lives up to its icon in the fiberglass giant fish menagerie outside—400 fish mounts, classic motors, lures and equipment. *West's Dairy* (www.westshaywarddairy.com, corner of 2nd and Dakota, 715-634-2244) has been around since the 1920s and serves excellent homemade ice cream, malts, sundaes and some sandwiches. Grab a coffee and some Wi-Fi here too.

WHITE WINTER WINERY

Founded: 1996
Mead Maker: Jon Hamilton
Address: 68323A Lea Street • Iron River, WI 54847
Phone: 800-697-2006
Website: www.whitewinter.com
Annual Production: 5500 cases
Number of Beers: 2 plus a lot of meads, ciders and a distillate or two

Beers:
» PREMIUM OAK BRACKETT (aged with oak chips)
» TRADITIONAL BRACKETT

Tours? Yes.

Samples? 3 free samples or the whole lineup for $5 (and you keep the glass)

Best Time to Go: Summer Festival (mid-June), Blueberry Festival (late July) in Iron River, and Oktoberfest. Sundays in the summer often host live music. Don't miss the Labor Day Weekend Sunday "Emergency Pig-out" with live music, pig roast, and more – to benefit local emergency responders.

Where can you buy it? Bottles on site and liquor stores throughout Wisconsin, Minnesota and Illinois.

Got food? Great fresh popcorn.

Special Offer: 10% off any White Winter meads, bracketts or hard ciders or other products made on site.

Directions: At the west end of Iron River along the north side of US Hwy 2, look for the winery set back from the road across a parking lot.

The Beer Buzz: Jon comes from a long line of beekeepers, and though his family lived in the Minneapolis area, his father kept an empty hive out in the backyard while Jon was growing up. Jon knew of mead since middle school when he would do his term papers on honey and bees. When he was older, he decided making this ancient fermented honey concoction was easier than sneaking into the liquor store. Just off US 2 at the west end of town, his winery offers a great variety of meads and ciders all made from local ingredients, but he also has a couple types of bottled brackett. This is the missing link in the evolution of beer, you might say. Fermented honey (mead) is believed to be the happy hour drink of choice with the longest history, and the Scandinavians came up with brackett which is a cross between mead and ale by adding malted barley to the recipe. Brewmaster Bo over at South Shore Brewery in nearby Ashland helps out with this one since a winery must otherwise get another license to brew beers. Mead is associated with Winter Solstice celebrations (daylight hours start getting longer after December 21, and you are hopeful winter might actually end in May this year instead of June). The winery name comes from the legend of Old Man Winter, who is a resident in these parts for all but those two weeks of road construction in summer. Just kidding. Sort of. Watch for Jon to start distilling in 2013. First up: *eau de vie!*

Stumbling Distance: For some excellent traditional diner fare and some very creative twists (baked puffy pancakes, baked omelets), head over to *Delta Diner* (www.deltadiner.net, 715-372-6666), southeast of Iron River on Cty Hwy H. You can't miss it—it's one of those classic shiny, aluminum-sided 1940s Silk City diners, restored and parked in the middle of the Northwoods. There are local bottled beers on hand and dishes are also made with many local ingredients. Fresh gourmet coffee right next door. Pick up some of Jalapeño Nina's Spicy Pickled Garlic while you're there too. *Oulu Glass* (www.ouluglass.com, 1695 W Colby Rd, Brule, 888-685-8969) eight miles west of Iron River features the amazing blown-glass work of the Jim and Sue Vojacek family from May 1 to January 5. Free demonstrations in November and December. Herbster, a town to the north, has sponsored an annual *smelt fry* every April since 1956, and it is a delicious taste of local culture. There are also many other area festivals—check with the Iron River Chamber of Commerce (www.iracc.com, 800-345-0716) for specific event dates.

Thirsty Pagan Brewing

Founded: 1996
Brewmaster: Allyson Rolf
Address: 1623 Broadway • Superior, WI 54880
Phone: 715-394-2500
Website: www.thirstypaganbrewing.com
Annual Production: 400 barrels
Number of Beers: 8 on tap plus a beer engine

Staple Beers:
- » Burntwood Black Ale (named after a local river; cool points if you can name which one!)
- » Derailed Ale (classic American Pale Ale)
- » Indian Pagan Ale (IPA)
- » North Coast Amber Ale

Rotating Beers: Lots of them! Rotation is frequent, often a new beer every couple of weeks or so.
- » Capitalist Pig Russian Imperial Stout
- » Oktoberfest
- » Pinta Colada (cream-style stout with coconut)
- » Saison
- » Some high-octane seasonals and monster IPAs as well

Most Popular Brew: Indian Pagan Ale

Brewmaster's Fave: "This is always that question no one really wants to answer, isn't it?" She's always been a fan of Burntwood Black Ale.

Tours? Informal ones by chance or appointment.

Samples? Yes, a flight of eight for around $7.

Best Time to Go: Open 3 pm–close. (Planning to open at lunch in spring 2013.) Tues–Sun nights host a variety of bands, Happy Hour is 3–6 pm Mon–Fri.

Where can you buy it? Only here and carry-out growlers.

Got food? Yes, quite literally the best pizza and toasted sub sandwiches.

Special Offer: A free 10 oz. glass of prune juice! No, I'm kidding—it's a beer.

Directions: Follow Hammond Ave south from the interchange with Hwy 53/I-535. Continue driving south to the first stop light, and take Broadway to the right (west). Or US Hwy 2 from the west becomes Belknap St. Take this to Ogden Ave and turn right north to Broadway where you will see the brewery on the corner of Ogden Ave and Broadway.

The Beer Buzz: In 1999, brewer Rick Sauer (now at Hudson Brewing) moved his Twin Ports Brewing to this 1910 creamery building on the corner of Broadway St and Ogden Ave. It's an unassuming place, still tiled like the creamery and all the feel of a northern town tavern. Local breweriana hangs on the walls. Steve and Susan Knauss took over and changed the name to Thirsty Pagan in 2006. Before this place, Superior hadn't had its own beer since Northern Brewing Co. emptied its tanks for the last time in the late '60s. They're serious about their beer here, but loads of fun to drink it with. The bar has expanded a bit adding space for forty more patrons. The restaurant side of the brewpub can seat larger parties.

Brewer Allyson is originally from Iowa and went to school in Mankato, but moved to Duluth in the early 2000s. She has always been a patron here and has a long history of drinking their beer. The beer inspired her

to start homebrewing. She spent as much time talking to other brewers as possible and even went into a few other breweries to just sort of follow people around and pick their brains. She read a lot. Finally, she did an internship under the previous brewer, Nate McAlpine. When he left, she stepped into the position. Her degree is in art, and while the job is not always about being creative, it's about being a maker. So whether it's a house brew that she makes the same way every time or something new, exciting and innovative, she feels happy to be producing something. Allyson is one of two female head brewers in the state (see Dells Brewing Co/Moosejaw in Wisconsin Dells).

Stumbling Distance: Dive into a dive at the *Anchor Bar* (413 Tower Ave, 715-394-9747) five blocks away. Burgeoning (yes, I really just used that word) with ship-themed paraphernalia, this cozy local tavern has many kinds of burgers—some weighing in at a pound—that are excellent, cheap, and inventive (*cashew* burger??). Take a growler of Burntwood Black Ale and get some fresh air at *Wisconsin Point* (Moccasin Mike Road), the world's largest freshwater spit (a sand bar with trees) with a lighthouse, Native American burial grounds, driftwood, agates, and many species of birds. History buffs shouldn't miss the *Richard I. Bong World War II Heritage Center* (www.bongheritagecenter.org, 305 Harbor View Parkway, 888-816-9944) where the ace of aces namesake is commemorated along with all the veterans of that war in an informative and sharply designed museum. A restored Lockheed P-38 Lightning fighter plane—the type of plane Bong used in his record 40 enemy kills—is on site.

BEER FESTIVALS

Ah, there is nothing quite like a beer fest. Brat tents, music, and copious amounts of great beer. Variety is the spice of life, and a good brew festival allows you to travel through a whole lot of breweries that would have required a much longer trip.

This is only a general guideline. New beer fests pop up all the time. Specific dates change from year to year as do ticket prices. Also, some festivals sell out the same day tickets go on sale, months in advance, so plan ahead!

JANUARY

Minocqua Ice Cold Beer Fest is around the second Saturday in January in Minocqua, WI. Tickets for the three-hour event are $15 in advance and $18 at the door. The Waters in Minocqua (www.thewatersofminocqua.com), a hotel with an indoor waterpark, is the site. Along with the beer, sample some gourmet cheeses and other fine foods. Contact Minocqua Brewing Co. for more information (www.minocquabrewingcompany.com, 715-356-2600).

Isthmus Beer & Cheese Fest is in Madison on a Saturday in January bringing over 30 Wisconsin brewers to pair beers with about 2 dozen artisanal cheesemakers' best stuff. (thedailypage.com/beercheese).

FEBRUARY

Milwaukee Ale House Mid-Winter Beer Fest is the first Saturday in February (www.ale-house.com, 233 N. Water St., Milwaukee 1–6 PM, 414-226-2337).

Fond du Lac Brewfest got its start in 2010. This event aims to be annual and breaks up a bit of winter blues with four hours of beer pouring from Wisconsin microbrewers, live music, and food. Tickets are cheaper in advance and cost around $25 (www.fdlbrewfest.com).

Food and Froth is Milwaukee Public Museum's fundraising fest, offering samples of Midwest and import beers, plus great local food. Tickets are $70 (cheaper for museum members) and $100 for VIP. (mpm. edu/events/foodfroth).

Oconomowoc Brewfest is hosted by the local Rotary Club and happens mid-February. Sample beers, wines, craft liquor, and help charitable causes. Tickets are about $40. (rotarybrewfest.com).

MARCH

Hops & Props brings in over 250 beers on a Saturday evening in early March. Hosted by the EAA AirVenture Museum in Oshkosh, the community benefit costs $60 (more for the VIP dinner). (800-236-1025, www.eaa.org/hops&props).

Blessing of the Bock & Milwaukee Beer Festival is around the second Saturday of March. The charitable event has gone on since 1989 and is hosted by the awesome newspaper Suds, Wine and Spirits. Only bocks are served. Locations vary. Tickets are limited and around $25 in advance and it goes from noon–4 PM.

APRIL

Northeast Wisconsin Beer Festival brings in 30+ brewers in early April. It's indoors since this could either be beautiful weather or the eternal winter depending on the year. There is wine, food and music on hand. Tickets go on sale February 1 and are $25 in advance. (800-261-BEER, homebrewmarket.com, stonecellar.com).

Superior Gitchee Gumee Brewfest (www.ggbrewfest.com) is the first Saturday in April. A $25 ticket gets you access to over 120 beers from 30 brewers.

The **Dairy State Cheese and Beer Festival** (kenoshabeerfest.com) benefits the Boys and Girls Clubs of Kenosha. Watch for it in mid- to late-April at The Brat Stop right off I-94 outside Kenosha.

Milwaukee Beer Week (milwaukeebeerweek.com) is a late April series of events around the Brew City which features a passport so you can keep track of where you've been and need to go. These can also win you prizes. Expect a beer/food pairing of the like at the Harley Davidson Museum.

MAY

Great Taste of the Midwest tickets usually go on sale May 1. The 5,000 tickets sell out in a couple hours (see August).

Madison Craft Beer Week is a 10-day (2 weekend) series of events around the city typically starting around the first week of May (or late April). Beer walks, parties, food/beer pairings, films, lectures—you name it! (madbeerweek.com).

Milwaukee Beer Barons World of Beer Fest is the first Saturday in May (www.beerbarons.org) and features over 250 beers from over 90 brewers. The Beer Barons also host a Monster Mash Homebrew Competition.

Oregon Micro Brew Fest is at the Bergamont Golf Club the second Saturday in May. Tickets go on sale March 1 or so and run $25 with a beer glass. Only 1000 tickets! (608-835-3697 or www.oregonwi.com) Live music, five hours of sampling from 20+ breweries/brewpubs, and great food being sold by area non-profit groups until 7 PM.

Wisconsin Micro Beer Fest in Chilton has been running since 1992 when late founder and masterbrewer Bob Rowland of Calumet Brewing Co. started a small event that quickly became the second largest of its kind in the state. Held in late May (Sunday before Memorial Day weekend), it features over 100 beers from more than 20 Wisconsin brewers. Sample these while enjoying good food and live music. Advance tickets only $25. Tickets go on sale at the end of March and sell out early. Held at the Calumet County Fair Grounds, Chestnut and Francis Streets, Chilton, 1–6 PM. Contact Rowland's Calumet Brewpub at 920-849-2534.

JUNE

Kohler Festival of Beer is a three-day fest usually held in early June and hosting craft brewers from around the country. Check akohlerexperience. com under Events for more information.

Milwaukee Ale House's Prosit & Paddle is a canoe/kayak race down the Milwaukee River, usually the first Saturday in June. Food, beer and live music. For more information: www.ale-house.com, 414-226-2337.

Door County Beer Festival on a Saturday afternoon in mid-June brings craft beer and local food together with live music, seminars, and more in Bailey's Harbor. Tickets are $35-40, plus a bit more for limited VIP tix. (doorcountybeer.com).

Eagle River's Great Northern Beer Festival is the second Saturday in June (www.greatnorthernbeerfestival.com, 715-479-4545). Tickets are around $30 and typically sell out early. Around 30 brewers turn up for this—many from Wisconsin but also several foreigners (from Minnesota and Michigan and the like)—and it grows a bit each year. Tribute Brewing founder Bill Summers also runs this festival.

International Bayfest in Green Bay, around the second Saturday in June, was once on the UW-Green Bay campus but has moved downtown to the park next to Titletown Brewpub. Lots of fun on the waterside and the usual suspects: beer, food and music.

Wisconsin Beer Lovers Festival in Glendale in mid-June features Wisconsin-only brews and their brewers, plus local chefs with foods to pair beers with. (facebook.com/BeerLoversFest, 414-963-8780).

Wisconsin Summer Solstice Beer Lovers Festival in Glendale features only Wisconsin beers. Tickets are around $50 and include about 100+ beers and some excellent local cuisine pairings (www.welcometoglendale.com).

JULY

Oshkosh Brews & Blues (www.oshkoshjaycees.org/bnb.htm) benefiting the Christine Anne Center for Domestic Abuse takes place around the second Saturday of July at the Leach Amphitheater, 303 Ceape Ave., Oshkosh. $25 in advance, $35 at the door.

Sprecherfest is mid-July at Heidelberg Park, Glendale (Milwaukee metro area) (sprecherbrewery.com).

Hub City Brewfest is also in mid-July in Marshfield, WI with music, pig roast, craft sale, games and activities for kids, and a car and antique tractor show (ci.marshfield.wi.us).

Milwaukee Firkin Craft Beer Festival highlights cask-conditioned beers, offering over 20 of them, and a total of about 100 beers all from Milwaukee metro breweries. Held on a Saturday in mid- to late July, tickets about $45 or $75 with VIP option. (milwaukeefirkin.com).

German Fest is a huge ethnic party at Maier Park in Milwaukee at the end of July. (germanfest.com).

Lac du Flambeau Lions Club Brewfest is held at the end of July on a Saturday in Minocqua. Over a decade old, the fest brings nearly 50 brewers together with food and live music to boot. $25-30 tickets, either ordered or at the gate. (lacduflambeaubrewfest.com)

Milwaukee Brewfest takes place in late July and features over 200 craft brews, live music, Wisconsin food for sale and sample, exhibits, games, and even the crowning of the Brewfest Queen. A great time right down by the lakeshore (milwaukeebrewfest.com, 414-321-5000).

AUGUST

Arts & Ales Festival in Columbus happens on a Sunday in early August and features music, food, arts and crafts, a homebrew challenge, and beer from Hydro Street Brewing and others.

Great Taste of the Midwest is sort of the big kahuna of beer fests and the second longest running craft brew festival in North America. Over 500 beers from over 100 brewers! All 5,000 tickets typically sell out in a couple hours and go on sale around May 1. The event itself is the second Saturday in August. Contact the Madison Homebrewers & Tasters Guild at mhtg.org. $30 and only in advance!

The Firemen's Catfish Festival in Potosi, home of the National Brewery Museum, serves up some the town's original beer for a massive fish fry. Friday through Sunday (second Sunday of August). Also features music, truck and tractor pulls, a euchre tournament, fireworks and dance on Saturday, and a parade Sunday followed by the catfish dinner. Call 608-763-2261 for more info. Look for Potosi BrewFest at the end of the month.

Brewerama in Reedsburg is the fourth Sunday in August and is hosted by Corner Pub (p. 84). This is a very local event with food, live polka music, more than a dozen brewers and about 50 beers. Tickets are $25 ($20 in advance).

West Bend Germanfest in late August (www.downtownwestbend.com) features two stages of continuous music, authentic food, dancing, Sheepshead tournaments and daily raffles. Friday hosts a Fish Fry.

SEPTEMBER

Clearwater Beer Festival (second Saturday of September) is a four-hour beer sampling with beers from a dozen or more area and national brewers. Tickets are $22.50 in advance. Check with The Coffee Grounds (www.thecoffeegrounds.com, 3460 Mall Dr Hwy 93, 715-834-1733) for more info. 600-800 people.

Wisconsin Rapids Lions Fall Brew Review Fund Raiser for Lion Camps and Leader Dogs for the Blind is the second Saturday of September at Robinson Park, Wisconsin Rapids. Reservations: 715-423-0669 $20 ($15 Advance). This is smallish and personable, just a few hundred people with 12 brewers (mostly Wisconsin), food and live music.

Oktoberfest 100 Bicycle Tour. Watch for this brewery ride affiliated with Potosi Brewery and the National Brewery Museum. Lengths are 20, 40, 65 and 100 miles. "Ride, Drink and Be Merry!" they say. Check the brewery website at www.potosibrewery.com.

Great Lakes Brew Fest is in the middle of September, third Saturday generally, several great hours in the afternoon with the beer of over 60 brewers represented and unlimited sampling right on the shore of Lake Michigan. Lots of food is served and various forms of entertainment are provided. It gets bigger and better every year. Festival Park in Racine. $25 in advance, $30 at the gate (www.greatlakesbrewfest.com, 800-272-2463).

Chippewa Falls Oktoberfest (chippewachamber.org, 715-723-0331) Northern Wisconsin State Fairgrounds (Hwy 124/Jefferson Ave), three days in the middle of September ($7–8). Lots of song, dance, sauerkraut eating contests and Leinie's beer. Good family event.

Angry Minnow Oktoberfest takes place mid-September up in Muskie-land at 10440 Florida Ave. in Hayward 715-934-3055.

Thirsty Troll Brewfest is around the third Saturday of September in Grundahl Park, 301 Blue Mounds St, Mt Horeb 608-437-5914. 15+ brewers sampling up to three beers each.

Septembeerfest is around the third weekend in September at the Oak Creek Community Center, 8580 S. Howell Ave., Oak Creek, 414-768-5840, www.occenter.com. $25 tickets.

Appleton's Octoberfest is late in September and draws over 100,000 people. www.octoberfestonline.org.

La Crosse Oktoberfest (www.oktoberfestusa.com, 608-784-3378) starts the last weekend of September and lasts nine days! Since 1961, the

event has been growing like a beer belly and draws thousands for beer, brats and parades. G. Heileman Brewing Co. had a hand in the idea at the beginning, but since its inception, Oktoberfest has been a community event. If you can't make it to Munich, this is the next best thing!

Quivey's Grove BeerFest is at 6261 Nesbitt Rd, Fitchburg, 608-273-4900, quiveysgrove. com and takes place at the end of September or in early October. This beer fest features 30 breweries, 60 beers, and great food. Advance tickets available at Quivey's Grove or by phone. Tickets are $27.50 and may be purchased in person at the Stable Grill or by phone with credit card.

Weissgerber's Gasthaus Oktoberfest at 2720 N. Grandview Blvd., Waukesha 262-544-6960 in late September.

OKTOBERFEST

Oktoberfest was originally a wedding celebration. Prince Ludwig of Bavaria married Princess Therese in 1810. They hosted a horse race outside Munich and 40,000 people came to watch. The event celebrated the marriage (I imagine it was open bar) but also was a sort of harvest fest, a religious thanks for the crops and such. Each year, parades bring together floats and bands, and of course BEER. Munich may be the home of the festival, but Wisconsin provides a nice variety of them, most notably in La Crosse. And the namesake beer, which is traditionally aged from spring until this event, is often available at non-October times as well. Check with your local brewer!

OCTOBER

Dallas Oktoberfest (no not Texas!) promises "beer, guns, live steel combat and polka music." How's that for a taste of Wisconsin? Seriously, Valkyrie Brewing Co. makes its home here and an unrelated group of Vikings often shows up to re-enact some marauding shenanigans in early October. Not huge, but worth the trip! "You never know who else will be there. Or how dangerous it may become." www.valkyriebrewery.com, 715-837-1824.

New Glarus Oktoberfest is in Village Park, New Glarus the first full weekend in October. New Glarus Brewery hosts a beer tasting and there is lots of live music, food and entertainment including kids' games (swisstown.com, 800-527-6838).

Sand Creek Brewery Oktoberfest (www.sandcreekbrewing.com, 715-284-7553) 320 Pierce St, Black River Falls, the first Saturday in October right on site in a huge tent with crafts and music all day and night.

Cystic Fibrosis Brew Madness—Prost to a Cure is held mid-October at Milwaukee County Zoo in Milwaukee. Make reservations: 262-798-2060.

Beers Around the World Tasting sponsored by the Lion's Club of South Milwaukee occurs on a Friday night usually in late October at Texx's Victory Hall in Cudahy, 414-769-8455.

Wisconsin Dells is home to **Autumn Harvest Fest** in October (a weekend around the 20th), a family friendly festival with a craft fair, farmer's market, hayrides and more. Moosejaw Brewing Co. hosts "Dells on Tap," the beer fest of this event, featuring around 25 local brewers, 800-223-3557.

NOVEMBER

Annual Bay Area Humane Society Beer & Wine Fest, Green Bay.

DECEMBER

I got nothing here. Get yourself a growler or a few six-packs of craft brew from the local brewer or liquor store and have some friends over for the holidays. Don't forget your lederhosen. Prost!

BEER, BOATS AND BIKES

BOOZE CRUISES

Sort of the malt and hops version of the Love Boat, or Gilligan's Island without the hole in the hull. Or the big storm. Or the Professor. Or Ginger. OK, *nothing* like Gilligan's Island. Here are a few boat rides with beer:

Madison

Capital Brewery serves the beer and Ian's provides the pizza on this boat cruise around Madison's lakes with great views of the Capital, the University, and one of the finest little cities in the country. Cost is about $20 per person, departs on Thursdays during the summer and lasts 1-1/2 hours. Reservations are required. Betty Lou Cruises (bettyloucruises.com, 608-246-3138).

Milwaukee

How about THREE brewery tours in one easy cruise? Saturdays and Sundays in Milwaukee, get on the river and take the hat trick brew tour to Lakefront, Milwaukee Ale House, and Rock Bottom. **Brew City Queen II** and **Milwaukee Maiden** set sail for a four-hour tour starting at Lakefront at 12:30 PM, Milwaukee Ale House at 1, and Rock Bottom at 1:10. (Do check these times when you make your reservation.) Tickets are around $29 and include samples at the breweries (no beer served on board, I'm afraid) and an hour at each brewery. For information or reservations, call Brew City Queen 414-283-9999.

Or just stay on the boat to drink and eat with the **Milwaukee Beer and Brat Cruise** aboard the Edelweiss. Enjoy a 1.5-hour cruise along the Milwaukee River and Lake Michigan shoreline while drinking Milwaukee Brewing Co. beer and eating (local) Usinger brats. Tickets are about $21 and include a beer and unlimited bratwurst. (edelweissboats. com, 414-276-7447)

GET ON THE BUS

Think of this as the ultimate designated driver option—you and a busload of other beer enthusiasts being carted around, beer in hand, to various beer destinations. Brewery tours, beer bars, sporting events with beer. Based out of Madison, **Hop Head Tour Co.** runs public and private group tours to small round-ups of regional breweries, sporting events in Milwaukee, and more. Tickets often include samples, meals, a guest host, and a souvenir of some sort (hopheadbeertours.com, 608-467-5707).

For something a bit longer, check out **GetAway Travel LLC** (getawaybeer.com, 262-538-2140), a leisure travel agency with an avid interest in Wisconsin craft beer. These bus tours are 3-day/2-night all-inclusive deals (bus, hotel, meals, beer tasting) and hit the breweries as well as a combo of Wisconsin distilleries, creameries, chocolatiers, or other local producers.

BIKING FOR BEER!

Wisconsin has a large network of bike trails, many of them former railway corridors, and what better way to end a ride than with a locally made beer? Here are some options for where to ride and where to take a break.

Where required, bicyclists ages sixteen and older must purchase a State Trail Pass which costs $4/day or $20/year. Often they can be purchased at self-pay stations along state trails.

Zone 1

The Glacial Drumlin Trail (920-648-8774) starts in Cottage Grove heading east and passes south of **Lake Mills**, home to *Tyranena Brewing Co.* and ends in Waukesha. Ambitious bikers may veer off the trail at **Delafield** for *Delafield Brewhaus* and *Water Street Lake Country*. Trail pass required. (Another trail, the Lake Country Recreation Trail, connects Waukesha and Delafield.) You may also ride bike-friendly roads west from the Glacial Drumlin trailhead to reach the *Great Dane's* Eastside pub at 876 Jupiter Dr., **Madison**.

The "400" State Trail (608-337-4775, 608-524-2850) starts in **Reedsburg**, home to *Corner Pub*, and heads north where it connects to the Hillsboro, Omaha and Elroy-Sparta trails. Reedsburg is 16 miles from **Wisconsin Dells** where you'll find *Moosejaw Pizza/Dells Brewing* and *Port Huron Brewing Co*. Trail pass required.

Madison has over 100 miles of trails in and around the city and special lanes in some streets just for bikes. With the high number of breweries in the city and the adjoining cities of **Fitchburg** and **Middleton**, you have a lot of options here. Capital City Trail winds around Lake Monona and passes within three blocks of the *Great Dane* off the Capitol Square, a block from *One Barrel Brewing* on Atwood, and within one block of the *Great Dane* Fitchburg location.

Military Ridge State Trail (608-437-7393) will take you from **Madison** (home of several brewers), through **Verona** (near *Gray's Tied House* and *Wisconsin Brewing Co.*) and **Mount Horeb** (*The Grumpy Troll*). The trail ends at Dodgeville and provides trails to Blue Mounds and Governor Dodge state parks. Trail pass required.

Cheese Country Recreation Trail (608-776-4830) connects **Mineral Point** (*Brewery Creek*) to **Monroe** (*Minhas Craft Brewery*).

Badger State Trail (608-527-2335) stretches from **Madison** to Freeport, Illinois, via **Monroe** (*Minhas Craft Brewery*) and within a few miles of **New Glarus** (*New Glarus Brewery*) down the Sugar River Trail. Trail pass required.

Sugar River State Trail (608-527-2334) starts in **New Glarus**, home of *New Glarus Brewery*, of course. Trail pass required.

Zone 2

Interurban Trail (800-237-2874) cuts through historic **Cedarburg**, home of *Silver Creek Brewery*. The trail crosses Washington Ave in downtown just a couple blocks from the Cedarburg Mill, Silver Creek's home.

Oakleaf Trail (800-231-0903) in **Milwaukee** is an asphalt trail right through the brew city and yet somewhat peaceful and secluded as it passes along the river. You'd have to venture into the streets to get to breweries though. (Also see Glacial Drumlin Trail in Zone 1.)

Zone 3

La Crosse River State Trail (608-337-4775, 608-269-4123) connects the Elroy-Sparta Trail to the Great River State Trail and **La Crosse** is home to *City Brewery* and *Pearl Street Brewery*. Trail pass required.

Old Abe State Trail (715-726-7880) ends in **Chippewa Falls**, home of *Leinenkugel's*. The trail ends right at the brewery. Say no more! Trail pass required.

Lucette Brewing Co. lies right alongside the Red Cedar State Trail (715-232-1242) in **Menomonie** and is about a mile away from *Das Bierhaus* farther into town. The Red Cedar heads south 14 miles to connect to the Chippewa River State Trail which could then get you to **Eau Claire** for *Lazy Monk Brewery* and *Northwoods Brewpub*. Trail pass required.

Work is still in progress to connect the Chippewa River and Old Abe State Trails so that Eau Claire, Chippewa Falls, and Menomonie would all be connected by a rails-to-trails bike system.

Zone 4

Bearskin State Trail (715-453-1263) starts south from (or ends north to?) **Minocqua,** home of *Minocqua Brewing Co.* Trail pass required.

See also Mountain Bay Trail in Zone 5. By the way, *Red Eye Brewing* in **Wausau** has a great number of cyclist fans who stop by after their rides each day. Brewer Kevin Eichelberger is also an avid pedaler.

Zone 5

Mountain Bay Trail (www.mountain-baytrail.org) connects **Wausau** in Zone 4 to **Green Bay.** This means *Red Eye Brewing, Bull Falls Brewing* and *The Great Dane Pub and Brewery* are connected to *Titletown, Hinterland, Cheeseheads, Stillmank,* and *Legends* in **Green Bay.**

Zone 6

Osaugie Trail (800-942-5313) starts in **Superior,** home of *Thirsty Pagan,* and heads east. This connects to the Tri-County Corridor Trail (715-372-5959) which spans the 61 miles to **Ashland,** home of *South Shore Brewing.* This one is pretty rough though for a biker. Mountain bike? ATV?

For up-to-date information and other state trails go to www.wiparks. net and click on Find a trail.

HOMEBREWERS ASSOCIATIONS

A.L.E. Club, Appleton Libation Enthusiasts

General club meetings are the third Thursday of even-numbered months at Stone Cellar Brewpub
1004 South Olde Oneida Street
Appleton in the "English Room"
www.thealeclub.org

Beer Barons of Milwaukee

Meets fourth Wednesday at Clifford's Supper Club
10448 W. Forest Home • Hales Corners
7:30pm, $5.00 per meeting fee
www.beerbarons.org

Beer Chasers

Ron Strobel
19555 W Bluemound Rd #26 • Waukesha

Belle City Homebrewers & Vintners

www.bellecitybrew.org

Bidal Society of Kenosha

www.hbd.org/kbs

Brew City Brewzers

Ricky Engstrom
2600 N 60th Street • Milwaukee

Bull Falls Home Brewers of Central Wisconsin

Meets second Thursday of the month at Bull Falls Brewery
www.bullfalls-homebrewers.org

Central Wisconsin Draught Board

Meets at O'so Brewing Company on the second Tuesday each month.
www.cenwisdb.org

Chippewa Valley Better Beer Brewers

www.cvbetterbrewers.org

First Draft

Steve Potter
5475 Marie Road • Oregon
608-257-2707

Frugal Homebrewers

Greg Snapp
228 W. Broadway • Waukesha

Green Bay Rackers

Mark Zelten
Box 247 • Green Bay
www.rackers.org

King Gambrinus Court of Brewers,

Art Steinoff
7680 Big Pine Lane • Burlington

LUSH, Lazy Unmotivated Society of Homebrewers

Meets second Thursday of each month at 7 p.m. at either O'Briens Pub in Eagle River or Minocqua Brewing Company
Eagle River / Minocqua area
northwoodslushinc@gmail.com

Madison Homebrewers & Tasters Guild

Meets two Wednesdays a month.
Bob Paolino
Box 1265 • Madison
www.mhtg.org

Manty Malters

Meets at Kathy's Stage Door Pub the first Thursday of every month.
Jeff Parks
1512 Jasmine Drive • Manitowoc
www.mantymalters.org

MASH, Marshfield Area Society of Homebrewers

Meets the first Thursday of the month at the Blue Heron Brewpub
108 W 9th Street • Marshfield
www.mash54449.org
marshfieldhomebrewers@gmail.com

Menomonie Homebrewers Club

Meets the first Monday of the month often at Stout Ale House in Menomonie
www.mhbrewers.com
info@mhbrewers.com

Milwaukee Beer Society
Michael Ratkowski
14835 W. Lisbon Road • Brookfield
262-782-5233

SOB's, Society of Oshkosh Brewers
Meets third Wednesday of the month.
Mike Engel
Oshkosh • 920-236-9080
mengel@realsob.org
www.realsob.org

Stateline Brewing Society
Meets at Suds O'Hanahan's Irish Pub on the
second Wednesday of each month. (Beloit)
www.statelinebrewingsociety.com

UWP Homebrewing Club
University of Wisconsin Platteville
groups.google.com/group/UWP_
HOMEBREW or on Facebook

Washington Heights
Milwaukee
www.washingtonheightsbrewery.com

HOMEBREW SHOPS

Brew & Grow
285 North Janacek Road
Brookfield • 262-789-0555
www.altgarden.com

Brew City Supplies
Milwaukee
Online only
www.brewcitysupplies.com

The Frugal Homebrewer
4866 S. Packard
Cudahy • 414-483-2937

The Frugal Homebrewer
238 W. Broadway
Waukesha • 262-544-0894
www.frugalhomebrewer.com

Grape Grain and Bean
816 S 8th Street
Manitowoc • 920-682-8828
www.grapegrainandbean.com

Homebrewing Depot
8008 West National Avenue
West Allis • 414-778-0781
www.homebrewingdepot.com

Homebrew Market
520 E. Wisconsin
Appleton • 920-733-4294
www.homebrewmarket.com

Hop to It
234 Wisconsin Avenue
Racine • 262-633-8239
www.dpwigley.com

House of Homebrew
415 Dousman Street
Green Bay • 920-435-1007
www.houseofhomebrew.com

Lake Geneva Brewing Emporium
640 West Main Street
Lake Geneva • 262-729-4005
lakegenevabrewingemporium.com

Market Basket
14835 W. Lisbon Road
Brookfield • 262-783-5233

Point Brew Supply
1816 Post Road
Plover • 715-342-9535
www.pointbrewsupply.com

Purple Foot
3167 S. 92nd Street
Milwaukee • 414-654-2211
www.purplefootusa.com

Wine & Hop Shop
1931 Monroe Street
Madison • 608-257-0099
www.wineandhop.com
www.facebook.com/
pages/The-Wine-Hop-Shop/129872203753403

Zymurgy Outfitters Homebrew Shop
5015 Netherwood Road
Oregon • 608-835-7370

GLOSSARY OF BEERS

Ale — Short answer: beer from top-fermenting yeast, fermented at warmer temperatures. Long answer: see Ales vs. Lagers in the History of Beer Section.

Altbier means "old" beer—as in a traditional recipe not a brew that's gone bad. It's a bitter, copper-colored ale.

Amber is that funny rock-like stuff that prehistoric bugs got trapped in and now makes great hippie jewelry or that pretty girl you were sweet on in middle school. But here I think they're just talking about the color of a type of American ale that uses American hops for a bitter, malty and hoppy flavor.

APA (American Pale Ale) is a pale ale using American hops. The hops flavor, aroma and bitterness are pronounced... exactly as they're spelled.

Barley wine is like precious gold wherever it's brewed. This ale jumps off the shelves or out of the tap. It is strong, sweet, a bit aged, and those who know are waiting to pounce on it.

Bitter is part of the family of pale ales, cousin perhaps to the IPA. Like folks in a small Wisconsin town, all beer is related in some way, I guess. This brew has a wider range of strength, flavor and color than the IPA. See "ESB." You'll be back.

Blonde or Golden Ale is a lighter form of pale ale usually made with pilsner malt. It's a popular Belgian style and gentlemen prefer them.

Bock is a strong lager darkened a bit and brewed in the winter to be drunk in spring. Monks drank it during the Lenten fasting period because it had substance to it, you know, like liquid bread? The name comes from the medieval German village of Einbeck. So, no, it does not mean Bottom of the Keg or Beer of Copious Kraeusening. (What IS kraeusening anyway?) Bock means goat in German. Thus the goats on so many of the labels and the popularity of headbutting at fraternity bock parties. Brewmaster Jamie in the Dells calls it the "chili of beers."

Brackett (also called braggot) is the first form of ale and a sort of beer and mead hybrid. It was first brewed with honey and hops and later with honey and malt—with or without hops added.

Cream Ale is a smooth and sweet American ale.

Doppelbock see "Bock" and read it twice. Seriously, just a bock with a stronger punch to it though not necessarily double.

Dunkelweiss is a dark wheat beer, a German style. "Dunkel" means dark.

Eisbock if you say it outloud is probably easier to guess. No, it's not beer on the rocks. Take a bock, freeze it, take the ice out, and you have a higher alcohol content bock.

ESB (Extra Special Bitter) see "Bitter" and add some more alcohol. Isn't that what makes beer special?

Gruit or **Grut** is a mixture of herbs that beer makers used to use before hops came into favor. It added bitterness and in some cases preservative qualities, and the unique blends offered a variety of flavors for beers. Some brewers might do unhopped beers and use things like juniper berries, chamomile, heather or other things that sound like lawn clippings.

Hefeweizen (German Wheat Beer) is *supposed* to be cloudy—it's unfiltered. Don't make that face, drink it. That's where all the vitamins are and stuff. See also "Weisse" et al.

Imperial Stout see "Stout" then drink it. The Brits originally made this for the Russian imperial court. It had to cross water as cold as our frozen tundra so the high alcohol content kept it from freezing. Expect roasted, chocolate, and burnt malt flavors and a strong left hook.

IPA (India Pale Ale) is what the Brits used to send to India. The long journey spoiled porters and stouts, and so this recipe calls for lots of hops. Did you read that part yet? About hops as a preservative? You can't just skip parts of the book. I'll catch you. And there will be a quiz. Don't say I didn't warn you.

Irish-style Stout is a dry version of stout, typically served under nitro for the creamy special effect. However, it's very dark and thus too difficult to dye green on St. Patty's Day.

Kölsch is just an excuse to use those little dot things—"What is an umlaut?" for those of you looking to score on *Jeopardy*—and a difficult-to-pronounce-and-still-retain-your-dignity name for a light, fruity ale that originated in Cologne... the city in Germany, please don't drink your aftershave no matter how nice it smells.

Lager — Short answer: beer with bottom-fermenting yeast, fermented colder than ale. Long answer: see Ales vs. Lagers in the History of Beer Section.

Lambic — Let's just call this the Wild One. It's a Belgian ale with wheat and it uses naturally occurring yeast, the kind that's just floating around out there. The brew is tart and may have a fruit element added such as raspberries or cherries.

Low alcohol — See "Near Bear."

Maibock is not your bock and if you touch my bock, there's gonna be trouble. This is the lightest of the bocks and is traditionally brewed to be drunk in May, but we're not always hung up on tradition and it is often around whenever you want it.

Märzen takes its name from March, the month in which this lager is typically brewed so it can age in time for Oktoberfest when it magically becomes Oktoberfest beer.

Mead is honey fermented in water. It ain't beer but it's good. And there's plenty of honey in Wisconsin to make it. The word "honeymoon" comes from a tradition of gifting a newlywed couple a month's worth of mead to get things off to a smooth start. From this you can guess why we say "the honeymoon's over" with such lament.

Near Beer — Let's just pretend we didn't hear this and move on, shall we?

Nut Brown Ale uses roasted malt, and a bit of hops brings some bitterness.

Oktoberfest is Märzen after the 6–7 month wait as it ages a bit.

Pilsner is a style that comes from Plzen, a Czech version of Milwaukee. Dry and hoppy, this golden lager is hugely popular and most of the mass-produced versions fail to imitate the Czech originals. Best to try a handcrafted version at your local—or someone else's local—brewpub. Also a term I use to describe residents of Moquah, Wisconsin which is also the Township of Pilsen where my grandparents lived.

Porter is not only a Wisconsin brewer (Tom at Lake Louie) but also a fine, dark ale made with roasted malt and bitter with hops.

Rauchbier is made with smoked barley malt. It may be an acquired taste, but if you like bacon…

MEASURE FOR MEASURE

A **growler** is a half-gallon jug, refillable at your local brewpub. Many brewers sell them to you full for a few dollars more than the refill.

One **US barrel** (1 bbl) is two kegs or 31 gallons or 248 pints, so you better start early.

A **keg** holds 15.5 gallons – this is the legendary half-barrel of the college party fame

A **Cornelius keg** is a pub keg, similar to one of those soda syrup canisters and holds 5 gallons.

A **US pint** = 16 oz. = a proper US beer. (Also defined as 1/8 of a gallon)

A **can** = 12 oz. = generally an improper beer of the mass-produced variety, but not always.

A **UK pint** = 20 oz. (lucky chumps) and there are laws protecting the drinker from improperly filled pints! Look for that little white line on the pint glass.

A **firkin** is a small cask or barrel, usually the equivalent of a ¼ barrel or about 9 gallons (34 liters)

Getting confused yet? I gave up at "pint" and drank one.

And don't even get me started on the whole metric vs. Imperial gallon vs. US gallon vs. 10-gallon hat conundrum.

Rye beer substitutes some malted rye for some of the malted barley. Remember in that "American Pie" song, the old men "drinking whiskey and rye?" Yeah, that's something else.

Sahti is an old Finnish style of beer, herbal in its ingredients, typically employing juniper berries but not always hops.

Saison is French for "season" (those people have a different word for everything it seems) and this beer was intended for farm workers at the end of summer. It's Belgian and the yeast used ferments at a higher ale temperature. It's generally cloudy and often has something like orange zest or coriander in it. While it was originally a low-alcohol brew so the workers could keep working, many American revivals of the style are packing a bit of a punch.

Saké — This is more of a trivia note than anything. It's not wine or rice wine; it's actually a Japanese rice beer. Odds are you won't see it brewed here but remember this to impress your friends next time you have sushi.

Schwarzbier is the way they say "black beer" in Germany. This lager is black as midnight thanks to the dark roasted malt and has a full, chocolatey or coffee flavour much like a stout or porter.

Scotch Ale or Scottish-style Ale is generally maltier than other ales and sometimes more potent. The FDA insists it be labeled "Scottish-style" as it is not actually from Scotland if brewed here in Wisconsin. Fair enough

Sour Ale is a variety of beer that uses wild yeasts and bacteria to get a brew that makes you pucker a bit. Beer can become unintentionally and unpleasantly sour when bacteria infect it. This is different; it's intentional and when done traditionally, it's kinda risky. A lambic fits the category.

Stout is so good we named one of the University of Wisconsin campuses after it. With dark roasted barley and lots of hops, it is a black ale most smooth. It can be bitter, dry, or even sweet when it's brewed with milk sugar (lactose). On occasion brewers add oatmeal for a smoother and sweeter ale and you have to start wondering if there is something to that saying, "Beer, it's not just for breakfast anymore." Imperial Stout is a strong variation on the recipe first done up by the English exporting to the Russians in the 1800s. The real fun of it is when it is on nitrogen tap. Look that up!

Tripel is an unfiltered Belgian ale that has a very high alcohol content. The combination of hops and large amounts of malt and candy sugar give a bittersweet taste to this powerhouse. Many brewpubs will only allow you to drink one or two glasses to make sure you can still find the door when you leave.

Wheat Beer is beer made with wheat. You didn't really just look this up, did you? Dude.

Witbier, Weisse, Weizen, Wisenheimer — three of these words are simply different ways of saying white wheat beer that originated in Belgium. They are sometimes flavored with orange peel and coriander and are mildly to majorly sweet. The fourth word describes the kind of guy that would write that Wheat Beer definition.

And what the hell IS kraeusening anyway???

BIBLIOGRAPHY

Apps, Jerold. *Breweries of Wisconsin*, 2nd Ed., University of Wisconsin Press, 2005.

Glover, Brian. *The Beer Companion: An Essential Guide to Classic Beers from Around the World*, Lorenz, 1999.

Harper, Timothy and Oliver, Garrett. *The Good Beer Book: Brewing and Drinking Quality Ales and Lagers*, Berkley Books, 1997.

Kroll, Wayne. *Wisconsin's Frontier Farm Breweries*, self-published.

Smith, Gregg. *Beer: A History of Suds and Civilization from Mesopotamia to Microbreweries*, Avon Books, 1995.

Swierczynski, Duane. *The Big Book o' Beer: Everything You Ever Wanted to Know About the Greatest Beverage on Earth*, Quirk Books, 2004.

Yenne, Bill. *The American Brewery*, MBI, 2003.

INDEX

Symbols

A

B

C

SIGNATURES

3 Sheeps Brewing (Sheboygan)

_____Date_____

10th Street Brewery (Milwaukee)

_____Date_____

Ale Asylum (Madison)

_____Date_____

Angry Minnow Restaurant And Brewery (Hayward)

_____Date_____

Appleton Beer Factory (Appleton)

_____Date_____

Big Bay Brewing Co. (Shorewood)

_____Date_____

Black Husky Brewing Co. (Pembine)

_____Date_____

Blue Heron BrewPub (Marshfield)

_____Date_____

Brady's Brewhouse (New Richmond)

_____Date_____

Brewery Creek Brewpub (Mineral Point)

_____Date_____

Bull Falls Brewery (Wausau)

_____Date_____

Capital Brewery (Middleton)

_____Date_____

Central Waters Brewing Co. (Amherst)

_____Date_____

Cheeseheads (Green Bay)

_____Date_____

City Brewery (La Crosse)

_____Date_____

Corner Pub (Reedsburg)

_____Date_____

Courthouse Pub (Manitowoc)

_____Date_____

Das Bierhaus (Menomonie)

_____Date_____

Dave's BrewFarm (Wilson)

_____Date_____

Delafield Brewhaus (Delafield)

_____Date_____

Esser's Cross Plains Brewery (Cross Plains)

_____Date_____

Fox River Brewing Co. – Fratellos (Appleton)

_____Date_____

Fox River Brewing Co. – Fratellos (Oshkosh)

_____Date_____

Furthermore Beer (Spring Green)

_____Date_____

Geneva Lake Brewing Co. (Lake Geneva)

_____Date_____

Granite City Food and Brewery (Madison)

_____Date_____

Gray Brewing Co. (Janesville)

_____Date_____

Gray's Tied House (Verona)

_____Date_____

Great Dane Pub and Brewery (Fitchburg)

_____Date_____

Great Dane Pub and Brewery (Hilldale-Madison)

_____Date_____

Great Dane Pub and Brewery (Madison)

_____Date_____

Great Dane Pub and Restaurant (Wausau)

_____Date_____

Green Bay Brewing Co. (Green Bay)

_____Date_____

Grumpy Troll Brew Pub (Mount Horeb)

_____Date_____

Hinterland Brewery (Green Bay)

_____Date_____

Horny Goat Brewing Co. (Milwaukee)

_____Date_____

House of Brews (Madison)

_____Date_____

Hudson Brewing (Hudson)

_____Date_____

Hydro Street Brewery (Columbus)

_____Date_____

Jacob Leinenkugel Brewing (Chippewa Falls)

_____Date_____

Karben4 Brewing (Madison)

_____Date_____

Lakefront Brewery (Milwaukee)

_____Date_____

Lake Louie Brewing (Arena)

_____Date_____

Lazy Monk Brewery (Eau Claire)

_____Date_____

Legends Brewhouse & Eatery (De Pere – Green Bay)
_____Date_____

Legends Brewhouse & Eatery (Green Bay)
_____Date_____

Lucette Brewing Co. (Menomonie)
_____Date_____

MillerCoors (Milwaukee)
_____Date_____

Milwaukee Ale House (Milwaukee)
_____Date_____

Milwaukee Brewing Company / 2nd Street Brewery (Milwaukee)
_____Date_____

Minhas Craft Brewery (Monroe)
_____Date_____

Minocqua Brewing Company (Minocqua)
_____Date_____

Moosejaw Pizza & Dells Brewing Co. (Wisconsin Dells)
_____Date_____

New Glarus Brewing Co. (New Glarus)
_____Date_____

Northwoods Brewpub and Grill (Eau Claire)
_____Date_____

Oliphant Brewing (Somerset)
_____Date_____

One Barrel Brewing (Madison)
_____Date_____

O'so Brewing Company (Plover)
_____Date_____

Pearl Street Brewery (La Crosse)
_____Date_____

Pigeon River Brewing Co. (Marion)
_____Date_____

Port Huron Brewing Co. (Wisconsin Dells)
_____Date_____

Potosi Brewing Company (Potosi)
_____Date_____

Public Craft Brewing Co. (Kenosha)
_____Date_____

Rail House Restaurant & Brewpub (Marinette)
_____Date_____

Randy's Fun Hunters Brewery & Restaurant (Whitewater)
_____Date_____

Red Eye Brewing Company (Wausau)
_____Date_____

Rhinelander Brewing Co. (Rhinelander)
_____Date_____

Riverside Brewery & Restaurant (West Bend)
_____Date_____

Rock Bottom Restaurant & Brewery (Milwaukee)
_____Date_____

Roll Inn Brew Pub (Chilton)
_____Date_____

Rowland's Calumet Brewing (Chilton)
_____Date_____

Rush River Brewing Co. (River Falls)
_____Date_____

Rustic Road Brewing Co. (Kenosha)
_____Date_____

Sand Creek Brewing Co. (Black River Falls)
_____Date_____

Shipwrecked Brew Pub (Egg Harbor)

_____Date_____

Silver Creek Brewing Co. (Cedarburg)

_____Date_____

South Shore Brewery (Ashland)

_____Date_____

Sprecher Brewing Co. (Glendale3Milwaukee)

_____Date_____

St. Francis Brewpub (St. Francis)

_____Date_____

Stevens Point Brewery (Stevens Point)

_____Date_____

Stillmank Beer Co. (Green Bay)

_____Date_____

Stone Cellar Brewpub (Appleton)

_____Date_____

Stonefly Brewing Co. (Milwaukee)

_____Date_____

Sweet Mullets Brewing Co. (Oconomowoc)

_____Date_____

Thirsty Pagan Brewing (Superior)

_____Date_____

Titletown Brewing Co. (Green Bay)

_____Date_____

Tribute Brewing Co. (Eagle River)

_____Date_____

Tyranena Brewing Co. (Lake Mills)

_____Date_____

Valkyrie Brewing Co. (Dallas)

_____Date_____

Vintage Brewing Co. (Madison)

_____Date_____

Water Street Brewery (Milwaukee)

_____Date_____

Water Street Grafton Brewery (Grafton)

_____Date_____

Water Street Lake Country Brewery (Delafield)

_____Date_____

White Winter Winery (Iron River)

_____Date_____

Wisconsin Brewing Co. (Verona)

_____Date_____

ABOUT THE AUTHOR

Kevin Revolinski is an amateur beer snob and born-again ale drinker with a writing habit. A Wisconsin native, he has written for a variety of publications including *The New York Times, Chicago Tribune, Wisconsin State Journal* and many postcards to his grandmother. His other travel books include the forthcoming *Michigan's Best Beer Guide, Backroads and Byways of Wisconsin, 60 Hikes Within 60 Miles of Madison, Best in Tent* Camping Wisconsin, Insiders' Guide Madison, *The Yogurt Man Cometh: Tales of an American Teacher in Turkey* and *The Wisconsin Beer Guide: A Travel Companion* (2006). He is a Packer fan by birth. Check out his website and blog, **The Mad Traveler** at www.revtravel.com. Or look for him at your local brewpub. (It's more likely he's at one of his own local brewpubs in Madison though.)

PHOTOGRAPH COURTESY OF TOM RISTAU

And finally, *what is kraeusening?*

Brewers can add a small amount of unfermented beer and yeast to beer that is done fermenting and being put into a bottle, keg or tank. The resulting bit of fermentation produces additional carbon dioxide which dissolves into the beer giving it carbonation. So I guess you could say it's a beer belch waiting to happen.